Where Two Worlds Touch

An Outsider's Memoir in England

Books written as L.R. Heartsong:

Ordinary Sacred: Farewell to the Soul Artist Journal
[**Nautilus Book Award winner**]

A Life for the Senses: Return to the Soul Artist Journal

To Kneel and Kiss the Earth: Inspiration from the Soul Artist Journal

The Bones & Breath:
A Man's Guide to Eros, the Sacred Masculine, and the Wild Soul
[**Nautilus Book Award winner**]

Advance Praise for *Where Two Worlds Touch*

"In this entrancing memoir, Faire encapsulates how true love knows no gender. [The author] writes ... as a mindful examination of the heart and soul, and its interconnection with the divine, nature, and mystery ... otherworldly in his careful attention to the dance between the earthly and ethereal with his lush portrayal of England's landscape ... not a bird, a lamb, or a fox escapes Faire's attention. ... Readers looking for traditional page-turners may find Faire's memoir elegant but meandering, but this is precisely the book's beauty. Faire can capture the intimacy in the mundanity ... A redemption of the soul, a second chance at love, and pursuit of transcendence despite fear and shame, this memoir explores the unorthodox ways of loving, and how a conscious and mindful relationship is the ultimate relationship worth having."

– **BookLife Reviews** by *Publishers Weekly*, **Editor's Pick**

"[A] charming and spiritual memoir ... Composed with immediacy and an old-fashioned whimsical tone, the narrative is underpinned with passion ... Faire's descriptions of the natural world are powerful and sensual ... indoors, too, where he delights in descriptions of food and cooking. Throughout the book, he navigates the chasm between the modern world and natural life ... reaching to refine what it means to be human."

– *Foreword* Clarion Reviews

"*Where Two Worlds Touch* is ... Faire's telling of his journey from 'happily ever after' to heartbreak and back again. Few writers have such keen self-awareness as Faire. [He] imbues each paragraph with an almost visceral sense of reality. Faire provides a unique perspective on reading the signs that life places in our path and ultimately following the intricacies of what the heart wants. An illuminating and bittersweet personal story of second chances."

– Independent Book Review

"[Faire's] prose is a heady blend of lyricism and affirmation-speak ... but those who share his enthusiasm for the magical side of life will likely find this work to be a touching portrait of a complex relationship. A heartfelt, spirituality-tinged rumination on love and healing."

– *Kirkus Reviews*

Where Two Worlds Touch

An Outsider's Memoir in England

For Josie,

All blessings, grace & magic of the mysterious journey, dear ... blessed be.

River

River Faire

Evolutionary Press • Bend, Oregon

Copyright © 2023 by River Faire

All rights reserved. This book may not be reproduced in whole or in part, stored in a retrieval system, transmitted in any form or by any means—electronic, mechanical, or other—nor used in any context related to AI, without written permission from the publisher, except by a reviewer, who may quote brief passages in a review.

Some of the names of people and houses in this narrative have been changed.

Evolutionary Press (an imprint of Hearthside Press)
PO Box 1232
Bend, Oregon 97708
Evolutionary.Press

Pages (69-70, 97-103, 166-169) contain an excerpt from *The Bones and Breath*, by L.R. Heartsong, updated and reprinted with permission of the author and Hearthside Press.

Cover image by Annie Spratt; hands photo by Brent Barnett
Cover fox by Erik McLean
Cover design and layout by Katie Boyer Clark (www.katielizabeth.com)
Author photo by Gary Calicott

First edition: 2023
Printed in the USA

ISBN: 979-8-218-25703-3 (paperback)

Library of Congress Control Number: 2023914550

For Robert

Je t'aime, toujours.

Contents

1 RETURN

17 REACQUAINTING

34 GHOSTS & TEA

52 HEDGEROWS & HAVEN

69 OUTSIDERS

86 REVELATION

104 AFTERSHOCKS

122 CONNEMARA

140 HIGHFIELD

158 EDGEWALKERS

176 LIGHT & SHADOW

194 WINTERSCAPE

212 STANDING STONES

231 THE FIELD OF POSSIBILITY

241 ACKNOWLEDGMENTS

243 ABOUT THE AUTHOR

RETURN

I NEVER INTENDED to return to England. On a frigid December morning, descending towards Heathrow airport after an overnight flight, as the drab sprawl of greater London comes into view through the plane's windows, delicate blue butterflies tumble and collide in my core with something close to happiness. How unexpected, this.

The things we do for love.

After waiting in a serpentine, bleary-eyed queue beneath fluorescent lights for Customs and Immigration, followed by the predictable Border Police questions regarding my UK residence visa—queries about work, home situation, partner—my American passport is finally stamped and handed back without a smile. Entry granted. Alone at the baggage carousel, surrounded by strangers, the airport ethnology submerges me; the clamorous international mix of arriving passengers and different languages, a current of people, noise, and emotions—energy, both psychic and kinetic—swirling all around. An olive-green carryon slung heavily over my shoulder, weighing me down, I await my luggage. Observing. Feeling anticipatory or possibly anxious, a distinct tingling throughout, on an interstitial level. Reflexively, I bite my lower lip. The recorded informational and security messages blaring overhead have British accents, genteel to a foreigner irrespective of the dull, official content. Surprisingly, their timbre and intonation comfort me, almost like a friend.

Two large black, battered suitcases in tow, I roll unhindered through the Customs checkpoint with nothing to declare, emerging through the metal

2   ◆ WHERE TWO WORLDS TOUCH

doors and strolling past a living wall of waiting drivers—bored-looking men of various ages and ethnicities in dark, cheap suits—each holding a sign with someone's name. No one will greet me today, and in my customary fashion, I proceed to Costa Coffee near the terminal's main entry. I don't eat on flights, and twelve hours have elapsed since my last meal, making me wobbly both from blood-sugar blues and the electromagnetic scramble of hurtling through the globe's atmosphere. My stomach grumbles like a bear emerging from its winter den, and a decent coffee will be necessary before the long cab ride to the house.

At the counter, my ear struggles slightly to catch and decipher the inflections of the Polish national working at the till, and I fumble in a pocket for the wad of newly exchanged currency. The blonde girl, boredom inscribed across her angular features, hands me the monetary change as well as a number placard to take to my seat. Staring at the once familiar British coins in my palm, I reacquaint with their respective shapes and values. White ceramic cup perched on saucer, weaving around customers to an empty table, luggage parked beside me, I loosen the dark grey cashmere scarf around my neck. A hubbub of voices and clinking of coffee cups surrounds me. Seated with double cappuccino, eventually a toasted panini of mozzarella and unripe tomato arrives; uninspired food at best, but the sandwich least offends of the pre-made, packaged options and will have to suffice.

Briefly, I attempt to count the times I've enacted an identical routine at Heathrow. Every step customary and normal, as if returning home but I'm not really. Or am I? Buzzing slightly from combined effects of travel, not eating, and an airport hive of activity and noise, underneath I hum with delight—thrilled to cross the Atlantic again. Removing the iPhone from my hand luggage, fingers tap a brief text: *Through Border Control, getting coffee and food, then cab. xx*

Message sent, a forgettable sandwich and coffee consumed, feeling slightly less shaky, I rewrap the exquisitely soft charcoal ribbon once more around my neck and button my dark wool coat. Slipping the mobile phone into a pocket, hoisting the much-too-heavy carryon over one shoulder, I wheel my bags through the building's exit doors. Freezing air slaps my face with an icy blow, and instantly I contract, pulling inwards for the warmth deep in my bones where winter's frigid hands will not find me, but escaping the assault isn't possible. Still biting my lip, I lower my head, as if to duck the cold wind as I cross to the taxi rank. This morning, the gods smile kindly, only a short queue awaits, and within mere minutes, I shove my bags into an iconic black London cab with its retro-style design.

Grateful for the car's warmth, from the rear seat, I relay the Wimbledon address to my driver. The portly man with an East End accent seems unsure how to get to my destination or the best route.

"Take Kew Bridge," I offer, opting for the most direct path across the river, slightly incredulous at instructing the cabbie. Thankfully, I know the way. Once again loosening the scarf and unbuttoning my coat, I add, "Go past Richmond Park towards Putney Heath. When we get closer, I'll guide you to the house."

"Right, then," he nods, pulling onto the roadway. "Live 'ere, do ya?"

A slight pause. Staring out the window at a grey morning sky, a low ceiling of hammered tin, I weigh my response.

"Yes."

"But yer American?"

"I am."

In the manner of taxi drivers, he recounts his single trip to the States several years ago, when he visited Florida and Las Vegas. Why do so many foreigners love the worst of what America offers? Why do they not go to Yellowstone or Yosemite, places which sing the soul alive with beauty, and be struck with wonder over the great parks and wild grandeur? We've become a society of cheap entertainment and distraction.

Even when not tired, superficial conversation and small talk rarely interests me, especially with a stranger. Ensconced in the rear seat, when occasionally asked a question while his narrative ramble continues, I reply with little more than monosyllabic, brief answers. Wordlessly, I consider the cityscape rolling by, the brick buildings, naked trees, and traffic roundabouts, all of it customary and every day rather than foreign.

4 ◆ WHERE TWO WORLDS TOUCH

Oh, London. Ancient and new, a silver-scaled hydra and iron machine. A tangle of stone and glass along the Thames. How tormented our relationship.

A mild jolt of realization. Almost exactly a year has ticked by since my departure on a British Airways jet rising through heavily burdened clouds, my heart broken open and life smashed apart. With a one-way ticket, I flew back to the States to begin life alone at the edge of forty, holding no tangible image of what such an existence might be.

A lifetime passing within a year. For both of us.

Boarding a long-haul international flight always triggers a quickening in my veins, the first quiver of excitement for new experiences ahead. Under my warm clothes and beneath my skin, a glistening, shifting stream of bubbly anticipation as the black cab makes its way toward the familiar streets of Wimbledon, south-west of central London. Traveling on the left side of the road, threading the sprawl of city on its dark web of curvilinear roads, noting the small European cars and generally uninspired architecture of the middle-class houses, everything feels familiar and unexpectedly welcome. The oppressive clouds and damp cold—diametric opposite of the turquoise sky and arid air of the American Southwest—this, too, is instantly normal. Oddly consoling. And the unanticipated happiness at Heathrow, the tingling lightness in my body, the sense of coming home catching me unawares and knocking me sideways a step, feels like a hand pressed warmly into my own.

One cannot fathom the mystery.

⁓

"I need a friend."

On the phone held to my ear, Robert's familiar voice sounds weak, not from distance or poor connection but from chambers of the heart. Laden with emotion.

"The doctor has told me to put my affairs in order and be in hospital within two hours."

Outside a modest adobe casita in Santa Fe, New Mexico, the dusty, pale earth shifts under my bare feet and falls away. For a moment, the world spins too fast and I've lost balance. Tightness grips my chest. My heartbeat feels irregular. From somewhere deep inside, a wellspring of hot tears surges up, refracting and blurring the blue October sky of the high desert.

"I'm on a plane tomorrow," I reply, voice cracking.

"No, not yet. What I really need is for you to stay in the States and be a support for my mum. She's crazy with worry right now and threatening to come here, even though she can't travel with her head injury. The last thing I need is my mother in London, thinking she can take care of herself here or be of some use. God, no! I don't need that stress. I have to put all my limited energy into fighting this . . . and trying to heal."

A moment of silence, pausing for a prayer or summoning courage.

"If I live through this . . . please, will you come?"

In the warming sunlight, I swallow tears like bitter medicine, choking them down quietly so he won't hear.

"You don't even need to ask that. I'd be there in twenty-four hours if you weren't telling me to stay for your mum."

The urban shaman in me surfaces unbidden, knowing the mysteries of illness and healing transcend the so-called physical realm. I offer Robert a meditation for the days ahead, inviting him to visualize the life-threatening infection surrounded with white-gold light, the destructive cells transformed or destroyed. He may doubt this will help, but what can it hurt? I, for one, believe in miracles.

"Thanks, love," he whispers, five thousand miles away.

We hang up the call and my mobile phone goes silent. I stare blankly at withered aspen leaves littering the patio enclosed by a rustic coyote fence of spruce-fir latillas, barely seeing them. Five minutes ago, the sparrows and juncos, my little friends, danced around my feet as I tossed handfuls of golden millet onto the wide, flat stones for them. Now, as if some unseen hunter crept down and took my bright joy, grief lives in my chest, heavy and dark.

~⌒~

6 ◆ WHERE TWO WORLDS TOUCH

Once again, life turns upside down and shifts course unexpectedly. An unforeseen return to the man I loved for sixteen years. A man whose own existence has capsized—spending more than a month in a London hospital, strapped to an intravenous drip feed of intensive antibiotics to combat the aggressive *streptococcus* devouring his mid-thoracic vertebrae and threatening to burst into his spinal cord. Had the bacteria succeeded in penetrating the barrier and entered the cerebrospinal fluid, the pathogens would have traveled rapidly to his brain, triggering first a coma and then death.

Over five long weeks, Robert defied a less-than-twenty-percent chance of survival. Released from hospital, frail and weak, he rests at home in the Wimbledon townhouse we shared, waiting for me to arrive. Leaving my newly fashioned life, I come to care for him, to assist his healing in whatever ways we may find. I circle back neither as lover nor partner, rather a closest friend, honoring the bond of love remaining between us—cords sorely frayed and stretched but somehow intact.

Serendipitously, the six-month lease ended on my eastside Santa Fe casita near the central plaza, and with the economy's collapse, the owners put the unit up for sale. At Robert's request, I will spend the next six months in England, potentially a year if required, helping him regain his footing. When he grows stronger, we will evaluate what the prognosis and landscape might be, yet this wandering gypsy knows better than looking too far down a winding road. Seldom have I ended up where I thought or imagined, nor stayed for long after arriving—ever a chorus of inner voices and fortuitous winds urging me onward.

Lacking adequate funds to ship my possessions back to the States— some antique furniture pieces along with boxes and bulky remnants of a life shared with Robert—my things remained in Wimbledon, stacked in a rear bedroom. By situation but also choice, I led a spartan existence in New Mexico, accumulating scarcely more than a futon, a folding kitchen table and matching wooden chairs, a couple of wool rugs, and a massage table. Supplemented by some kitchen essentials and a set of Riedel wine glasses. Along with a bench for the patio on which to sit, read, and talk to the birds while contemplating a wide sky.

Keep it simple.

When it became apparent Robert would survive the infection, his impending discharge from the hospital drawing near, I quit my spa therapist job, said good-bye to a few private clients, entrusted two boxes with a friend, gave away the rugs and meager furnishings, and sold the bodywork table. I packed my bags, the same ones which departed London, and tucked a few long-cherished items inside: an Asian-style, celadon porcelain teacup with lid and removable infuser; a cherry wood tea scoop; the world's most special Laguiole corkscrew, its grip crafted from an ancient fallen yew tree in the Queen's Grove at Versailles; a green leather pouch, my *medicine bundle*; and a curvaceous black, earth goddess figurine. Wearing a chunky silver Navajo cuff and Māori whalebone pendant, the two pieces perpetually attached to my body during waking hours, I stashed an assortment of rings, necklaces, and trinkets into the well-traveled, olive canvas carryon, accompanied by trusty Parisian fountain pen, a small journal, and my MacBook.

Learn to journey lightly, but carry your treasures.

﹏

Arriving Wimbledon, my cab passes the famous tennis complex with its impressive new, retractable roof over Centre Court, under construction when I left. Co-piloting the driver through a maze of tight residential streets, we slow to a stop in front of a narrow, multistory Edwardian terraced house with a tall hedge. Nervously, I fiddle with the silver, inch-wide cuff, turning it on my wrist. Fingers tap restlessly on one knee. I stare at the dark blue front door with stained glass window, my pulse beating faster than normal. The twirling blue butterflies morph into a whirlpool of anxiousness in my gut, but I step from the vehicle into December's harsh chill, set luggage on the footpath, and pay the fifty quid fare.

The taxi drives off. I open the waist-high, wrought-iron gate, steering the two cases onto a tidy terrace of vintage black and white tiles bordered by the deciduous, mostly bare hedge. My eyes sweep the well-known scene, noting the lavender shrubs I planted in matching green ceramic pots have died. The cheerful annuals in ornate terracotta window boxes have also perished and gone. In a painful flash, Kona, our little Italian Greyhound, stands on the patio beside me and my heart knocks loudly behind ribs, threatening to burst from its cage. A salty sting of tears kisses my eyes.

So many memories, so few of them good. Ghosts and sorrows linger in this tall, white brick house. With an effort, I push the wreckage from my mind and turn to close the low gate. Then I inhale a calming breath to settle the churning within, wriggle toes inside black boots, and rap the front door's brass knocker.

Minutes pass in a tumult of heartbeats before I knock again. Finally, a shadow of movement darkens the stained-glass window, followed by familiar clicks of the latch. The cobalt door swings open and Robert, impossibly thin, scarcely resembling the man I know, stands just inside, wavering slightly. Dark blonde hair cropped military short, his skin pale as bleached bones, the normally bright blue eyes resemble flat stones in winter. Unsteady on his feet, dressed casually in jeans, a navy-blue, zip-up sweatshirt with Hamburg in white letters across the chest, he wears thick wool socks. His unanticipated, wraithlike appearance punches the wind out of me. Stomach tight, my throat constricts. For a moment, I can't move. I steel myself to reveal nothing of my dismay at the shocking alteration. Wordlessly, we regard each other across the threshold, unsure how to bridge the distance between us, a year of estrangement.

"I didn't hear the cab arrive," he apologizes in a fractionated voice.

I maneuver luggage inside the door with a clunk and thud, stationing the bags on the grey-blue carpet, and push the portal shut to its signature loud *click*. Turning, I take him gingerly in an embrace.

"You came," he whispers, words choked with emotion. Sobs begin, face pressed against the shoulder of my black wool coat. I hold a trembling ghost of flesh of blood, nothing but a wisp in my arms. What happened to the dynamic, driven man I knew, the one to whom I said goodbye in this exact spot a year ago?

"Yes, I'm here." He cannot see my tender smile in his ear as he weeps and convulses mildly. "I've loved you a long time, Robert. You are my family and best friend . . . you always will be. *Of course*, I came."

From a coat pocket, I withdraw the travel packet of tissue and hand it to him, pulling away and glancing briefly around the entry foyer with its steep, carpeted stairs to the upper two floors. Like everything greeting me, the scent of the house stirs memories. An old, vaguely musty smell of a residence long inhabited but curiously vacant. A staleness I kept at bay with open windows whenever possible and resinous sticks of incense; endeavoring to create a pleasant, olfactory sense of sanctuary instead.

Decimated by the antibiotic regime in hospital, the man nearly needs a walking cane. Bypassing the stairs, together we step into the front salon, the *reception* Brits call the main living room. Little is different from when I departed. A compact space crammed with our furniture brought from the States, the glass-topped coffee table with ornately woven inlay of rattan and mahogany still sits sandwiched between the fat green couch and matching loveseat. Atop the chimneypiece of the blocked-off fireplace with its metal insert, a new array of pictures, primarily of Robert and his younger Welsh cousin, Stephen. Tall, chalk-white walls with their ornate cornice moldings give the room a bit of breathing air and grace, yet in the squeezed salon, like this entire dwelling, my own breath feels shallow.

Folding doors to the dining room remain propped open, revealing a space similarly crowded by rectangular table and chairs too large, including two showcase cabinets made from reclaimed teak, purchased from Lombok in London shortly after our initial arrival. One displays a collection of antique Blue Willow China, the other contains wine and cocktail glasses from our bygone days of entertaining. Pleasingly, the house feels moderately warm, not chilled as my memory of it, and once again I unwind my charcoal scarf, tossing it along with English coat on the overstuffed sofa.

"Sorry it took so long for me to answer the door," Robert mumbles. "It's an ordeal to get up and down the stairs. Actually, I'm sleeping in the front guest room, because it's just too much to get all the way up to our bedroom . . ."

He recovers the verbal slip, averting his eyes.

10 ◆ WHERE TWO WORLDS TOUCH

"My bedroom. If it's alright with you, I really need to lie down for a bit."

Seeing this ebullient, expressive man's *élan vital* wicked away, his very lifeforce sapped, rattles me through.

"C'mon, then," I slip an arm around his gaunt frame. Together we slowly ascend the stairs, one step at a time, as he clings to the century-old wooden banister for additional support.

"I'm sorry there's no food in the house. I was going to ask Matt and Rich if they could get me a few things but . . . "

"Don't be ridiculous," I hush him. "I'll take care of it this afternoon."

"Sorry, love, I know you must be knackered from the long flight. We can have dinner delivered if it's easier on you . . . "

"Stop fussing, Robert. I'll take care of everything."

"I know . . . you always do," he says weakly, breathing hard and clutching the rail.

At the top of the stairs, we pause. Winded, leaning upon me, he considers his next action.

"Will you help me to the top floor? I'd rather sleep in the big bed."

Leadenly, we go up the narrower steps to the uppermost floor, a refurbished loft with master bedroom and miniature *en suite*. Large skylights in the sloped ceiling pivot open for fresh air, offering a view over the rooftops and wintry, bare trees of Wimbledon. In the distance, a ceaseless aerial parade of jumbo jets descending towards Heathrow. The room appears much the same as before, with the canopied teak bed at its center, now sporting an unfamiliar botanical print duvet cover. Photos of us on the side tables and dresser have disappeared. And other men have slept here since I left.

He rests on the edge of the bed, exhausted from the effort of climbing both sets of steep stairs, his chest heaving. I help him get recumbent, swinging his legs up. For a second, I hesitate, unsure, then lie down alongside. My right arm around his emaciated body, and left limb crooked beneath my head on the feather pillow. Long minutes pass resting together silently. Breathing in, breathing out. Familiar and odd to hold this man once more. My body still vibrates with a gentle buzz from a dozen hours of air travel to reach the other side of the globe. Ungrounded and airy. Further unraveled by the shock of my ex-partner's condition, and haunted by ghosts lingering beneath this roof.

Cradled by the quietude of the house, the rustic charm of Santa Fe and vast expanse of my beloved high desert seems a world away. Here, the low drone of the metropolis surrounds us, millions of people living in proximity. I *feel* it acutely. Lying beside my friend, tiredness weighs heavily in my limbs and eyelids, yet an inner voice prods me to get up and go for provisions. Having not eaten during the flight, if I eat at normal mealtimes today here in England, and stay awake until evening time, tomorrow I'll be suitably on Greenwich Mean Time without any jet lag. A slightly challenging travel protocol but works like a charm.

"I'm so sorry, River," Robert whispers, tears starting again. "Sorry for everything."

Only twice have I heard him use my middle name to address me, the name I started using last year after leaving for New Mexico. His recognition sounds slightly out of place, almost formal, as if addressing a stranger. Despite facing away from me, I detect the sincerity—an opaque truthfulness in the tone—and regardless of what has transpired, he remains a good man at heart. Crisis, in its dramatic way of transformation, forced him to confront his own soul. And his once impenetrable shell cracked open.

"I'm going to go get us some food," I say, rousing myself from the comfortable mattress lulling me toward tempting sleep.

"Where are you going? Not far, I hope . . . "

"No, probably just to Sainsbury's. I've missed England's lackluster grocery stores."

"Do you have any money? There's cash in my wallet by the front door. And your key is in the drawer of the hall butler . . . "

Placing a kiss atop his severely trimmed head, I rise and pull the folded duvet from under his feet to cover him, then make my way down the carpeted stairs.

Reaching the middle floor, I pause, drawn by an unvarnished pine door.

12 ◆ WHERE TWO WORLDS TOUCH

Turning the old-fashioned metal doorknob, peering inside, floral blue curtains still hang in the window, the ones I wanted to remove, and my campaign desk sits in place, overlooking the rear garden.

Here rests all I sorted, packed, and then waited long months for. My favorite books and cookbooks, *batterie de cuisine*, artwork, and treasures. Until the day I surrendered any time schedule or agenda for Robert shipping them, and simply went on with life. In light of my Zen-like existence the past twelve months, the room piled with cartons strikes me as practically absurd. Other than camping gear and a marble mortar and pestle dearly missed, contents of the boxes constitute a minor mystery. Memories and attachments of a previous life, stacked as brown cardboard cubes.

I shut the door and descend to the ground floor, my suitcases patiently waiting at the bottom of the stairs. I'll haul them up later. At the rear of the townhouse in the minuscule kitchen, the fridge stands bare: a container of pesto pasta salad from Marks & Spencer, a packaged medley of grapes and cut melon, a couple of strawberry-flavored yoghurt pots. No surprise, really. Even if Robert hadn't been in hospital for five weeks, he doesn't cook. A "friend" came by and tossed out anything too old or rancid. On the nearly empty shelves, the few lonely jars of condiments are brands I would never purchase. Nothing organic or *bio* in view, and the tub of whipped butter-substitute insults this Paris-trained chef. I require *real* butter in my house. Who knows the last time the man ate a decent meal, poor chap.

Conducting a quick inventory of the cabinets, I check for spices, olive oil, pasta, whatever may be found to assemble a meal. Not much. I've stepped into a house hardly lived in. A lucid dream, familiar and unfamiliar at the same time.

I used to joke despairingly the bathroom had more space than this kitchen. Larger galleys exist on sailboats. Outfitted in cheap, green IKEA laminate cupboards and countertops with a postage stamp-sized metal sink, the world's smallest dishwasher lives here, which I initially mistook for a trash compactor until opening it. As a cook's zone, perhaps the only redeeming grace is the petite hob and oven aren't electric but gas. I'm a tidy and organized chef, but the first time I prepared dinner for four in this closet, I nearly lost my mind.

The old door with etched glass accessing the rear terrace remains blocked with a wooden kitchen trolley I purchased to have additional storage and room to work. Beyond the window, the rear garden lays forlorn, not merely from winter's chill. Dormant brown grass, ragged and soggy. Patio furniture and large barbecue from John Lewis hulk silently under tarps, awaiting sunnier days and happier times. The lone pear tree leans nakedly bare, the cherry and apple trees similarly denuded along Mrs. Marshall's new wooden fence. To the back, the ivy-covered, ever-damp shed where the bizarre, electric hovercraft lawnmower dwells. Gazing out, I half expect the twittering birds who gathered daily on my patio, first in Taos and later in Santa Fe, will appear at any moment in a thrum of wings. Alas, they do not, and a stone of blue sadness weighs in my gut. Amid the tight grid of the city, absent too is any feeling of the wildness enfolding me the past year; my wanderings in rugged solitude, alive to my core with senses cast wide, catching the flash of sunlight on a crow's ebony wing.

I have returned to a house biding time: hoping for animating breath, the warm scents of good cooking and gracious meals, laughter, and conversations. *Healing*, in a word. In an eerie way, this residence personifies being overfed yet undernourished, so typical of our modern consumerist world; despite being stuffed full, it feels lifeless and empty. Want amid plenty. The knife of dear Kona's absence twists painfully in a barely closed wound in my heart, suddenly reopened and beginning to bleed. Too many slow, sad hours I stared forlornly through these windows, watching cold, dark rain streaming down the glass like tears as it drummed the terrace with ten thousand fingertips. A requiem of rain and grief.

Robert's same Mulberry wallet of fine brown leather rests on the mirrored hall butler, a piece we brought from the States. Two tall umbrellas, corralled by curved wooden side arms of the stand, lean lazily towards the wall. Looking into the silvered glass, I face my tired, forty-year-old reflection in the narrow mirror, contemplating the grey in my dark hair and goatee, shadows under my brown eyes. Have I aged since living here? Pulling open the drawer and picking up the set of house keys once mine, now with a different ornament dangling from their ring, I place them into a pocket of my trousers.

Garbed in *de rigueur* black wool coat, I wrap the cosseting cashmere scarf snugly, stash some English currency bills into another pocket, turn the brass lock on the front entry, and step out into the cold. The door closes behind me with its recognizable loud click. I cross the tiled patio to the small iron gate, swing it open and shut as I pass through, reacquainting with its rusty squeak, and from the shelter of the tall hedge emerge onto the street and turn left. Boot heels strike pavement with a solid, rhythmic cadence in the midmorning air—black Chelsea boots which, until a blur of hours ago, I've not worn since leaving London.

Familiar, this. Every bit of it.

Against all odds and expectation, I have returned to England, once again walking through a historic, densely populated neighborhood on my way to purchase groceries and a bottle of wine, thrown back in time.

Such strange fruit of circumstance. The currents of fate never fail to mystify me, elusive whispers of a larger plan. An *empath* and a banker, reunited. Ever the unlikely pair—the introverted, earthy neo-pagan-quasi-Buddhist and the extroverted, bright-eyed businessman—two men from different realms. What does it mean in the bigger picture, the enigmatic machinations of the cosmos.

I shake off my pensiveness and inhale a deep breath. Travel weary as I am, thoughts leap ahead to supper tonight. Cooking sets things right, particularly when a day goes sideways and awry. The sensory ritual of good fare tethers me securely in the moment. My professional-grade cookware remains packed in boxes upstairs but, no matter, I'll make do with whatever pans and tins I left for Robert in the kitchen. Tonight, and most nights going forward into the dimly foreseeable future, we will dine on simple, fresh, and reassuring food. Comforting. A free-range chicken possibly, its skin rubbed with butter or olive oil and roasted until bronzed and crackling, served with crusty, herbaceous roasted potatoes alongside. A salad of baby rocket topped with generous shards of well-aged Parmesan and red jewels of hothouse cherry tomatoes, if any worth eating at this time of year may be found. Robert almost never drinks wine, but it complements my dinnertime, so I'll pick up a bottle of something Old World—preferably French but perhaps Spanish. Making a proper dessert is out of the question, so we'll nibble on some fine dark chocolate like Green & Black's Espresso bars, addictive as sin.

My dear Robert. Unbelievably wounded in body and soul, in need of healing. His heart, too. Mine, as well. If we can find our way to forgiveness, then this strange return will prove something more than a mercy mission and serve a greater good. Invoking the best of our humanness seems a worthy aspiration.

A tear wets the corner my eye, and I quickly wipe it away, unsure whether the emotion arising is grief, joy, or an amalgam of both. At least we will begin our new chapter with a slow-cooked meal to nourish body and soul. A hot supper *à maison* with flickering candles and pleasant wine will be precisely right. Noisy ghosts in a weathered, narrow, and crammed house notwithstanding.

I pick up my pace to leave phantoms behind. Muscles purr contentedly at walking after interminable hours on the plane, eager to move and be in motion at foot speed—*soul speed.* The freedom from closely confining walls revives me, and another deep inhale helps clear my thoughts. Never mind the air smells of exhaust rather than fragrant juniper and piñon. Robert is undoubtedly asleep. I'll have a good walk and go farther to the High Street and shop at Bayley & Sage, the upscale grocer I used to like. The one with gourmet items, good vegetables, decent cheese, and a perpetually dour, unfriendly staff.

The wind feels cold but not arctic. Glancing up, expecting a pale moon or bright sun, no vista or painted horizon receives me. Somber clouds press down upon the tile roofs of timeworn buildings in all directions. Winter's light shines weak and anemic. My soul has landed incalculably far from the wild, fragrant mesa I love to roam; a barefoot dreamer with a foot in two realms, wishing upon the twinkling diamond stars.

Such a jumble of emotions, simultaneously longing *and* curiously content.

Packing up and starting over. Always bittersweet. The colorful gypsy wagon routinely rolls on to some hitherto unrecognized destination, but so it goes. I've no clear vision how this latest unforeseen twist of fate will unfurl or where we will end up, either of us. Healing must be summoned here, drawing upon the tenderness of a man's heart, where everything feels fragile and crystalline. Fraught with uncertainty.

With a dash of luck and helping of mysterious grace, somehow or other, things will turn out for the best.

Welcome back to jolly old England, River.

REACQUAINTING

THE INITIAL SHOCK of my arrival, confronted by Robert's shattered condition, gradually dissipates like foul weather. Both our lives are completely rearranged in a reality wherein everything feels delicate, yet the new scenario is held within contours of a familiar existence in greater London. These first weeks in December mark a gentle process of reacquainting, not merely with each other but similarly the routines and rituals which once comprised my days here.

Bit by bit, I reinhabit the narrow house and its dormant rear garden. I have not missed this dwelling. Never warm nor welcoming, the cold walls remain draped with the grey silk of sadness. Kona's absence strikes at my heart, catching me in undefended moments when I detect movement in my peripheral vision and turn, expecting him there or near my feet, standing on his long, graceful legs or sitting with one paw uplifted in a slightly affected but endearing gesture, those sweet dark eyes gazing up at me. Repeatedly, I attempt to ignore the voiceless ghost, wiping away a tear and resuming my task at hand, but his shade does not easily dispel.

In the Harry Potter cabinet under the stairs, sits the small front-load washing machine requiring hours to do even a modest load of laundry, ceaselessly spinning and humming. I have not missed this machine, either. The house lacks a clothes dryer, having just a clothesline, typical of much of Europe, and as before, routinely I must dash out to grab still-wet items whenever the clouds burst. Dozens of times, I departed on errands, or a trip into central London via train or Underground, on a clear day, only for

18 ◆ WHERE TWO WORLDS TOUCH

rain to arrive and soggy clothes greet my return, often wetter than when initially hung on the line. Reinhabiting a house with collapsible laundry racks for airing, and damp shirts hung over the corners of doors, while silvery precipitation falls outside, I casually accept it all.

Wimbledon has a distinctly different soundtrack from Santa Fe, to say nothing of the jewel box casita on the river in Taos where magpies cackled and called, peppering the wind among trees above a meditative gurgle of rushing waters. Here, my ear reacquaints with the morning parade of mothers pushing wheeled prams and shepherding uniformed children, noisily passing in front of the house on their way to school and day-care. The tall hedge on the front terrace provides a screen of visual privacy, but one hears the tapping of suited and booted heels along the sidewalk, an occasional *clickety* rolling of a suitcase going by, and the rumblings of diesel engines or delivery vans in the street.

As if it were an unpleasant neighbor, I avoid the car whenever possible, and the German sedan rests on the street a couple doors down. Robert mastered left side driving early on, whereas I found the challenge surprisingly stressful, my blood pressure rising, especially in the compressed confines of the city. Utterly content with him as my competent chauffeur, and in light of his preference to drive, the arrangement suits us both—though presently his frailty prevents him from even leaving the house.

Having a car requires tedious weekly parking permits, purchased from the local borough council, and the necessity of having a valid one displayed inside the windscreen. Autos sit parked tightly on both sides of the street, facing either direction, leaving only a narrow passage of road, and if a driver encounters an oncoming vehicle, one must reverse to a place where the other can pass. The first time moving the car on my own, needing to relocate it for a parking permit issue, as feared, I met a delivery truck, forced to retreat backwards along the slender street and then parallel park on the unfamiliar side, like doing everything backwards or in a mirror. Completely flustered, when I finally wedged the sedan in its new spot, back inside the house, I promptly poured myself a glass of elegant, flinty Sancerre irrespective the day hadn't quite reached noon.

A tactile sensualist navigating the world by heart, my *atelier* is the kitchen, the center point for tending hearth and home. I reclaim the minuscule space, after unpacking the boxes upstairs containing my culinary possessions, their contents returned to previous stations in the cheap IKEA cabinets and drawers. Given the limited countertop, and my aversion to clutter, only a few key tools and items earn the special privilege of being out on display, ones I employ regularly but also for their aesthetic appeal and *feel*. Accompanied by the wooden block of well-honed German knives, the select assemblage—two mortar and pestles, a half-liter glazed earthenware bottle from Huilerie J. Leblanc holding good olive oil, a classic-style cranberry-hued pepper mill, and two palm-sized bowls cupping different salts—reveals a certain French-schooled chef has returned and delicious things will be enjoyed once more at table.

All strangely familiar, as if I never left.

Three former rituals are distinctly absent this second round of living in London. On Fridays, we usually went to Piccolino or the Fox & Hound in Wimbledon, celebrating the end of Robert's workweek and giving me a night off duty in the kitchen. Now, we stay snugly in the relative warmth of the house on a winter day or night, where I read books and my friend rests. Come suppertime, the dining room invites us graciously with a couple of flickering candles and soft music playing. Far more tranquil and cozier than any restaurant, and with food equally appetizing, if not better.

Missing too, my daily walks with Kona to the open expanse of Wimbledon Park, where we circumnavigated the perimeter, stopping to observe the ducks he found fascinating, or children from a distance, much more distressing. Part of me feels gratefully liberated from this domestic duty, seated comfortably indoors in unkind weather, yet I secretly miss our excursions—and our dear little dog more so.

During the final months of our earlier life, most evenings I sat alone in a depressing ritual of dinner growing cold while awaiting Robert, late as

20 ◆ WHERE TWO WORLDS TOUCH

usual. Dejectedly, I stared at a dark sky mirroring my mood, watching pewter rivulets streaming down the French doors of the dining room, poured myself another glass of wine, and eventually dined solo—rewarming my mate's portion when he ultimately arrived. The embers in my heart faded, steadily burning down into white ash.

Whether the house, the absence of Kona, or simply returning through space and time to a life left behind, a hovering melancholy stalks me—like a faint scent in each room I enter, or a disincarnate entity trailing alongside, brushing my cheek or nape of the neck with a chilling touch. Since the morning of my return, an abundance of memories exists here, taking up space, but only a handful bring joy or a smile.

Desperately, I want to create new, brighter ones.

⌒⌣

Most significantly, the first weeks yield an opportunity to reacquaint with each other. On extended medical leave from his West End role with Lloyds, unable to work, Robert rests on the sofa, wearing his blue Hamburg jumper, as Brits casually call sweaters and pullovers. A diligent overachiever, via phone he checks-in daily with his team; ignoring their protestations, their encouragements to rest and heal, their assurances English banking can survive without him a while longer.

As the financial world crashes in scandal, my former partner is not among the ranks of investment bankers raking-in obscene salaries and bonuses; the ones escaping prosecution for their criminal behavior, who, with pockets and portfolios bulging, will be discreetly relocated to Hong Kong to escape the hastily implemented, so-called *bankers' tax*. Wedged firmly in the middle tier, managers like Robert and his colleagues daily endure the public's wrath, and ultimately take the fall for the greedy ones higher up.

His position feels secure, overall, despite being tied to a work visa and contract. Robert's health crisis manifesting in England is a curious wrinkle of mystery and grace; the combination of national medical and private supplemental insurance covered nearly all the expenses for his five-week stay in a single-occupancy hospital room. Had his illness occurred in America, the astronomical, unregulated costs would be crippling, and probably he would have lost everything, job included.

Our initial days together feel easy and effortless, the way our connection usually felt until the final months. In all the long years, we seldom quarreled or stood at odds. Early in our coupling, we learned effective, interpersonal communication—a cornerstone for any solid relating—along with some basics of developmental character strategy; an understanding of how a person's behavioral patterns and belief systems form through childhood, and the dynamic ways those interact and create systems in relationship thereafter. Emotional attunement—a *felt* sensitivity for the other's experience, mood, or emotional affect—another fundamental aptitude, which, like skillful communication, generally must be learned, came easily enough for both of us. Indeed, for an *empath* like me, it's simply an innate ability. And while these skills and maps didn't resolve all our issues or make everything perfect, as tools they helped immensely.

Decidedly not strangers to each other, both of us have transformed during a year apart. Beyond his physical transformation to a pallid wisp, Robert is a man gravely altered; slowly emerging from an Underworld journey—the sort in mythic adventures where the hero descends, willingly or not, into the shadowed realms to face an impossible task. Dismembered, possibly. A quest from whence he or she returns profoundly changed, curiously reborn, and perchance carrying some boon or talisman bestowing extraordinary powers. Or, similarly, in pan-cultural traditions of the oft-termed *vision quest*, when an individual spends extended time alone in nature as an initiation or rite of passage, abstaining from food to purify and to facilitate entering a state of higher awareness, the experience changes them. Something essential—a gift or aptitude, a spirit being or guide, a vision—reveals itself. Further, society understands the one who returns from the mountain *is not the same as the one who went out.*

Other than his very life, what this dear, changed man has returned with, only time will reveal.

December days pass sitting together in the cramped reception, each with our respective books and cups of tea, the single radiator by the front window cranked high but the room barely warm. Robert falling asleep repeatedly on the couch. He is tender and breakable, just emerged from a chrysalis or womb. Wet and exhausted from the trauma and tremendous effort of birth, like a newborn in need of nurturing and protecting. More acutely sensitive than ever before, too much coarseness or shaken abruptly, he would promptly fall apart. Even as an *empath*, I can hardly imagine his ordeal: alone in a hospital bed for weeks, facing his mortality in a foreign country far from primary family, with only an occasional visit from his distressed cousin in Wales or a single nervous friend. Indubitably, the trial has realigned his soul's compass.

I too am rearranged after stepping away from sixteen years together— recast by a solitary existence in the high desert of New Mexico. Under a bright dome of sky, across a vastness of rugged, pastel-hued land, I roamed through gnarled piñon trees and scented sagebrush for hours upon end, bearing my heavy grief. Elemental voices of wind called me while giant ravens swept above with guttural laughter, as my tightly sutured self split open. Lost was a long-term relationship, cherished dog, and my identity. Enfolded by an arid, untamed landscape, my spirit roused from a fitful slumber; an ineffable part of myself first discovered years ago living in a shaman's adobe tower on the juniper-clad mesa west of the Rio Grande gorge. Something non-domesticated. Vaguely magical. Unapologetically nonconformist and counterculture.

Departing London, a bone knowing guided me back to my haunt of Taos as the place to start over. Practicality be damned. And when I arrived at the foot of the sacred mountain, the dancing ground of the sun, in choosing to walk a wild, difficult way, I knew solace and healing would find me. I stepped into the inner fire of *soul initiation*, surrendering to the rough, timeless hands of nature in an uncivilized embrace, reclaiming and awakening my most authentic self.

Together in the Edwardian townhouse once more, both of us wish to welcome the fledgling part of each other, understanding one needs time to

REAQUAINTING ◆ *23*

find their wings. Or perhaps, like a slender, pale shoot, planted gently and watered to take root and grow.

"You're wearing your wedding ring," Robert observes on the third or fourth day of my return.

A glance down at the flashy band purchased ten years earlier when we moved from Colorado to the Big Island of Hawaii; a bespoke gold circlet inlaid with three squares of luminescent, blue Australian fire opal alongside three diamonds.

"It's a stunning piece of jewelry. I enjoy wearing it, but it doesn't fit on my right hand," I shrug nonchalantly. "Sometimes I wore it in New Mexico just because. I guess now it symbolizes a commitment to help get you back on your feet."

A tear glints at the edge of his eye, but he turns away so I won't catch the full measure of feelings. Much remains unsaid between us. Subterranean rivers of words and betrayals. We both walk gingerly, one measured step at a time, testing the waters. The old wounds lie barely beneath the skin, ready for release and forgiveness.

A day or two later, he too is wearing his ring again.

On a freezing and dreary afternoon, each cradling an English blue and white porcelain cup filled with malty tea, Robert's with milk, I share my clairvoyant vision.

"Shortly after you rang me in Santa Fe with the fateful phone call, I sat down cross-legged on the shaggy white rug in front of the kiva fireplace in my casita, where my nightly piñon fire crackled. I conducted a long-distance healing session for you, energetically connecting to your etheric template while The Team did their work. As I held the connection intently, *seeing* you resting in a hospital bed, thousands of tiny white bubbles—as if all the marauding microbes were encapsulated—rose from your spine and floated clear of your physical body. And in those seconds, I *knew* you would live."

Emotion floods his blue eyes.

"The pain of your leaving, the intense ache in my back, spending five weeks alone in hospital contemplating my own death or the possibility of it

... all just shattered me. This infection lodging in my thoracic spine, right behind my heart, it's no surprise, really. I knew it was my grief manifesting in a powerful, dramatic way."

Post-hospital X-ray and CAT scans reveal the invasive bacteria wreaked havoc on his upper mid-back. Two intervertebral disks are mostly eaten away, along with considerable damage to the vertebrae itself. His primary doctor advocates surgery to fuse the spine and speed the mending process, but after many years married to a stalwart advocate of alternative medicine, my comrade is dubious of the surgical approach and seeks other, less invasive options.

"It should fuse eventually on its own," another specialist says, delivering a ray of hope, "but you're going to have a year or two, perhaps longer, with considerable pain."

Currently, only a high level of opiate-based medication dulls the knife of agony and intense throbbing in his back. Seeking to support a fragile Robert in every way, I regularly encourage him.

"You can get to the other side of this without surgery. When you're ready, I'll give you some bodywork ... maybe we can even find a warm pool for Watsu and aquatic sessions."

Too soon for massage on his back, he protests. Yet gentle hands-on work and mild stretching holds the key to escape from the cage of a chronic pain cycle, which I foresee may trap him. Nevertheless, I back off from my agenda and let the matter wait until he feels ready.

At times, helping him up the stairs, or when leaning on me for stability as he dresses, he says weakly, "You're my savior."

Each time he utters the proclamation, I shake my head in disagreement, a visceral tightening in my gut.

"No, I'm not. That's way too big a projection for anyone to carry, and I am certainly not taking it on. Much as I want to be virtuous and noble. You've come through the abyss on your own, *mon ami*. Now you just need to heal."

We sleep together each night in the uppermost bedroom in the great teak bed, me holding him gently, but our connection remains strictly platonic. He is too feeble for sex, regardless if one of us desired it.

"I'm not interested in being lovers," I decree one rainy morning, sitting with our bowls of organic yogurt and muesli for breakfast, giving him an unsparing look. "I want to support and help you mend and rebuild, as a best friend, not an intimate partner."

A cluster of seconds slips away as he considers this pronouncement, silently contemplating the contents of his white cereal bowl.

"I know, love. I understand and truly appreciate what you're doing. You didn't have to come and be with me. Honestly, sex is the furthest thing from my mind. And I'm just so weak, I doubt my willy even works right now."

Reacquainting continues. Over and above the rituals comprising my previous life here, past customs and rounds beyond the house invite and beckon. At the Wimbledon Park farmer's market, I buy flowers from the smiling old gent wearing a rumpled sports jacket, no matter the weather. The modest assemblage in a school's car park constituted one of my "survival rituals," a term adopted from Marlena de Blasi, an American chef and food writer who moved to Italy to marry a Venetian, and subsequently penned lush memoirs of gilded prose. Standing behind collapsible tables arranged with local vegetables, fruit, jams and jellies, or whatever they sell, the vendors unwittingly helped my vessel stay upright in the currents of my aloneness in a foreign place, an oar and rudder guiding me back to the haven of the kitchen.

The humble gathering no longer feels like my survival ritual but a small, weekly source of delight—a personal connection with the food we eat, warming my soul in a way the anonymous big shops cannot. Not much selection in winter, even less *bio* or organic, but I go anyway, if only to support the vendors in some token measure by purchasing a few things: onions, carrots, turnips, chard, flowers. Ever since culinary school in Paris years ago, *la cuisine du marché*, market food, is my preferred way to cook; seeing what's available and fresh, plotting a course from there. Heirloom

26 ◆ WHERE TWO WORLDS TOUCH

varieties of produce particularly delight me, alluring with intrigue and character, encouraging more sensitivity in their preparation. Admittedly, the Wimbledon setup pales in comparison to the multisensory pleasures of the weekly *marchés* in France, or the glorious Santa Fe Farmers Market, my cherished weekend custom until only recently; a battered, woven French basket in hand, empty at the outset but brimming full and heavily laden with seasonal bounty on my return to the casita. Smiling, already scheming good things to cook and eat.

Be here now, River. Have gratitude for what you've got.

Bundled in black wool jacket and luxurious scarf, as before, the rattling District Line on the Underground ferries me to the bustle of High Street Kensington and my urban oasis: Whole Foods Market in the historic Barkers Building. A thirty-minute passage to central London via the Tube, each trip finds me lugging the limits of what I can tote in my sturdy jute bags.

Out and about on errands, I perch somewhere with a double cappuccino or a *flat white*, content to sit a while and observe. Absorbing the scene of London, mixed accents, and close-fitting, tailored English fashion, normal to me like I'd never left. I reacquaint with colorful, hustling Chinatown in SoHo, shopping for slightly obscure Asian ingredients not found in mainstream shops—tamarind pulp, black rice, galangal, makrut lime leaves, shrimp paste—momentarily pausing amidst the noisy swarm to marvel at living here again, a swirl of energy in my core. A slight elation, a faint flush to my cheeks and a little smile on my face, if also feeling overly stimulated. London endures as one of the world's greatest cities, but regardless of history and charm, throughout the earlier round of residence I shuttered my heart to it. As a *sensitive*, the teeming capital overpowered my nervous system. Even a brief foray into the crowded labyrinth compelled me to retreat in a mild stage of activation. Communal and claustrophobic, the flurry and hubbub of London itself became my opponent, pummeling me with fists of loud sound and diesel fumes.

Long on the run from dissonance and noise, moving to the largest city in Europe seemed something of an odd choice. Yet Robert's recruitment by Lloyds Bank brought opportunity to our door, and off we went on an international adventure. The blonde boy who grew up in southern Germany, and the dark-eyed Paris-schooled chef, carrying bundles of bright dreams and tattered disappointments, the two of us drifting apart but braided and bound together.

Intense is still the word for this city, all the buzz and commotion of a hive constructed of concrete and stone. Rather than tightening musculature and breath, pulling into my invisible shell, I strive to remain open. Breathing into my belly. Tensile instead of rigid. Submerged in chaotic energy, multilingual crowds, and the rumble of red busses, I lean into it—an intention made easier by a pair of wired earbuds plugged into my iPhone, weaving a sonic cocoon of music. Insulating me.

Flow, River, don't retract or constrict.

Sheltered in the relative tranquility of the Wimbledon townhouse, at the dining table I sit with a few well-read friends—*cookery books*, they're called here. My favorites celebrate the cyclical turn of seasons as a delicious, sensual affair. Celebrity compilations, the sort with superfluous, posed photos of the author on every page or so, I find distasteful. Far preferable are the cooks and chefs reflecting my love of understated, unfussy fare, even for dessert; the ones who let best-quality ingredients shine as themselves without excessive mucking around. *Fresh* wins me every time. My palate appreciates bold flavors, particularly with intriguing notes added by semi-exotic additions such as *harissa, sumac,* and *za'atar,* which I first encountered here. Seated with a steaming cup of tea beside me, feeling pleasantly civilized and at ease, I disappear contentedly into the familiar ritual of gathering culinary inspiration. An ongoing love affair with books. Finding delight in the simple, mundane moments, recognizing them as the quicksilver joys and sorrows of one's life. In the quietude, with Robert asleep, as I contemplate what simple, tasteful things might be put together for a meal—a life attuned to *making* rather than *doing*—the clamor and drama of modern existence fades out. All seems well in the world, at least in this tiny corner of it, my companion's broken condition notwithstanding. And delicious things, shaped and formed by my hands, will appear on the table to savor.

～

Like storm clouds appearing in an otherwise sunny sky, a penetrating sorrow for what took place in our first London round often overtakes my ex-partner.

"I'm so sorry." His eyes look puffy and bloodshot, as if from crying, and he stares down at his hands, repeating his penitent mantra. A wounded soul seeking forgiveness or salvation.

Usually, I shush him when he says this, dismissive, finding no point in reliving the past or wallowing in regrets. One day, however, at the end of lunch, he will not be silenced or dissuaded.

"I was such a fool . . . " he says from a misty place inside, "but I couldn't see it until you left. Not until that final night when you sat here at the table crying, and I realized for the first time you *really* loved me. I felt consumed by work, trying to figure things out and stay afloat at the bank where no one wants to help the gay American or see him succeed. Swimming with sharks, that's what it is . . . or having a target on my back."

Walking down some lonely street within himself, his blue eyes fade into grey melancholy. Outside the French doors, an ill-tempered and icy wind shakes the naked trees of the rear garden. Remains of a baguette sandwich sit on our plates: roasted red capsicums layered with creamy young goat cheese and fresh rocket, the toasted bread's cut surface smeared with pungent homemade *aïoli* and chipotle-olive tapenade. Warmed in the oven briefly, served with a pile of kettle chips, for a boldly flavorful, vegetarian lunch on a gloomy day.

"I was chasing money and the good life, the one that seemed finally within reach. Meanwhile you hated it here, hated everything about this place."

Pulled into the past, he shakes his severely trimmed head, dragged down by an emotional undertow for a minute, until he resurfaces and finds my steady, clear gaze.

REAQUAINTING ♦ *29*

"I really thought *you* were the misguided one with his head up his arse, sleeping in the dirt of the wilderness on one of your *vision quests*, when actually I was on the wrong track all along."

"It's rather bitterly ironic," I concur, one eyebrow arched and a wistful, weak smile.

"In the hospital, what kept going through my head, over and over, was how much I didn't want to die in cold, grey England . . . alone. And I didn't wish to be without you. It was so clear—and incredibly painful—I had made the biggest mistake of my life. And you were gone, a world away in New Mexico and never coming back."

He swallows another wave of emotion, briefly looking away. The air of the room hangs dense and silent, the walls and teak cabinets leaning close to listen. Some part of me relishes his words, vindicated. Yet our situation was undeniably a two-way street, and I played a significant role in the complicity. The pressures of living in London—both of us outsiders, Robert struggling to succeed in his high-profile role while I twiddled at home alone without work or friends—these were merely the catalyst. Or the crucible, perhaps. And only after leaving, in my hermetic time of introspection, after many years of pointed criticism not only of Robert but of myself, masking my own buried anger, did a crucial insight enlighten and humble me.

Criticism doesn't build love, only erodes it.

"Maybe you're judging yourself a bit too harshly." I reach to touch his pale, dry hand. "We've always gotten stuck in the pattern of trying to take care of each other."

"That's true. I think I finally decided, to hell with it, I'll just do my own thing, even if it breaks my heart, which was already quietly breaking, anyway. I would go on and grab the golden life in London I wanted, and maybe you would get your act together and share in what was offered to us here . . . or not."

Fixedly, I hold him with my eyes across the gleaming, dark wood table, half-registering the unfinished bit of sandwich and crumbs on the plate before him.

"You broke my heart into a hundred pieces, Robert. It's such a sad

30 ◆ WHERE TWO WORLDS TOUCH

mystery our journey together as partners somehow carried us in opposite directions. The blue-eyed opera singer I fell in love with so many years ago was abducted by a corporate businessman in a suit—a banker, no less. Your sight became fixed on the dangling prize, wanting to make a comfortable life for us and help your mom in her old age in a way artists can almost never achieve. Some people would say your ambition was noble, or, at least, the way of the modern world. Yet *my* path continued to be about healing and the soul. The deeper, mysterious journey of being alive—the relevance of personal transformation and *individuation*, as Jung would call it. I've loved you for years, but things simply reached the point where we could no longer authentically support the other's directive. That's the crux of it, I think. Our goals and dreams became mutually exclusive, and neither of us wanted to go where the other was headed."

"You were on the right journey all along."

Such a huge admission on his part, testament to the powerful changes overtaking and breaking him open. Validated, at last, I feel my abdomen relax and breath deepen, unlocking a conducive state for an honest exchange.

"I'm not sure there is a *right* journey," I shrug, brown eyes limpid, "other than the one at our feet, calling us forward. And there's no villain in our story. I still believe you were *meant* to be in London, and if I hadn't agreed to accompany you initially, you wouldn't have come. Somehow all this . . . " hands gesturing wide to the dining room's glass doors and chilled winter garden beyond, "our breaking apart, losing Kona, your illness and 'dark night of the soul,' it too was meant to happen."

Gently, I enclose his hand resting closest to me on the table, thin but warm within my own. For an extended minute, silence gathers its robes around us. Robert nods in agreement.

"Do you think there's a chance for us in the future?" he asks in a tone lodged somewhere between lament and hopefulness. "As partners, I mean . . ."

With a light squeeze, I release his hand and draw back.

"Probably best to not look very far down the line. Let's just focus on getting you strong again and back on your feet without raising the stakes."

Sadness darkens his face as he retreats into an inviolate place somewhere deep inside. My response isn't what he wishes to hear, but within the confines of a squeezed, tall house, I'm speaking my truth.

～

In a southwest borough of London, sequestered within old brick walls, a sedate rhythm guides the drab December days and our incipient weeks together. Television, that blatant and rude intruder, we banished long ago from our house, but occasionally we watch a movie. Keenly sensitive, Robert desires nothing of violence or drama, neurotic people, or cheap humor—effectively ruling out the bulk of Hollywood offerings. Mostly he wishes to go to bed early.

Following dinner, after I've done the washing up, I go upstairs to the guest bathroom to prepare him a healing soak. Opening a glass-front wooden cabinet holding an assortment of pure, top-grade essential oils, I concoct a *synergy*, pulling upon my background as a trained aromatherapist—blending scent-ual potions and balms for private clients, including the exclusive Four Seasons Resort on Maui. On my own skin, one might detect lingering bass notes of favorite woods, resins, and roots—Atlas cedarwood, frankincense, spikenard, vetiver, sandalwood—chosen not simply for pleasing scent but their grounding and centering qualities.

Factoring Robert's physical pain but likewise his emotional stress, my selection differs nightly but nearly without fail I reach for the high-altitude lavender from the Alpes de Haute Provence, an adaptogen and all-around balancer. Moreover, it *feels* right for him. Citrus, too, for a zesty, energizing note, and he is fond of sweet orange, a powerful sedative but also uplifting. His therapeutic mix calls for an analgesic, possibly chamomile, both the Roman and German varietals, marjoram, rosemary, cypress, juniper, or eucalyptus. Something warming, more often than not. And though I draw from a mental and medical knowledge of distillations and their properties, an inner guidance also directs me: picking up the bottles wordlessly *calling* to me as if pushing forth in the cabinet for choosing. I swirl drops of aromatic, volatile oils into the hot water, inhaling the vitality of these plant essences and offering a silent blessing into the fragrant vapors.

After his steaming soak, skin flushed pink from the heat he adores, Robert haltingly ascends to the top floor bedroom. Tucked into the canopied bed, I read to him until he falls asleep, rarely more than five or ten minutes, and then lie awake beside the Underworld hero, the one returned from the edge of death. Flickering light from a bedside candle illuminates the appliqué white linen draped above us, and I stare up at shadows cast upon the creases and folds, seeing them as long, straight sled tracks in snow. The placid rasp of his breath becomes a meditation. Outside the sheltering walls, the low hum of the city drones on. Musing on this unexpected new life and the one I've left behind, gradually I succumb to dreamtime alongside a wounded man.

What dreams do we carry? The ones not laid aside or buried along the challenging road, thinking them too impossible or burdensome to shoulder any farther. Mine are shifting, briefly nearer but then receding into the distance. Dear old Taos and Santa Fe, my cherished *soul places* where, until mere weeks ago, I envisioned building a handcrafted existence—dwelling in a rustic, earthen house surrounded by pungent sage and chamisa beneath a blue sky, my hands and fingers weighted with Native American-fashioned silver and turquoise—that vision slips away. Caring for my once-mate, I have returned to a cold and wet island-nation in the frigid northern sea. Drifting once again. Unmoored.

Much of my life, I've followed an invisible but glimmering thread, unsure where it leads, knowing only I must keep ahold of it for my soul. At times, distracted, I lose sight or drop the filament completely, briefly lost until a whispering voice or the reassuring touch of something says, *yes, this direction*. And the body, ever knowing, has strangely guided me, often with a gut sense, a visceral tightness and restriction, or openness and ease— like a cosmic antenna attuned to something much larger than what I can detect or grasp. Trusting such intuitive and somatic impulses as my *mode de vie*, I find a way through thickets and brambles, making a path when one can't be found or followed. And thus, I've fashioned a life with my hands; laying them upon other people to lessen their constrictions and pain, and, for a while, as a chef for the rich and famous, creating beautiful meals. Only recently cognizant the golden thread weaves the spirit of *nourishment*, both of self and others.

Yet what is mine to bring to the world? My search continues, turning over stones to peer underneath, wandering amid noble trees, and contemplating distant constellations. Surely, I have more to offer than bodywork and healing arts, or the eco-depth-therapy of wilderness-based *soul work*. But where does the mysterious thread lead beyond this moment? I can't yet see or even guess.

Am I more myself in England, or less? Less, I think. My soul still roves a high desert and rumpled mountains far from here. Whether it will answer a summons home to my heart on this side of the Atlantic remains undetermined. Too long asleep and contained in familiar patterns, at the edge of a wild mesa, I woke to a sense of freedom. The raw, powerful land itself was the prime conspirator, prying open my restrictions and *dreaming* me with curious visions.

If I were able to summon it, unlikely the untamed part of me will stay alive in London. Possibly, I'd rediscover my wild, barefoot nature hiding behind hedgerows along a winding lane in the verdant English countryside. Once upon a time, Robert and I aspired to move out of the city when he better established himself in his role at the bank; settling in a quaint village or town from whence he would take a train into London for work while I tended things in a landscape more deeply nourishing to my overall being. Like City Mouse and Country Mouse in the children's story, one day we would find a precious in-between house. Instead, everything fell apart for us. And despite a rural landscape relatively close to hand, we remain city locked. Breath shallow and tight.

In the dark depths of winter, even for an *intuitive*, the future remains a mystery.

GHOSTS & TEA

BENEATH A LOW, encumbered sky, an ornery wind bullies me with gusty breaths. My ears sting from the harsh bite of frigid air, so I pull the silky warmth of scarf more tautly around my neck, bemoaning not wearing a hat, and lean into the aggressive zephyr as it darts between the naked trees. No child of winter am I.

Only a fool would be outdoors walking, grumbles the part of me who greatly prefers ease to hardship. *I should be tucked in a warm house, curled up with a good book and a pot of fine tea, contentedly civilized . . . but no.*

Leaving the muddy path behind, I head across an open stretch of Wimbledon Common, the semi-domesticated thousand-acre tract amid the sprawl of London's southwest region. A haven of relative wildness where unpaved footpaths interlace through stands of trees and open clearings, a scrubby heath, and public golf course. Here, between the leaf-bare copses, I find more room to breathe than the streets nearby of shouldered, orderly rows of Edwardian terraced houses where we live. No right angles or straight lines, no trimmed hedges or tidy gardens, only the jumbled interplay of nature's intricate order and interconnectedness. Living earth underneath my soles, not entombed in concrete, yielding with a mild spring to each passing step. Ignoring the distant but unceasing noise of vehicles, and the steady drone of giant planes descending towards Heathrow some fifteen miles away as the crow flies, one might briefly forget a sprawling metropolis of eight million people surrounds.

Just a few weeks ago, I was a native creature roaming alone for hours in a dramatically different landscape, my tan skin and greying hair scented with sagebrush and dust, nostrils flared to the fragrance of an afternoon thunderstorm building over aspen-clad peaks. Denizen of a locale to which I belong more than any other thus far.

Beneath my shoes, the sodden ground moans, slurps, and belches with too much water, and scouting for less boggy patches, I hop from one spot to another like a tall, two-legged frog in a puffer jacket. Considering my lack of Wellies or waterproof boots, the footpaths would be less treacherous, flooded areas notwithstanding. Yet rarely do I abide by their well-trafficked, rigid lines, heeding my allurement instead, meandering among the watchful trees and less-traveled spaces, because life brings interesting things when we depart the track.

My youthhood spent in greater Los Angeles as a well-groomed and uptight preppie twink, my soul awoke during my early twenties on an untamed mesa west of Taos. On a self-imposed, indefinite retreat from love and the world, dreaming of writing a novel, living in an adobe tower built by a Native American *medicine man* of Cherokee descent, surrounded by thousands of acres of the Carson National Forest, I befriended my inner hermit. Rather than penning anything worthwhile, however, an unanticipated seduction by the forms and forces of nature—the Wild Beloved—transpired in an epic unraveling. My self-contained, well-kempt existence, and tidy notions of reality fractured and expanded. A *sensitive* since childhood, unexpectedly the mystic nature of things—energies, entities, and voices—pressed forward to greet me at every turn. An awakening, of sorts, or a door opening within myself, never fully closing since.

Subsequently, no matter where I dwell, only by rambling in nature do I come home to my authentic being. Stepping out from customary structures, whether physical or mental, letting other senses guide me, walking somewhere wild or semi-wild, I wake, even briefly, from the consumerist, industrial trance holding the human world spellbound. On foot, immersed in the living milieu, I escape from the consensus reality.

Wimbledon Common is hardly *wild*, certainly not in a wilderness

36 ◆ WHERE TWO WORLDS TOUCH

sense, and long ages have passed since the mythic occupied this domain, the faerie folk and elementals. Regardless, I have immeasurable gratitude for its wordlessly sighing presence and moody expanse. Open space feeds the spirit. Returning to these ungroomed acres compares with meeting a good friend, albeit an unhappy one haunted by ghosts.

I yearn for my rugged, soul-stirring mesa, or the consolation of fields and woods beyond the city, but walking here, undeterred by the cold air and omnipresent hum of the modern world, my core expands. I'm closer to my wild, essential self—something more feral than fashionable—as if peering under my tailored shirt I might find tawny coyote fur instead of bare human skin. Traversing a blurred edge between the domesticated and non-domesticated, senses cast wide, I come home to myself once more.

For those of us who don't fit in, who know the difficulty of living with a foot in two worlds—sensing energies and entities, detecting the shimmering *aliveness* of things, knowing magic still exists but hidden within mundane forms—how keenly we feel the solace of unspoiled, untrodden places. Necessary to the spirit, I say.

Like a lover, Wimbledon Common draws me regularly. In the depths of winter, the open spaces and paths are uncrowded, and I walk for at least an hour, warmly attired in a winter coat, cashmere scarf, and wool cap rolled snugly down over my ears. Boots crunching loudly in an unhurried tempo along the gravelly paths. Breath forms clouds in the frosty air, and scent has disappeared in the cold. I punctuate my aimless rambles with periods of sitting pensively on frigid wooden benches, listening to the timeless ballad of the wind, until feeling too chilled and needing to move limbs again. How comforting this place, home to all manner of wild ones including owls, ducks, frogs, rabbits, foxes, crows, and uncountable birds—falcons, even—though here, too, the memory of Kona lingers.

Within two days of his disappearance, I have alerted north Wimbledon, Southfields, and Wimbledon Park that a fawn and white Italian Greyhound

GHOSTS & TEA ◆ 37

is missing. Robert goes reluctantly to work, distraught and distracted, while I affix notices with our darling dog's photo on every corner lamppost and traffic signal within two miles of the house. Singlehandedly, I push eight hundred adverts through the mail slots on the nearby streets in our neighbourhood. And I stand at the entrance to the Wimbledon Park farmers market for the entire duration of business hours; a corkboard with Kona's photos beside me, handing out flyers with our contact details, hoping someone has seen him.

For the first two days, calls come from people who have spotted our dog near a certain place, and I rush—desperately drive, even—to the vicinity and scour it. Timid, traumatized, and afraid of people, he keeps to the alleys between the rows of terraced houses. Calling his name, forcing my way through narrow, overgrown passages strewn with rubbish and debris, I meet only startled red foxes disturbed from their hiding places and dens.

On the third day, our lost companion is sighted on the Common, thus he has crossed several dangerous, busy roads. People report him running scared near the windmill—no collar, evading humans—and seeing the flyer I posted outside the Windmill Tearoom, they ring me. Long hours of cold days I spend roaming the heath, woods, and golf course, calling loudly, his favorite plush toy in hand, squeezing it repeatedly to make the distinctive bugle sound, hoping he will hear and recognize it. Heart torn from my chest, pockets bulging with dog treats and snot-soaked tissues, I sob for him, alone, scared, and hungry in the cold. Too, I weep for my own pitiful life ripping painfully at its seams.

A phone call from someone walking Putney Heath, north of Wimbledon Common and the busy A3 motorway, reporting our dog near the pond close to Roehampton Lane. Flying the distance in the car, I search the area for an hour. The day hangs grey and cold, with hope fading steadily. Dejectedly retracing my steps along the unpaved track to where I parked the car, still hoarsely yelling his name, an inner voice instructs me to turn around. A hundred and fifty yards behind me, a small but distinctive head peers out from behind a tree, looking in my direction. It's Kona, I'm certain. My heart pounds like a drum. I call out and start walking back, wanting to run his direction but sure it will scare him off now he has gone feral. The canine visage disappears, and I sprint down the path, keeping my eyes on where he appeared. Reaching the spot, I stand at

38 ◆ WHERE TWO WORLDS TOUCH

the edge of the trees, pinching his squeaky dolly in my hand as a beacon, calling him in a coaxing voice. He is gone. Gutted, I spend another twenty minutes in the area, crying, looking, and hoping. Begging whatever gods may exist, knowing this is my last chance to rescue him.

My grief at returning alone to the crammed but empty townhouse is nearly too much to bear. Mobile phone remains glued to hand, but no more calls come. Life goes quiet, dark, and cold.

We never saw him again.

During the weeks following the disastrous day in early October he was inadvertently locked out and scared off by the construction work next door, Robert and I driven even further apart, in the black pit of desolation, I envisioned Kona as the Little Master. Somehow our ultra-sensitive, precious dog had departed on his journey to propel me to finally embark on mine—the great leap I was reluctant to make. An outlandish thought, but what if his higher purpose was something more than merely a pet; rather a *soul agent*, with a contract as a catalyst. Just possibly. Even in my crushing sadness I wouldn't leave London, him, or his other daddy without an extreme event or soul crisis, so he gave me one.

Bless you, Little Master.

How we resist cracking open. The shredding of one's fibers never unfolds as a pleasant or painless experience. Yet sometimes no other way exists to emerge from a life too small other than breaking apart, gently or violently. Love will either shatter or build us into something greater, but often an initial wreckage is required.

More than a year later, roving the Common where I scoured stands of bare trees and muddy stretches for my lost dog, the searing agony slowly fades, though like a scar, the memory will never fully disappear. If there were a place less woeful to walk and nourish my wild soul I would but zigzagging through Wimbledon's open acreage is the only option close at hand. And despite a clinging heartache, the greater soul of nature mirrors my own changeling shape in tangled branches, ribbons of sunlight upon water, the lilting song of a meadowlark, or a raucous crow. Reluctant mystic that I am, the more-than-human world consoles and uplifts me.

GHOSTS & TEA ♦ *39*

England doesn't feel like home, though I'm unclear exactly what home means anymore. Perhaps it's only *hiraeth*, a wistful longing for something I may never find or recapture. The tall, squeezed house feels utterly familiar but strangely not my own, like a shirt outgrown that I gave away, or as if I'm only a guest—which in some ways rings true. Missing the *soulscape* of my recent life on an elevated mountain plateau in the American Southwest, wearing a pair of vintage, deerhide hand-stitched Taos moccasins when indoors at the townhouse, stalked by an indigo sadness, I carry a slight heaviness in my chest. Strangely interwoven with this, I feel an odd contentment, and focusing on that, my breath becomes easier with a gentle expansion. Can I simply inhabit the space of uncertainty and not belonging, without needing to change it?

Don't look too far down the road, River.

As an *empath*, I navigate almost solely by *feeling*—the invisible but entirely real messages of energy, mood, and sensation in my core. A more intuitive, curvilinear, and heart-centered guidance than a mental, linear, or rational one. From the mists of time, steeped in a sentient realm fully alive—versus a strictly material world reduced to inanimate objects—intuition served as a primary mode of knowing. Only in the past two centuries have the deductive intellect and reasoning become the vaulted method of determination—our seat of identity placed in the head rather than the heart. Smug in our anthropocentric naïveté, the power of reason has suppressed the world of mystery.

I've long wrestled with the labels of *clairvoyant, clairaudient,* and *clairsentient,* as people with my non-ordinary gifts are frequently called, whether by themselves or others. Such terms feel clunky, and often sticky with ego-inflated, pseudo spiritual self-importance, hence my preference for "intuitive." Or "empath." Moreover, I believe this *high sense perception* is simply a circuitry all humans possess innately; some of us are born with the circuits turned on whereas others aren't, but anyone can learn to activate them.

In spite of my perennial wandering and uprootedness, a relaxed knowing in my gut tells me things are right, exactly as they stand. At least for now.

Life has rearranged Robert and me. Irrevocably and for the better, I trust.

Most of my life, regardless of my sensitivity, I rarely cried. Rent asunder, from a bottomless well of grief I wept at losing a dear little dog *and* my long-term relationship within three cold months of each other. An unforeseen train wreck, both of us thrown in different directions, and one of us flying back across the frigid grey Atlantic. Nowadays, I suddenly become teary-eyed at the beauty of a thing, the preciousness of life and its fleetingness, touched by a luminous yellow rose, a dying bird, or a homeless woman on the street. Willingly devastated by the beauty and cruelty of the world. Celebrating through my senses this brief, sensual, and miraculous existence. Apparently, in the great breaking, I shed my protective armor, too.

Sharing space with Robert, irrespective of the past wounds we inflicted upon each other, a deep affection engulfs me, wide and true as a green river in springtime. My gaze softens as I observe him resting, or simply when together. A little smile on my face, leaning in closer to listen as he shares thoughts or a story. Laying a gentle hand on his knee or shoulder, with a friendly, caring squeeze. And a further lessening of my old judgements of him. His struggle—the daily pain, his ongoing weariness—evokes my compassion and empathy. Meanwhile, the first measures of improvement show themselves. Incrementally stronger, he reaches the upper floor on his own, surely an outcome of meals cooked with love and feeling nurtured instead of alone.

Now and then, a dysfunctional pattern briefly snags like a low-hanging branch or a submerged log, threatening to pull us into murky water. Still, we commit to neither reliving nor rehashing the past, and not dragging out the old hurts like tortured prisoners of war. Forgiveness is fundamental and essential. My genuine desire is only to support his recovery in whatever ways I might, and both of us wish to make a new start within the undefined parameters of dwelling together again these months and beyond.

Commotion outside in the night awakens me, disturbed by the now-recognizable bark of fox voices and a crash of breaking pottery. A fight or fucking. Both, maybe, in foxy fashion, and soon enough I fall back asleep. Come morning, opening the front door to put a bag of rubbish into the bin on the terrace, the pretty garden pot lies smashed, soil scattered across the vintage black and white tiles, with odiferous scat on the threshold. The wild ones have greeted me since my initial arrival in London—the very first night in this house.

In the darkest hours, I wake to a strange cry. Again, it repeats. My sleepy mind places the disturbance outside or perhaps next door. Nothing to worry about. A curious sound, decidedly non-human. Was I simply dreaming? No, once more the stillness breaks, something between a bark, a rasp, and a plaintive wail. Again, I hear it, and then again. I rise from the warm cocoon of bed, naked and fumbling for my eyeglasses, and peek through the window blinds to the shadowed street below.

At first, I see only stationary cars along the road, but movement catches my eye. From beneath a parked VW Touareg, an animal emerges. Larger than a cat, with upright triangular ears and a bushy tail, reddish brown in the ochre glare of the streetlights. Groggy from international travel, disoriented, my brain takes a minute to connect the dots. Fox! Heart skips a beat. The creature turns its head and sniffs the air, then calls out with the non-human voice that roused me from deep slumber. Trotting down the empty street, the four-footed transient disappears, leaving me nude and peering through the window, grinning at such a marvelous way to arrive in London. A fox at our doorstep. How brilliant.

Canids aren't overly popular in England, many people regarding them a nuisance. Nowadays, the traditional fox hunt, a gentlemen's pastime with hounds and horses, is outlawed. Their numbers and ability to survive in the city amazes me, even more so than the adaptable and resilient coyote in

America. They reside in the rear of gardens, underneath sheds, and in junk-filled alleyways between buildings, where I met several during the desperate days of looking for Kona. From time to time, our bins get knocked over at night, their contents strewn across the terrace tiles and down the street, but personally, I admire the creatures' resourcefulness. And they like takeaway dinners as much as everyone else.

Mirroring my previous London round, I encounter foxes regularly. Indeed, it's uncanny how often one crosses my path, as if a spirit guide or messenger. On my journeys out, commonly one disappears round a corner, a final flick of its tail catching my eye. While I wait on the platform at Wimbledon Park station, one will wander alongside the tracks farther down, sniffing around. And from train windows as I pass, they scratch and sun themselves beside bramble patches.

The shaggy coyotes *yip yipping* outside my Taos casita, laughing and singing at the silver moon, similarly leaving shit on the doorstep, have been swapped for tenacious foxes in the urban grid. In world myths, both animals are clever tricksters and storytellers, though feasibly Fox is marginally slyer and more magical than his American cousin. A fair trade, and their presence uplifts me with a bit of nonhuman wildness in the city.

"Bless their furry paws," I mutter, a pail of sudsy water in hand to wash away the rank fouling on our terrace.

~

Wild ones aside, my rituals comfort. The unassuming daily ceremonies, whether deemed the *survival* sort or otherwise, which, for me, comprise the *art of living*. Deliberate acts to nurture *bodysoul*, like cooking a meal to please loved ones, a stroll outdoors through autumn's painted leaves, or puttering in the garden and feeding the birds. A nourishing life doesn't happen of its own accord or by accident, nor only with financial abundance, but through cultivation and tending. And for years now, my old-fashioned soul has deliberately built a hand-crafted life—a mindfulness and attention to detail, attuned to texture, taste, sound, ambiance, and overall feeling—a life for the senses, always an eye towards soulful nourishment. In our rushed and harried society, choosing to pause for a moment, allows us to step out from the currents of busy doing and frenetic gratification.

Prior to our move to England, I already drank tea religiously; a devotee of whole, loose leaves of *camellia sinensis* brewed in a teapot, or the "cut, torn, and curled" leaf pellets simmered on the stove for authentic chai. Many of my first London explorations were forays to locate decent teashops, something akin to Mariage Frères in Paris, always dear to my heart. Finding my way to Chelsea, Notting Hill, and the West End, bombarded by the bustle of the city, what I found mostly disappointed me. I imagined a world of fine tea, thus how sobering to find London is a realm of coffee drinkers: Costa Coffee, Caffé Nero, and the ubiquitous Starbucks everywhere. Adding insult to injury, green or white tea—appreciated for the delicate, almost ethereal taste of less-oxidized leaves—is unpopular, and a challenge to find any of real provenance. For most Brits, "white tea" means their standard brew loaded up with milk. What a pity. Tea may be the national beverage but, overall, a lowly sort, brewed from cheap sachets of broken-up remnants of better-quality leaves. *Tea dust*, producers call it. The crushed bits yield a brew high in tannins, and to draw out the flavor, the infusion steeps too long and turns bitter, requiring milk and sugar, consequently all nuances lost. *Builder's tea*, so termed for the blue-collar workers who chug the strong, tannic brew all day long, is decidedly not my taste.

Green, white, and oolong varietals, loaded with antioxidants and health benefits, offer their own sort of ritual when brewed in an Asian-style vessel and sipped from a round, handle-less cup. Nevertheless, I find a genteel charm in English tea service, even if it's really an excuse to eat something sweet. At home, both in the morning or afternoon, tea marks a time to set aside my troubles—or continue steeping them, maybe. A pot of quality, intact leaves, skillfully brewed, delivers not only a less-acidifying cup than a mug of coffee but also an experience more soothing than stimulating. An opportunity to sit and imbibe the moment, contemplating the sky outside or emotional weather within. Inviting breath to settle into my belly with an exhale and sigh. Shoulders softening and dropping down in relaxation.

WHERE TWO WORLDS TOUCH

My mate wasn't a tea drinker until arriving in London, whereupon he swiftly learned the beverage is unquestionably regarded as an indispensable part of the workday. A line item in the department budget, no less. Tea is required at any staff meeting, and Julia, his assistant, routinely pops into his office to enquire whether he would like a "cuppa."

For the first month of my return, with Robert at home, we enjoy teatime together. Cake with tea borders on national obsession, and the list of British favorites is lengthy, but traditional, frosted confections seldom tempt me. Too cloyingly sweet. A bit of seasonal fruit dolled up with flaky, golden pastry will *always* score my interest. Much as I enjoy baking, I'm not always inspired to do so, and we generally have buttery shortbread biscuits stashed in the cupboard. Purchased and convenient.

Placing the kettle on the hob, I arrange half a dozen Duchy Organics gingerstem biscuits on a plate, fill a dainty porcelain pitcher with milk, tumble some French cubes of unrefined sugar cane into a small bowl, and set the lot alongside two blue and white porcelain cups on matching saucers on a battered wooden tray. My buddy prefers his brew milky and sweet, accompanied by something to nibble on for a treat.

"I love teatime," he grins daily, munching a round of shortbread, blue eyes sparkling. "It's one of the very best things about living here."

"Agreed," I nod, sipping my cup of unadulterated, amber brew. "Now if only we could have a bit of sunshine."

"I hate to tell you, but that's not bloody likely."

Alas, probably not, so let there be tea. And sweet little biscuits.

Improved from wraithlike but still thin and frail, definitely not ready to face the office but determined to do so, Robert returns to work. Less for any real concerns of job security or being on sick leave too long, more for a need to reconnect with his team and fulfill his leadership role. The Good Boy Scout, I've called him, an inner character in myself, too. I'm gravely concerned the bank will quickly steal the modest measure of strength he has regained. Given the damage of two intervertebral discs eaten away, the compression from sitting or standing more than a short period brings extreme discomfort, and he consumes high amounts of pain medication. How on earth will he manage at his desk job?

"I think mostly I'll stand," he says weakly, tightening the knot of a conservative blue and red tie around his neck. For a brief flash, the strip of patterned silk is a hangman's noose cinching up tightly. I read the pain on his face, the hunched shoulders, restricted chest, and shallow breath. A deep-set reluctance and grim resignation.

Bless him.

With my comrade gone back to the bank's regime, the tightly jammed house feels eerily lifeless and cold. In my earlier life here, Kona kept me company. Having no one to focus on except myself, wrapped in quietude, once again I have the gift of *time*; more than needed for usual errands for provisions, roaming the Common, and preparing our meals. Unquestionably, my wide-open schedule constitutes a luxury, free of the demands of seeing clients or even real work other than supporting Robert a few months longer. London offers a wealth of interesting attractions and diversions, and I appreciate what the city offers, particularly for gourmet food and fine restaurants, excellent bookshops, arts and culture. Yet despite a newfound willingness, the city still feels intense to my finely-tuned nervous system, so mostly I remain at home other than for specific runs and searches.

No stranger to silence, I have long thrived on solitude. Sporadically, however, I muse how pleasant it might be to have a friend, even an acquaintance nearby, who would call in for a *cuppa*, delivering friendly, human company during an otherwise hushed day. For better or worse, no one knows me here. I lead an outsider's existence where, apart from Robert, my only social interactions are exchanging money at the till of the supermarket or a coffee shop.

Wimbledon Common. My ritual of walking amongst barren trees. Hungry for sunlight and warmth, beneath the ever-leaden sky, I encounter first heralds of spring: the small white flowers called snowdrops, followed

46 ◆ WHERE TWO WORLDS TOUCH

a few weeks later by pixie cups of purple and gold crocuses, and at last the trumpeting daffodils—cheery as sunshine on a stem.

One cold and windy day, holding a tall, fastened umbrella in hand mimicking a gentleman's cane, a blue melancholy circulating in my veins, I stop to gaze at a chorus of the golden bells on their lanky stalks in a tangled patch of brown briars. Concurrently, a phalanx of geese passes overhead calling loudly, evoking a stanza of words from "Wild Geese" by the Pulitzer prize-winning American poet, Mary Oliver. *You do not have to be good. You do not have to walk on your knees for a hundred miles in the desert, repenting. You have only to let the soft animal of your body love what it loves. Tell me about despair, yours, and I will tell you mine.*

Hearing the words in my mind, *despair* seems too strong a descriptor for my mindset in this new passage, though shadows gather at times. Aloud, I speak the poem's closing lines to the listening trees, ribbons of thorns, and the turmeric-hued daffodils.

"Whoever you are, no matter how lonely,
the world offers itself to your imagination,
calls to you like the wild geese, harsh and exciting—
over and over announcing your place
in the family of things."

Snared in a geometric web of city streets, even here on the Common a loneliness encircles me for the untamed earth. Acutely, I miss wandering the chamisa-strewn plain bordering my elegant casita on the Rio del Ranchos de Taos; under an impossible expanse of cerulean sky, unsheltered and untethered, my breath commingled with alluring scents of juniper, piñon, and sunbaked earth. Exiled from the Land of the Thunderbolts, a vastness of undisturbed nature at my doorstep, summoning me to receive the timeless blessings of trees and rainstorms. In flying across the sea to aid my former partner, I've severed from a soul-infused life where I took my tea with a party of little birds, followed cougar prints through the snow—wondering who was stalking whom—and delighted in the antics of loudly zooming, iridescent hummingbirds. Finding my way into the heart of the world. Gathering sun-bleached bones in washed out arroyos or finding them scattered beneath a gnarled and squat evergreen tree—carrying pocketsful of intriguing stones and skeletal bits back to my brick patio, arranging them by the front door like some shaman's hut, a portal between realms. An evocative threshold of life and death.

Only bones remain.

Something of a malcontent, in following the mysterious golden thread, I've frequently longed to be elsewhere, a profound unsettledness in my core. A sense of home eludes me. For years, Robert and I half-joked "On The Road Again" was the theme song of our relationship, searching for where we wished to grow roots, frustrated that any place beckoning one of us didn't call or speak to the other. Crisscrossing the tidy Common, seeking solace for my wild soul, even as the earth wakes from dark winter dreaming, I most desire to escape the hum and buzzing energy of the city.

A stab of memory. A few months previous, riding out a particularly rough stretch of the journey in Santa Fe. Working two jobs and my body under strain from doing deep-tissue massage at the spa, as well as too many *vinyasas* in ashtanga yoga, both wrists wrapped in supportive braces, I repeatedly asked—urged—myself: *can you say yes to your life even when it's breaking you open?* If I trust the splintering serves a greater purpose and ultimate good, can I lean into it?

Yes. I can. I will.

Challenges often become our greatest teachers, I've learned.

In the manner of new shoots rising from dark earth, the weeks feel tentative and tender, but mercifully the harbingers of spring appear everywhere. The two cherry trees in the rear garden stand adorned in ruffled pink blossoms. Buds swell upon the lone, leaning pear tree. Wherever I walk, even along the rain-slicked city streets, I spy delicate green leaves on naked branches. Life awakens once more. Blessedly, blue skies arrive occasionally amongst the days of onerous, wet grey—teasing or offering hope, hard to say which. Extremely timely this seasonal shift, and each of these humble gifts I welcome gladly, uplifting my restless heart. A lightening of limbs and heavy thoughts. We will emerge from the long darkness yet.

48 ◆ WHERE TWO WORLDS TOUCH

Reaching the end of an interminable workday, when Robert boards the Underground near the Thames, he sends me a text message. Expecting him, the full-sized umbrella under my arm, I walk to the Tube station and await his District Line train, seeing the long metal, illuminated caterpillar approach. Garbed in requisite London black wool coat, shiny black shoes, and a striped scarf knotted tightly around his neck, my companion's face looks ghostly pale and severely drawn—utterly exhausted both from the day and tightly-packed commute. One needn't be an *empath* to sense his struggle, how he pulls upon a subterranean reserve of will.

Cold and damp make no friends with him, exasperating the throbbing ache in his spine. When I take his briefcase and hold the generous umbrella over our heads, he voices no protest, and slowly we walk home from the station, arm in arm, with him leaning slightly upon me. His return to the office devours every ounce of strength and resolve, thrust back into a soulless realm as the entire financial world roils and rocks, the glass towers wavering upon their foundations. A difficult and unpopular time to work as a banker in America or Britain—to say nothing of foreign and openly gay in a staid English establishment, where some of his colleagues secretly hope, even not so discreetly, he will fail.

In the tight, spindly house, dinner awaits. Or nearly so. When Robert has changed his clothes, seated at the table we eat by dimmed lights and flickering candles, mellow music playing in the kitchen via Bose speaker docked to an iPhone. For my part, I prepare dishes he specifically enjoys, meals to fend off the unfriendly temperature outside: a warming risotto; *coq au Riesling*; fish fillets with *beurre blanc*; plump, juicy *bratwurst*; pork chops with apples, thyme, and cream; penne with broccolini, garlic and lemon, showered with *pecorino Romano*; a chicken pot pie; potatoes *dauphinoise*; Puy lentil stew with caramelized onions and pancetta. Occasionally, I cook a fragrant curry or *pad Thai*, seasoned mildly for his palate, additional fiery condiments to satisfy my own. During our time apart, he came to rely upon takeaway from a nearby Indian restaurant, and every so often, at his

GHOSTS & TEA ◆ 49

request, I ring them up to order his preferred chicken *tikka masala,* with spicy vegetarian dishes for me, delivered to our doorstep via motor scooter.

Faites simple. Keep it simple.

Can anything be more nurturing than the grace of the table? Beyond the sustaining nourishment of good fare itself, humans have connected with each other for ages and eons over shared meals, exchanging stories and weaving threads of connection from the heart. For both Robert and I, the ritual we missed most dearly the past year apart was our mealtimes together.

My counterpart hasn't much strength for conversation most nights, so I recount the details of my day, trivial as may be. Something humorous observed while out, a new shop I discovered, or a bit of wildness encountered while roaming the Common—a heron, a falcon, a throaty chorale of frogs. Quite frequently, a fox. Shared observances on the British and American cultural differences elicit a chuckle. Intentionally, I bring a dash of mirthfulness to distract him from his pain and possibly ease his burdens somewhat. A bit of *joie de vivre* to lift his spirit.

"You've always made me laugh; I love you for that."

Laughter brightens blue eyes into unpolished sapphires, and despite his struggle and endurance, a faint new lightness glimmers in him. He grips his work role less tightly these days, the ego slightly relinquishing command, once again hearing soul whispers of the musician-artist he formerly was.

Still, his recovery is incremental, slower than either of us would have predicted or hoped. Whilst he could function on his own in a couple more months if I depart for the States, life would be difficult for him. The pressures of work, the peak-hour commute, and the cheerless environment of banking drains his essence. Were I to go away, his existence would be bleak.

We dine tonight on a fragrant stir-fry of diced organic chicken and mushrooms, redolent with Asian-esque lemongrass and ginger, a helping of smoky hot chilies for my bowl. A glass of crisp German Riesling *kabinett* alongside as a perfect complement.

"Would you consider staying longer?" he asks delicately, a young boy in

50 ◆ WHERE TWO WORLDS TOUCH

his face, measuring the risk of such a request.

Nothing urgently calls me back to America other than my ongoing apprenticeship with an organization in Colorado conducting wilderness-based, eco-depth-soul programs. A requirement to fulfill a couple of intensives and group-based *vision quests* a year, along with retreat gatherings where I reconnect with my long-sought, soulful tribe. Currently, apart from intuitive bodywork, such work is what I foresee myself doing one day, at least in part, specifically for gay men, an evolution of the men's groups I led previously.

Wooden chopsticks in hand, I pause, a gentle smile turning up the corners of my mouth.

"Yes," I nod, "that feels right, somehow."

Immediately, an invisible weight rises from his stooped shoulders. He sits slightly more upright, a glint of pearl in his irises.

"I was thinking, when the lease expires in March, we could move out of the city. I want someplace tranquil and quiet where I can heal . . . where you'll be happier too. You *need* nature, otherwise something withers up inside you. We *both* need it."

Reaching for my wine, fingers on the crystal stem, I swirl the glass a couple times before lifting it to my nose and catching the crisp notes of tart green apple. Thoughtfully, I take a sip, considering both the vintage and his oh-so-tempting idea.

"Really?"

"Yes, it's time to escape London. More than time, really. If you're willing, we could begin looking for a nice little house. Maybe on the weekends, we take the car and go out towards Sevenoaks or Royal Tunbridge Wells to meet with estate agents. It just has to be somewhere there's a direct rail line to Charing Cross or Waterloo."

His suggestion doesn't need repeating or consideration. With the utterance of a few words, my wanderer's heart has swiftly found its wings. We will flee the noisy, crowded confines and finally leave the ghosts of this chilled, cramped house. Dinner sits momentarily abandoned. My earlier grin spreads ear to ear, bright as spring. An urge grips me to get up and dance around the room, and I could almost hug and kiss the pale, thin man for sheer joy.

With a bit of grace, City Mouse and Country Mouse may find the dear, in-between house after all, with birdsong outside the windows rather than autos and passersby. The restorative balm of countryside and open spaces, where the breath is easy and full, the spirit uplifted.

What an unexpected gift of the Mystery, one to embrace with wild abandon.

HEDGEROWS & HAVEN

MOVING DAY ARRIVES. Four months after returning to England, following several day trips of scouting potential areas to reside, and then traveling repeatedly on my own via train during the week to meet with estate agents to view various properties, we've rented a nicely renovated old farmhouse.

The location is farther from London than we initially considered. One night, I woke in the dark hours with a compelling directive: *find a house with a pool.* If the water were heated to a suitably warm temperature, Robert could receive Watsu, the aquatic bodywork I practiced back in the States. Supported by the therapist's arms and assistive floats, effectively weightless, a client is gently cradled, stretched, and slowly moved through a series of Tai Chi-like poses in the water for a profoundly relaxing and healing result. A perfect modality for mobilizing the spine.

The next morning, after browsing several UK property websites, I narrowed in on a few rentals in our price range; some with enclosed indoor pools, others with outdoor ones. Locating them on a map, all were too remote from London and thus impractical, save one in pastoral Kent whose photos immediately attracted Robert and me. Pictures showed a rectangular swimming pool bordered by tall hedges at the rear of a brick house. Albeit unusable in winter, the pool's smallish size might feasibly be heated to 35°C/95°F, the required temperature for Watsu, hopefully without costing the earth, maybe just a couple days a week. Contacting the agency, we arranged to drive out on the weekend to see the place.

HEDGEROWS & HAVEN ◆ 53

Ease fills me from the moment of our arrival. The vacant farmhouse is chilly, but stepping through the heavy oak front door onto wood floors gleaming like warm honey, I've unexpectedly returned to a house I already know. Waiting for me. Something clicks somatically, the key to my heart turning in its lock, followed by a gentle expansion. Those invisible, silvery wings, perhaps.

The spacious dwelling feels more than ample for two inhabitants, almost absurdly so. A sizable cloakroom adjoins the foyer, and the main reception boasts a brick fireplace and shiny brass chandelier. Accessed through double glass doors, the second reception has a vaguely Mediterranean ambience with terracotta tiled floors, a Kilim-style rug, and wall sconces fashioned of forearm-length, red clay roof tiles from some faraway land where sunshine reigns. We admire the formal dining room with carved stone fireplace and forest green walls, a carpeted study next to the kitchen, and then four large bedrooms upstairs, including a master bedroom with *en suite* and a generous shower to rival a hotel spa. A proper bathroom at last.

"There is no gardener," warns the joyless, heavyset estate agent with a stern look. The owners have recently moved abroad to Switzerland, the husband maintained the garden, and they won't pay for groundskeeping. The Savills representative clearly does not approve of their money-pinching measures, shaking her head and remarking how highly unusual for this sort of property to not have such service provided, stressing it will be our full responsibility to care for the garden adequately. Smiling and nodding, we both enthusiastically assure her of my keenness and aptitude for taking care of things; an assertion, from the dubious stare, she doesn't quite believe. As queer Americans, in her eyes we stand already suspect; our capacity as gardeners is apparently even more doubtful.

Beyond the modest lawn out front, a few decorative shrubs and roses under the windows, the garden at rear is principally the pool flanked by a moderate patch of grass, bordered with several long flowerbeds. Surveying the scene, the task looks manageable to say the least. Welcome, even.

The pool, too, falls under the tenants' responsibility to manage and care for, the dour agent adds in further warning. Close to a reprimand. In another age, she would have made a commendable if punitive schoolmistress.

"Not a problem," I grin. "The pool is the reason we're here."

Again, a skeptical look. Likely we are oblivious rain falls twelve months of the year in her fine country, that only slim opportunity exists for enjoying the outdoors and swimming in the water. Rain is perpetual in the estate agent's world, I suspect, indoors and out.

While indeed the prospect of a Watsu pool has lured us, the glorious kitchen nearly sweeps me off my feet. Once a brick workshop or milk shed, separated from the original farmhouse by a dozen feet or so, various expansions and renovations incorporated the outbuilding into a rear annex with a separate gabled roof of local slate. As with the rest of this genial home, it oozes Old World charm, touched with a slight patina of wear around the edges. Nothing too polished or picture perfect.

An old-fashioned Rayburn oven, icon of British cookery, occupies the imposing inglenook fireplace. The fridge is large, at least for European standards, and within a walk-in larder, beside the boiler, rests an American-style washer and tumble dryer—the sight of which nearly brings tears of joy. Above the doublewide, vintage porcelain country sink, a leaded-glass picture window frames a view of the rear garden, and an antique, bifurcated barn door opens to the stone terrace, where resident Mallard ducks waddle noisily on their way to the stream bordering the front driveway. In sum, a near perfect escape from the eerily lucid dream still holding us in greater London, an opportunity to step instead into an idyllic setting in the English countryside. Not a sliver of hesitation troubles either of us.

⌒〰

The day of the spring equinox finds us packed, our household goods loaded into a removers' lorry and heading to Kent under blue skies—as if the gods themselves have smiled. An auspicious day for new beginnings, with the hours of daylight becoming incrementally longer than night. The new residence is an hour's drive, and Robert has gone ahead in the car to meet the agent for the keys and perform a detailed move-in inspection.

HEDGEROWS & HAVEN ◆ 55

Remaining with the crew, after their departure I drift through the emptied rooms, feeling able for the first time to extend my arms and fully inhale within the close, cold walls. Freedom looms imminent, and lightness fills my entire being. Farewell to Wimbledon, the Common, ghosts, and dear little lost Kona.

Leaving both sets of house keys on the chimneypiece, I shut the cobalt blue front door behind me with a brassy *clack* for the last time, and without a backward glance, stride down the street, buoyant enough in body and spirit to whistle or hum a jolly tune. When I reach the Underground station, my journey will carry me into central London, and from Waterloo Station onward to Kent via overland train.

Robert is waiting with the car when I alight at Headcorn. We motor through the village with its few shops, turning onto a smaller road, which, after a mile or so, narrows further into a winding country lane flanked with green hedgerows and tall trees on either side. The distance makes four miles, station to front door. London lies behind us, and as if I were resting in a shady hammock on a warm day, with a long exhale, my body settles into a soft relaxation. Gratitude, embodied.

Rounding a bend near the farmhouse, cottontails dart along the embankment, a long-established warren under the twisted, deep-rooted rhododendrons. Riddled with countless small tunnels, their home is safe from foxes, and dozens of them hop nervously about, ears twitching, retreating from the rumbling of the German diesel engine.

"It's like Watership Down here," smiles Robert, slowing the car. Blue eyes wide, a sweetly childlike affection for *bunnies* lights his face.

Not having traveled this way from the station before, I quietly absorb the lane. Drinking in the landscape of trees with their limbs newly sprouted in electric green, the wild rabbits, and pastures dotted with fluffy sheep.

"Actually, I was thinking *The Wind In The Willows*, myself . . . but yes, it's wonderful whatever it is. Simply lovely."

The removers' truck sits parked in front of the nineteenth-century farmhouse with its Kent peg tile roof, neat patch of lawn, and detached, brick two-car garage. A slender willow freshly robed in emerald makes a graceful watchman at the gate, standing beside the irrigation stream flowing through a culvert under the lane and tracing the edge of the property. How wonderful to arrive here, a gentle happiness tingling in my hands, and an energetic swirling in my solar plexus saying *yes*.

Irrespective of its unassuming front and exterior, the dwelling is gracious, somehow dignified and casually elegant; conjuring a sense of goodness and home, regardless we are merely renters. As a dear in-between house for City Mouse and Country Mouse, in virtually every way, the farmhouse exceeds anything I dreamed. Even with all our belongings placed and unpacked at the end of the day, the rooms are but partially furnished. What irony we recently jettisoned the olive-green couch to give ourselves more breathing room in the tall, squeezed townhouse, and kept the smaller loveseat. Now we have abundant space, and the sofa would be useful, even if terribly American in its overstuffed, lazy styling. More than double the size of the Wimbledon residence, with the enclosed garden and pool at rear, the spread seems to us almost a country estate, and the monthly rent amount is the same.

The one apparent drawback of the farmhouse is the sole tub, located in the bathroom on the stairwell landing. *Tiny* is an inadequate word. A wine barrel probably holds more volume. Robert requires a hot soak each night to coax tight spinal muscles into relaxing and to help reduce his pain cycle, but he barely squishes his frame inside.

"It's a hobbit tub," I shake my head, lamenting for him. "Your mother is the only person I know who would fit comfortably."

Knees drawn up to his chest, sponging warm water over his back, the man is a good sport, but the diminutive bath doesn't befit a grown adult. Clearly, the pool must be heated up. Soon.

The house *feels* energetically different to me from the outset. More inviting. The original residence, long since remodeled and changed multiple times, significantly predates the Edwardian townhouse we've left, and arguably more souls have dwelt here. Yet oddly it feels less cluttered or *heavy* on a psychic level. Fewer impressions come, arriving as they do, cloaked like memories, at other times a weight or chill in my body. Not as many entities and energies lingering about. Aptitude notwithstanding, I've no desire to be a spiritualist *medium*, and closed the door long ago on spirit communication, but their presence is often still felt. Like it or not, I live at the edge between realms.

Fundamentally brighter, light fills the farmhouse. Not solely from windows all around versus only front and rear, but a spread of countryside outside the walls rather than tall, urban houses. Too, the days grow longer, if still cloudy and cool. Equally pleasing, the musty smell of the townhouse has been replaced by a lighter, more elusive note I find much more agreeable.

"Hello, house," I whisper aloud, a warmth in my chest as I touch the walls along the upstairs hallway, or when entering a room, acknowledging the unknown lives long-since past and forgotten hands which built this place. If I cared to tune-in, the wooden beams, old bricks and mortar holds lifetimes—centuries—of impressions.

My splendid cooking space delights utterly. I feel happy and alert whenever I enter the room, almost bubbly with cheerfulness, my outlook instantly brightened. Redemption at last from the uninspired, average, and utilitarian kitchens I've inhabited previously. I have won the cooks' lottery—a culinary atelier lifted from pages of English *Country Life* magazine—tailor-made for my earthy nature, right down to the terracotta tiled floor, reminding me of Santa Fe. A sensualist's kitchen. Here is the warmly beating heart of the house, in spite of its location at the rear. The minute we signed the rental contract, I moved into this room, knowing the bulk of my days would pass looking out at the terrace with its shifting moods of light, the upper half of the barn door ajar in all sorts of weather. Even if I never cooked a damn thing. For the first time since coming to the UK, inspiration finds me.

I've dreamt for years of a fireplace, open hearth, or a wood-burning oven in the kitchen, and though the inglenook is fitted with a rusty Rayburn, it holds a certain allure. Initially fueled by wood, at some point the black cast-

58 ♦ WHERE TWO WORLDS TOUCH

iron beast was converted to kerosene. Even before we unpacked, I imagined how the intense, radiant heat from all sides of the cooking chamber would transform my hearth-style *pain au levain*, delivering a burnished, amber crust that cracks and shatters perfectly. I have not baked bread since returning to England; the tiny Playschool oven in Wimbledon wasn't suited. By our second day in the farmhouse, a new "starter" is underway; a slurry of organic wheat flour and water, which through a daily series of additions will gradually develop a symbiotic colony of local yeasts to flavor and leaven a rustic, traditional French sourdough.

I station the sturdy wooden kitchen trolley in the center of the generous space, wheels locked in front of the aging Rayburn. Perched alongside in a chair brought from the dining room, with a porcelain cup of tea and a small plate holding something sweet, I contentedly gaze out the diamond-paned window and open barn door. Writing. Reading. Simply being. Weather allowing, from time to time, I stand and walk barefoot onto the cool grey flagstones of the terrace or amble unhurriedly around the garden. Silently observing. All senses cast wide. Gathering the rustle of a breeze in the trees, the voices of sheep, the rumble of a distant tractor. Talking to the ducks.

A couple of these waterfowl are fond of waddling from the stream at front—or flying with a great squawking tumult and ungainly landing—to the rear of the house and sitting on the pool's thermal cover. The newly warm water underneath makes the blue plastic expanse an inviting place to rest, and I routinely dash out to chase them off it; employing a harmless watery blast of the garden hosepipe since their little brains deduced I cannot reach them from the rim. On principle, I welcome nature's denizens with whom I share a patch of earth, and I wouldn't mind the ducks' presence on the cover except they defecate on it. Retracting the great sheet onto its large roller at the pool's edge must be done with utmost care to keep their muck from fouling the water. Often, the orange-footed, noisily endearing troublemakers come to the kitchen door when it stands open, curiously peering inside with cocked head and glassy eyes.

"If you cross the threshold, you're dinner," I warn, raising a chef's knife or cleaver to further enhance my point. "I'm a French-trained cook and I love eating duck. *J'adore le canard. Vous comprenez?*"

⌒〜

Early on weekday mornings, Robert and I drive to the rail station for his hour commute. We have settled a far enough distance from the city he usually gets a seat, an unlooked-for benefit to our somewhat remote location. The stations grow more crowded closer to London, and had we chosen a house near Tunbridge Wells or Sevenoaks, as first intended, he would have been forced to stand the entire journey.

Solo, I pilot home along the increasingly narrow roads and hedge-lined lanes to the farmhouse. As if I were a new driver, the journey always feels stressful, and my absurdly high percentage rate of meeting a speeding delivery van or oncoming car on a blind curve is almost comical. *Almost.* Parked safely in the drive, shaking off the white-knuckle tension and knot in my stomach, I make a beeline for the kitchen to brew either a proper cup of tea or a pot of spicy chai on the hob—warming notes of cinnamon, clove, and cardamom wafting into the air—and set one of my fresh-baked cranberry and ginger scones on a plate.

The Brits would never consider a scone in the morning; it's simply not breakfast fare. Outsider status, however, grants liberty to make my own rituals and traditions, and these scones have won the favor and praise of everyone who has tasted them. Assuaging my jangled nerves with tea and a tasty bite to eat, I swing open the bifurcated door and sit, contemplating the rear garden. Breathing in, breathing out.

Bless this house.

Tunes of songbirds play to my ear, accompanied by the quacking of ducks and bleating sheep in the near distance. And something akin to *contentment*—expansive, warm, and sunny—purrs in my innermost self.

⌒〜

The spacious farmhouse feels hushed. Devoid of intrusive television and radio, quiet as an old library, the space is too much for one person to inhabit

60 ◆ WHERE TWO WORLDS TOUCH

or fill. Ten hours will lapse before I fetch Robert from the station, thus my day becomes a blank canvas. Apart from tending to chores of cleaning, laundry, mowing the lawn and working in the garden, my grocery runs to Tenterden, and the evening ritual of making dinner, few real demands press upon me. My hours of solitude in Wimbledon were fewer in number, and frequently I was out and about, traveling by rail or Underground, on foot and occasionally in taxi, exploring London and searching for whatever thing called me. Poilâne's sourdough bread on Elizabeth Street near Eaton Square. Household items at the flagship John Lewis on Oxford Street. Whole leaf tea from the Tea Palace. Extraordinary British and Irish artisan cheeses from Neal's Yard Dairy in Seven Dials. A crunchy, sugary *palmier* and a perfect, long-extraction *flat white* from Monmouth Coffee Company. Browsing the green-carpeted refuge of Hatchard's, booksellers since 1797. A trek to High Street Kensington and Whole Foods Market. An occasional lunch with Robert in Covent Garden near the bank.

More so than in the city, I'm slightly adrift. Partly for diversion, partly to acquaint with new surroundings, but mostly to nourish my untamed soul, daily I go walking. A battered, wide-brimmed hat atop my head, gaily I traverse the winding country lanes, stepping animatedly with arms swinging. Admiring the budding trees and relishing the fresh air, stepping aside for an occasional car, delivery van or, better yet, horse and rider. One day, just down from the farmhouse, hearing a *cloppity cloppity* of multiple hooves approaching behind, I slow and turn toward the sound. Moments later, a double horse-drawn carriage comes into view, pulled by two attractive sorrels with a high, proud gait. Holding the cart reins, sitting erectly, a silver-haired gentleman sporting a hat much finer than my own. He nods slightly in polite acknowledgment when his handsome team passes me. *Oh yes, this is* exactly *what England ought to be like*, I smile as they round the bend and disappear, leaving me filled with giddiness and bouncing on my toes.

Enfolded in an animated, breathing scenery, the novelty of the countryside thrills me in uncountable ways. Nevertheless, I soon tire of walking along roads and lanes where cars speed noisily past leaving me in a wake of exhaust. The occasional signage of various footpaths, seemingly trails leading across fields, intrigues me. With a bit of investigation I learn, although they cross private land, such paths are technically public rights of way.

No longer forbidden, enthusiastically I explore ones located near the house, but repeatedly a track disappears at the edge of a wide field and where it resumes on the far side cannot be determined. Some are overgrown from disuse. Occasionally, a gate marked No Entry blocks a path, putting me at a loss. Too frequently, I retrace my aborted course, stymied, having met an obstacle or losing the way entirely. Even when the route is apparent, it's difficult to shake the feeling of trespassing; half-expecting some resident farmer to emerge with a shotgun and angrily order me off his land.

One early spring day in Tenterden, on my shopping run to Waitrose, after sauntering down the main street and appreciating a blue sky, while browsing a bookshop, I discover a rack of Ordinance Survey maps. In the blink of an eye, my world expands. Long before satellite images and Google, every segment of this time-honored country was charted down to its fields, footpaths, and streams. Similar to the topographic maps I used for hiking and backpacking in the States, these are more specific. A frisson of excitement flutters through me with a quiver, and I purchase two OS maps detailing our section of Kent. Keys to the kingdom placed in my hand.

A happy conspirator, I plot new routes for traveling further afield. Map tucked into my pocket or rucksack, when I reach an obscure section of footpath, or it disappears completely, out comes the folded graph to show me the way forward. Brilliant.

Old-fashioned maps have won my heart. Liberated from walking along roads other than to cross them, my outings transform into proper countryside rambles of several miles, generally following a circular track, heading out from the farmhouse along the lane in one direction and arriving back a couple of hours later from another, pleasantly tired, but enlivened in limb and spirit.

Rucksack strapped to my back, its main compartment holds my water bottle, folding umbrella, a bag of raw almonds, and a crisp, tart-sweet

62 ◆ WHERE TWO WORLDS TOUCH

organic apple. Tucked in another compartment, my trusty Paris fountain pen and a small black notebook. Should weather permit and be warm enough, I remove my soft-shell pullover, stash it inside the pack, and walk less encumbered by outer layers. Crowned with my ivory-canvas walking hat from Taos, threading across pastures, when I come near the flocks of unshorn sheep with orange numbers spray-painted on their muddy coats they scatter nervously. My approach startles up ring-necked pheasants, launching noisily into the air with a whistle of wings from where they've been hiding crouched in the grass, and rabbits who dash quickly back to the shelter of hedgerows or warren of tunnels. The air sparkles with birdsong and a spritely breeze plays amid the fields. I pass through orchards, neat and well-tended, others neglected and overgrown—abandoned even—but all of them adorned with blossoms and iridescent green leaves as life surges forth in another cycle of renewal and growth. Genesis, encore.

Immersed in a living milieu, being on foot bestows a sense of at-one-ment with the awakening around me. Gone is the melancholy that stalked me in Wimbledon, and in freedom from walls which contain, nature restores my essence. Eyes are bright, movements fluid and energized, and my heart opens to the world. Everything about this domesticated green realm is diametrically opposite to the sage-strewn mesa I previously roamed; never am I out of sight of a farmhouse or barn, and humankind's presence is everywhere, having shaped the landscape itself. Still, a similar soaring lightness animates my bones and breath as when I walked beneath walked beneath an azure sky in the Land of Enchantment. Nothing is *wild*, not even the copses of trees, but perhaps a civilized countryside is enough for my soul to find peace. Time will tell.

Breezes shimmer across expanses of new wheat, the tall grasses swaying silver-green like vast schools of fish flashing through a liquid jade sea, and I meet sleek horses, some of whom follow me from a distance. On a blustery day, bisecting a large field and lost in my reverie, watching herds of puffy clouds migrate above, I realize the pasture's lone inhabitant is an imposing black bull with impressive horns. I slow, weighing the options, my pulse quickening. Breath goes shallow. Looking back over my shoulder and then

HEDGEROWS & HAVEN ◆ *63*

forward to the far fence line, I am equidistant between them.

Walk calmly, and then run like hell if necessary.

Sometimes large, barking dogs are decidedly unfriendly, growling and lunging behind fences as I pass alongside, a tight fist of fear in my gut, and adrenaline pumping through my system. A sturdy walking stick might be prudent, and should I happen across a suitable staff, whether a rustic one waiting for me along the way or hand-carved in a shop, I will pick it up. For now, I go on rambling.

Robert's company in the evenings brings gladness, the warm glow of human companionship, yet my days are anything but lonely. In seclusion and silence, away from the din of the modern world, whether walking or in the garden, I draw near to things and ponder their detailed beauty up close, losing myself to gentle rhapsody and wonderment like a lover will do. A honeybee loving a flower.

Often the simplest, most ordinary things are the most beautiful.

Possibly, my delight in such incidental encounters arises from the embodied practice of *mindfulness*. In mystic traditions, the more a person is truly awake, distinctions between the earthly and the spiritual, the mundane and the sublime, cease to exist.

As with pleasure in simple things, I confess to a longstanding love affair with trees, and the majestic English oaks enamor me with their stateliness and presence. Is it any wonder the ancient Druids revered them as sacred and magical? Sometimes, I approach one to rest my palms upon its rough grey bark, like touching the craggy and sun-parched skin of some African rhino or dinosaur. Through my fingers, a streaming of energy close to a shiver or a rippling up the arm to my heart. An exchange of unspoken communion. Subtle but real. Great trees uplight the soul, offering something ineffable to the human spirit, and we as a species are impoverished by their loss whether for "resources" or so-called development. Meeting a centuries-old oak, feeling its distinct *presence*, reminds me once more: everything we encounter is a relationship—consciously or not.

Count me among those such as C.G. Jung and notable others who have reflected upon the loss of our emotional and mythic connection to nature—estranged from the darkly tangled woods, full of spirits and magic, and to remarkable beings like an ancient tree. The disenchantment of the modern world bears consequences on the psyche, I think. Moreover, in our disconnection, along with a growing enslavement to technology, we're toppling headlong into a collective, trancelike *un*consciousness. A new generation is born directly into the trance, and our increasingly artificial and toxic world is more and more traumatizing. Riveted to illuminated screens and devices, addicted to social media, medicating our angst and depression, how will anyone wake—or discover a re-enchantment of life—but for nature, curious interventions of grace, and a wild imagination.

Healer is another sticky, self-important word I wrestle with and try to avoid for myself, knowing true healing is mysterious, and comes from something other than techniques, skill, or even *energy*. In my observation, nearly everyone has a *soul sickness*, the direct result of lives out of balance and a culture trapped in psychosis—a distinguishing hallmark of which is a person doesn't recognize their own disorder. Not only is he or she totally unaware their behavior is strange in any way, but they are unable to determine what is real and isn't real. And while they might ascertain delusional behavior in others, they cannot perceive it in themselves. A fairly accurate description for most of the modern world, I think, an unsustainable society and materialistic culture conscripted to social identity and ego, blindly chasing money as the path to happiness.

One method to heal and begin recovering, "waking up" individually, is to *rewild* the body and soul. Unplug from technology and go out walking. Befriend a terrain intimately through our senses and greet the other-than-human ones we meet. Get our feet and hair wet outdoors, and in the words of American poet Gary Snyder, learn a "wild etiquette" of freedom. Indisputably, the inestimable gift of rambling on foot is coming home to an essential, latent part of ourselves. Put another way, counterintuitively, in getting lost we may just be found.

A couple of years ago, in my late thirties, I met my birthmother for the first time after a long search to find her. I was the second of two children she gave away, and our adult relationship felt challenging from the outset. She carried a host of harsh judgments and bitter anger like a chef's bundle of knives, and my homosexuality—a word she used with pointed distaste, nearly disgust—was intolerable to her, despite having a queer sister. Yet in her own way, she was something of a mystic. At the age of seven, at the Oregon coast, wandering off a little distance from her family, she "walked over the dunes and into the arms of God," as she put it—struck with a divine relation of Source as the ultimate fountainhead of love, glory, intelligence, creativity and *beingness*—and spent the rest of her life seeking such an experience again, never finding it in any church, religion, or spiritual path. She only drew close, at moments, when alone and surrounded by nature.

Shortly after we met, already driven apart in our relating, she learned from one of her two sisters about my solitary, barefoot walks in Forest Park among the noble, watchful trees—exactly as she had done throughout her early adulthood in Portland in the same woods, before her mother committed her to an asylum for electric shock therapy.

"You carry the mark," she told me via email, "and I will share something with you. The mystic's dilemma is that she or he wishes only to draw closer to the One, yet their work is to be *in* the world, and not retreat from it."

Her words immediately struck me as truth, knowing my own deep yearning for the wilder places, drawn outward in an expansive, kinesthetic communion with *other*, feeling a palpable sense of my own greater soul mirrored in nature. The soul of the world, perhaps.

Yes, this is who I am.

Not long after my arrival back in England, just months ago, in a different way than her gay sister, she took her life, ending the struggle with cancer along with bipolar disorder. Yet I carry her insight in my heart like a final gift bequeathed to me, curious guidance bound together with a darkly haunted lineage.

As a reluctant mystic, wandering in nature, following my allurement, whatever strange destiny draws me or I'm headed toward, only time will

66   ◆ WHERE TWO WORLDS TOUCH

reveal.

⌒

Evening time. In his usual way, Robert sends a text message once he catches a train at Waterloo East, and an hour later I greet him at the station; one of dozens of cars in queue fetching husbands returning from work, a scene replicated at every rail station within two hours of London. We swap places at the wheel, and he drives back to the house, unspeakably weary in his banker's dark suit and tie. While he changes clothes upstairs, I finish any last details for dinner, artfully arrange our plates, and light the tall candles. The hour is nearly eight o'clock when we sit down, much later than I prefer to eat. *C'est la vie.*

The rusty Rayburn, even when not cooking, radiates a welcome heat, and most nights we dine next to its warmth. *À deux*, two chairs pulled up to the wooden trolley, the kitchen feels homier than the formal dining room with our large table. I yearn to light the fireplace of that salon to make a cozier and inviting space, but Robert doesn't wish to sit in chairs for long. He needs to soon retire to the more comfortable loveseat, and thus the carved stone hearth remains cold and unlit.

My companion is stronger, but the pain has not lessened. Working at his desk is punishment, so he stands or circles around the office regularly. Yet regardless of the day's interminable hours and the tedious commute on a crowded train, coming home to the gracious farmhouse among orchards and fields—a haven amid hedgerows—is undeniably affirming and healing to his spirit.

Worn down, running on empty, Robert must push himself to join me but, if rain isn't falling, after dinner we bundle up and step outdoors. I gather his arm gently in mine and we amble slowly north along the tranquil lane, serenaded by a demure rustling in the shadowed trees overhead. Breathing the unconditioned air. Gently recharging body and soul. Admiring the erratic twirl of bats against a violet sky. Not far do we go, maybe two hundred meters to the mini hamlet of charming brick houses from the seventeen and eighteen hundreds, each set behind wide wooden gates and surrounded with well-tended gardens. At the edge of the first wheat field, we turn back, he hasn't strength for more than a very short walk. Complementing the grace of the table, our little stroll makes a soul-nurturing connection at the end of day—rejoining with each other and whispering nature under a fading sky, held by the bigger dream of life.

Closing my eyes, the soul of the world, the *anima mundi*, hovers indescribably nearby. I *feel* it somehow, a faint, ethereal expansiveness, almost a porousness of being, defying explanation or reason. Just possibly, a faint glimmer of magic enfolds us, as well.

"I love it here. Thank you for finding us such a nice house, it's so calm and peaceful. It feels *healing*. You know, it's actually hard for me to go into London and work. When I pass through the long tunnel shortly after Sevenoaks, the one where you lose mobile signal and then emerge into the outer ring of the city, my whole body constricts. It's like everything presses in on me . . . and it brings up anxiety. Does that sound crazy?"

Pulling his arm more snugly, I draw him closer beneath the darkening heavens as we reach the farmhouse gate left open.

"This you're asking the fellow who lived five miles down a dirt track in a shaman's haunted tower on the mesa west of Taos, the guy who could barely wait to get out of London because of the buzz and energy . . .?"

"I knew you'd understand," Robert smiles, returning my squeeze of linked limbs.

"I'm very glad to be where we are, too. It's lovely . . . simply lovely."

"It's only lovely because you're here."

"Oh, now don't go sentimental on me, you old softie."

"I can't help it, I'm highly sensitive these days."

"You are indeed, thank the gods. That soulless, hardened, and uptight banker act was, well, a bit dull. Good riddance to bad rubbish, I say."

He chuckles crossing the front lawn, his laughter warm and bright in the cool spring evening.

Yes, how very good this is.

The general madness and ugliness of the world seems pleasantly far away.

We wake to birdsong and a neighbor's chickens rather than the hum and traffic of the city. The haunting ghosts are left behind, and I feel surprisingly myself in a genteel country house with a fabulous kitchen and ducks at the door. Roaming the fields by day, communing with trees once more, and savoring quiet evenings with Robert in a place of tender beginnings. A fresh start in a new season as spring unfurls vividly in irrepressible splendor.

Lovely. Simply lovely.

OUTSIDERS

THE OLD FARMHOUSE is still unfamiliar in the dark, the creak of its floors a language different from others I have learned and since forgotten. Outside, the tranquil green countryside of Kent stirs to daily waking far differently than the buzzing urban congestion of London. Gone are the cars and drone of the city, a cadence of suited and booted heels clicking on pavement. Here, instead, the dawn chorus of birds awakens me each morning, the most jubilant avian celebration since we dwelt in the windward rainforest of the Big Island of Hawaii.

After a long night of enigmatic dreams, the happy *cluck-clucking* of the neighbor's flock of tawny chickens and the insistence of a full bladder conspire to wake me. Throwing back the fluffy bulk of feather comforter, I slide from the warm bed and stumble groggily naked into the bathroom. Without eyeglasses, I'm nearly blind. Not yet thinking clearly, hovering at the threshold between worlds.

Unbidden, Jelaluddin Rumi, the thirteenth-century poet and Sufi mystic, reaches out to me through time and space in a whisper. *The breeze at dawn has secrets to tell you. Don't go back to sleep. You must ask for what you really want. Don't go back to sleep. People are going back and forth across the doorsill where the two worlds touch. The door is round and open. Don't go back to sleep.*

Dreamtime pulls with heavy hands on my shoulders, and bizarre story fragments illuminate my mind like streaming meteors. In the borderlands of sleeping and waking, what is real or isn't? Turning away from the toilet

70 ◆ WHERE TWO WORLDS TOUCH

to return to bed, my blurry gaze passes briefly through the diamond-shaped windows where, in the pale dawn light, a peach-colored mist drifts across the fields. The hazy world is draped in an apricot-hued prayer shawl of dreams and birdsong. Beyond the front lawn along the lane, the tall trees, still gracefully nude from their own winter dreaming, are silhouetted against a brightening sky. The bare sentinels stand silently, their branches reaching upward, and I suddenly *see* them as spirits cleverly disguised as trees. A thousand slender fingers fanning out to touch the heavens. Letting go of the dreaming stars and celebrating Creation itself.

They are *singing*.

The moment shivers with veneration, infused by wonder in the dawn's glowing light. Everything is holy. Awe fills me in a tremulous breath, my chest expanding with gratitude. Whether an ultrasonic or infrasonic exultation, I don't know, but the reverberation echoes in a range outside normal hearing. In my expansive, liminal state, somehow, I *hear* the soundless sound as the very earth sings praise.

Struck by sonic lightning, my reality has cracked open with magic and possibility.

Don't go back to sleep.

~

The bifurcated kitchen door stands ajar, and tumultuous breezes cavort like invisible spirits on the terrace and in the garden, randomly dashing indoors. The morning feels moody, a petulant child temperamentally tossing clouds above Kentish fields, bringing scents of rain, plowed earth, and muck. Birds twitter and sing, embellishing a chorus of sheep in the neighbor's field. The Rayburn, a rusty lord presiding silently on the old hearth, warms the room despite the open door. Today is bread day; a multistage process of mixing and kneading, shaping, resting, and allowing my *pain au levain* to ferment and rise.

Admittedly, the loaves could be built simply with a series of "turns"— folding the dough upon itself over a period of hours, and letting it rest

OUTSIDERS ♦ *71*

between each manipulation—but I *enjoy* kneading. Working the bread with my hands, rocking slightly on my feet and engaged in my core, brings me home again to my body. Eyes closed, a smile crosses my face for the humble gift of *being* while engaged in an ageless, tactile ritual of creating nourishment.

A ribbon of green-gold olive oil drizzled inside the large ceramic bowl employed solely for making bread, I place the wet, sticky dough in its concave womb to rest, spin it once to lightly coat the surface, then drape the container protectively with a linen tea towel and set it to rise. The natural yeasts of the *levain* will work their leavening magic, and later I will punch the airy pillow down, dividing the mass in two.

A high hydration ratio yields loaves with an open-holed structure and "crumb" I desire, but also makes the dough challenging to handle. Using quick, deft movements of my palms—cupping, turning and dragging to generate surface tension and create a taught, smooth skin without tearing—each spherical *boule* is then placed in a round willow *banneton* for "proofing." At a further indeterminate point, when they have risen again and feel right to my touch, I cover and transfer them to the refrigerator to *retard* overnight—slowing the fermentation process and intensifying the loaves' flavor. Tomorrow morning, they will bake in the cast-iron stove on a stoneware slab, emerging with a gorgeously bronzed, dense crust and hunger-inducing aroma.

The dough relaxes in its covered vessel. I brew a pot of Assam tea and turn my attention to the green world of the garden—now fully waking from its winter hibernation with cohorts of purple and gold crocuses, accompanied by undeniably cheerful daffodils. The orange-footed Mallards are elsewhere, wherever ducks go. Standing at the wide, farmhouse sink, glad and grateful for the vivid eruption of spring, my gaze travels to the forbiddingly twisted old apple tree draped in ivy and crowned in mistletoe, a gnarled being I call the Shaman.

The day Robert and I first considered the farmhouse and walked through the rear garden, this unusual tree signaled my attention and curiosity. Its trunk rests horizontally along the ground like a shaggy slug or some ivy-cloaked salamander, and then rises in a contorted question mark, from whence the main branches—budding into delicate bloom—are twisted horns. Like a dark cave beckoning above a trail, enticing passersby to climb up and discover its shadowy treasures or terrors, a numinous energy emanates from the venerable, mythic tree. Building a relationship with it, I place small, worthless treasures at the base; a bronze Chinese lion, a leather bracelet and battered silver ring, a beeswax candle, along with the dried, fragile remnants of flower *leis* from Hawaii, draped upon knotted protuberances and limbs. If I had any colorful ribbons, they would adorn the tree too. Call me *pagan*, I won't be offended. Nature, wilderness, and magical, mythopoetic things like the longstanding apple tree conjure an upwelling in my soul.

Sipping my aromatic *cuppa*, contemplating the hunched and wizened Shaman, an exchange passes between us in an acknowledgment or summons. A wordless intonation or primeval chant, reminding me the soul defies domestication. Much as I uphold the small rituals which nourish, like hearth-baked loaves fashioned by my own hands and a pot of best-quality tea, something of a split exists in me: untamed *and* civilized, shadow *and* light. The seeming contradiction of being a wild soul and urban sophisticate, a barefoot bohemian yet also an aesthete. Two worlds ever at odds, sharing an uneasy truce.

Nature, soul, and magic all reflect the embodied imagination of the universe. In a disenchanted world, we have lost our magic; first banished by religion, then mocked by science. And despite that we *are* nature—right down to our microbes—we are losing our connection in a wider sense. Alas, in the disappearance of the magical, mystic, and wild sacred, we have cleverly lost our way. And when lives are out of balance, when people no longer live in right relationship with their own *bodysoul* and a larger story, sickness arises, individually and culturally.

Magic still exists, the Shaman whispers across the garden. *Step outside and come home to yourself.*

OUTSIDERS ◆ 73

Springtime weather is marginal, but I turn up the pool's electric heater until the water is warm enough for a Watsu session with Robert. Likely this venture will cost a king's ransom, yet if aquatic work helps my suffering comrade, then all will be worth it. Ethereal wisps of steam rise from the surface into cool air, and I descend the steps at the edge to immerse myself in a liquid embrace, exhaling with an audible *aaah*.

My first experience of Watsu came through a friend who was a practitioner. Immediately, the intimate and profound modality captured me. The receiving person's ears submerged barely below water line, a session is silent, and cradled in the therapist's arms, one gradually loses all sense of time and separateness. A profound repatterning is possible. Manually kneading a client on a massage table, confined by gravity and weight, became Paleolithic, whereas holding them weightlessly in warm water is an aquatic ballet and pure grace. Already a bodyworker for fourteen years, I plunged into the certification path, traveling across the USA to learn from various, highly regarded teachers.

Eager to get in the water, eyes dull from pain, the freedom from gravity and gentle movement will help Robert's wounded spine immeasurably. An aficionado of this art, he knows its graciously healing power, and with floats affixed to his calves, he lays back in my arms for stretching and movement, but unexpectedly, any sideways motion, even slight, provokes nausea. Options in the session become limited. Other than supporting and massaging his back, I can do little else without him feeling sick and needing to exit the pool.

Seated on the top step feeling queasy, a towel wrapped around his shoulders, my companion's face is sullen and downcast. Our shared disappointment feels like a heavy, wet blanket, making ribs tight and the heart sink. Most likely, something in his inner ear or an impinged nerve causes the issue. Perhaps the stretching and movement of Watsu is out of the game for now, but I will find a way forward with his healing. Aquatic sessions indubitably hold the key to gently elongating his paraspinals,

74   ♦ WHERE TWO WORLDS TOUCH

easing them from their chronically constricted state locked in a pain cycle.

Deflated but not beaten, lowering our expectations, we try again the next evening. Retracting the blue thermal cover onto its hand-cranked roller, silver clouds of vapor rising from the bath-like water as bats spin dizzily above in the dusk sky, I float my counterpart naked in the healing waters. Embracing stillness. Applying no lateral movement or stretches, my hands gently work his back and spinal muscles. Ever so slightly, a faint relaxation sequences through his entire body, musculature softening just perceptibly. His breath shifts with a sigh, triggering mine to do the same.

Going forward, the warm, healing pool becomes our new ritual after dinner. Once Robert's back has received sufficient therapy for the session, I place a buoyant neck support pillow under his head and release him to simply float. With a couple floatation devices supporting my own body, together we drift in the titan's bathtub, nude beneath the evening firmament. Ears under the waterline. A silent, aquatic meditation at our private spa. *Peacefulness,* embodied.

The neighbor's wooden house, originally the barn for this farmhouse, stands near the tall box hedge bordering the rear garden. Barn conversions are popular throughout rural England, and I've glimpsed spectacular ones in magazines, as well as online when searching for our London escape. From the upper floor, our neighbors can see the pool. Floating serenely unclad in the twilight gloaming, I don't really care. If peering out their window and observing a forty-year-old naked man—or two—gives them a thrill, or possibly a flash of awkward embarrassment, who cares.

⌒

Returning one day from a long ramble on foot, elated in spirit if slightly tired in body, at the front door sit two bottles of organic apple juice and a carton with half a dozen eggs. A handwritten note accompanies, outlining the days for rubbish and recycling collection on the lane, instructing us to take our bins to the drive and set them outside the gate; the juice is the commercial brand they produce and sell from their orchards, the eggs courtesy of their hens, and the signature reads Sara and Paul.

As gay men relocating to a new place, in the countryside no less, predictably we feel a twinge of hesitation about unmet neighbors and locals. Will they be open-minded, accepting, and friendly folks, or Bible-thumping Fundamentalists? Ranks of the latter are blessedly thin in England but one never knows. Holding the message in my hand and opening the front door, bringing the gifts inside, the kindness of this gesture charms me. A secret relief washes through my body in a ripple, a softening of the belly. An exhale. We are outsiders, yes, but perchance not entirely unwelcome.

Both farmhouse and barn share the gravel drive, and the neighbors must stop in front of our garage to open the gate to their property. Robert has briefly met the husband, who frequently comes and goes in his green Isuzu truck. A lean, middle-aged man with a clean-shaven but weathered face, Paul has tough craftsman's hands. Cordial, if not overly friendly. What does he think about two queer Americans living next door, I wonder.

Poof, there goes the neighbourhood.

His wife is pretty in her late forties, with blondish hair cut to her shoulders, and drives her convertible Mini Cooper like a sports car. Considering the rounded, curling script, undoubtedly, she has left the note and goods on our doorstep.

As a thank you for the friendly token—and for not being dreadful from the outset—I bake one of my signature desserts to give them: a crave-worthy, just-slightly-sweet torte made with ground walnuts, accompanied by a rosemary and honey-infused whipped cream. The Beltane Faerie Cake, I've dubbed it, because it seems deliciously Old World; the sort of rustic thing to leave a slice of outdoors on a pagan sabbat as an offering to the fey folk. In light of their three large, black dogs regularly at the gate, a mild anxiousness grips me at the thought of taking it next door, but hopefully the cake and I won't come to a bad end. Fingers crossed.

～～

The ache in Robert's back is continual, and the high dosage of potent medication he consumes daily disconcerts his doctor. Bones knit gradually, but the news that two years may elapse before the vertebrae fully fuse and his pain lessens discourages us both. Slowly and surely my former partner gains strength, yet he is still only a slim fragment of his former, vibrant self; the chatty and animated opera singer I fell in love with many years ago.

On weekends, what he earnestly wishes to do is rest in bed; horizontal rather than vertical to ease his discomfort. Nonetheless, summoning an inner strength and resolve, he rallies, and we head out for day excursions to nearby sites owned by the National Trust. Founded in the late 1800's, the legacy organization stewards historic properties across Britain for cultural preservation and public enjoyment. Much as I find contentment in my own company—walking, writing emails and journaling, cooking, taking care of the garden—and evenings with Robert, escaping our farmhouse den on Babylon Lane for a change of scene makes a pleasant diversion. The various homes, estates and castles, gardens and parks owned by the Trust, offer a perfect means to explore some of the countryside heritage in Kent and East Sussex, gleaning a bit more of England's storied past.

We live not far from Sissinghurst, the world-famous garden of Vita Sackville-West, a poet, author, and aristocratic lover of Virginia Woolf. Irrespective of weekend crowds, the enchanting garden with its Elizabethan brick tower—all that remains of a once grand manor—becomes a favorite destination for us, the living display in themed outdoor "rooms" changing continually as new flowers come into bloom.

Other days out take us to Scotney Castle, notable for the old keep on a petite island amid a parkland of stunning rhododendrons; medieval Bodiam Castle, set within a moat, recognized from multiple Hollywood movies; and Hever Castle, childhood home of Anne Boleyn, second wife of Henry VIII, with its Italianesque gardens and manmade lake installed by a more recent owner, William Waldorf Astor, once the richest man in America.

We visit Knole, a massive estate nestled within a thousand-acre medieval deer park, where I spy a rare, all-white stag; Ightham Mote, a fourteenth-century moated manor house oppressively dark with unhappy spirits; Chartwell, the residence of Winston Churchill; and Bateman's, a seventeenth-century Jacobean manor house in the wooded Sussex countryside, home of Rudyard Kipling, author of the classic *The Jungle Book*. Daylong excursions lead us to the seaside town of Rye, as well as Dover to view the iconic white cliffs. Descrying the misty outline of Normandy across the English Channel, my heart smiles and quickens its beat. *Ma chère France,* so close and yet so far.

Robert enjoys the castles, manor homes, and their art collections, intrigued by the details of past owners' privileged lives, but such places soon bore me. I find them cold and lifeless in rigor mortis, all much the same: gilded relics of a bygone age, haughty testimonials left by the elite and wealthy. Interesting architecture and fine craftsmanship always hold appeal, but beyond a childhood fascination with ancient civilizations, history seldom interests. Let me walk with shoes off among the trees and gardens, a breeze upon my face, any day.

Occasionally, I appreciate the kitchens of grand estates when such rooms are open to the public, relating more to the "downstairs" of the working-class servants' world than to the grander, main floors of the gentry. Some of the sculleries and kitchens impress with their size, equivalent to a modern hotel kitchen, and their respectable *batterie de cuisine* of copper pots and culinary tools sets my thoughts to lavish dinners and banquets. What a hub of activity these rooms once were, clamorous with sound, toasty from the ovens, a boisterous and bubbling scene of people, smells, and food.

Heedless of unpredictable weather, I load up our recently acquired wicker hamper to bring along. Leather straps inside hold two porcelain plates in place, along with metal cutlery and proper linens, as well as a pair of short wine glasses in a padded case which we use for San Pellegrino *limonata*. Its belly packed with simple fare—homemade sandwiches, a container of cut fruit, kettle-cooked crisps, a slice or two of leftover tart or a bar of dark chocolate—I stash it in the boot of the car. Alongside, a quilt for sitting on the grass of whatever site we may be visiting, savoring our modest meal amongst the other picnicking Brits—all of whom have a small

78 ◆ WHERE TWO WORLDS TOUCH

square, requisite blanket and some type of hamper.

By comparison, the large patchwork quilt is oversized. How typically American. Yet the lovely tradition of a casual lunch on the lawn we gladly adopt. Decidedly nourishment for the soul. Even on cool days, I shed my shoes to walk barefoot in the grass, relishing the spongy green carpet under foot; a move garnering sidewise glances from those nearby, one that straightaway marks me as a probable foreigner. Typically contained, most English don't seem keen to bare either sole or soul. Mores the pity. They might find benefit in loosening up and having their toes in the dirt.

Spring is fickle in disposition, and rain frequently falls on our weekend excursions. More than once, we eat our picnic in the car. Each National Trust site we visit has a tearoom or modest restaurant, and after touring the respective property, Robert and I sit at a table so he can rest. The tea is pedestrian and lackluster, meant for drinking with milk, sugar, or both, and I'm equally underwhelmed by the requisite scones, though jam and clotted cream helps. Nevertheless, parked together on our day out, we have a fine time of people watching.

Beginning when the clock strikes three in the afternoon, and reaching its peak at four, an orderly stampede descends upon the tearooms of every public site across the country. The crush of teatime, with the Brits' ever-restrained but palpable excitement, their brow-wrinkled concern over finding an open table in the crowded room, the lengthy and genuinely pained deliberation over which cake to choose, never fails to amuse us in a good-hearted way. The teatime ardor strikes me as endearing and genteel, equally with their unabashed love of gardens.

One Saturday at Sissinghurst, observing the English garden patrons in rapture over the latest colorful blooms, visitors bending down to read respective placards with a particular cultivar's name, Robert turns to me.

"Now I understand why my grandmother, who came from Kent, loved gardens so much. It was simply in her blood. When I was a child, any time we went to a place with a garden, she was thrilled."

Here and there, we spot or hear other Americans. My sidekick, Mr. Congeniality, a Southerner by birth and ever friendly, usually engages them in a conversation, enquiring where in the States they hail from. Reticent, much more reserved than Robert, I keep my distance, not saying a word, instead wandering off to examine an alluring flower, or remaining quietly at my hard-won table in the tearoom.

Confessedly, even in America I felt apart from the herd, gay or straight, and, somewhat embarrassingly, I find the clichés about our countrymen ring true: we are loud, overly casual, and poorly dressed. Noticeably overweight. Short on worldliness and appreciation of others' customs—an ignorance arising partly from the States having only two geographic neighbors, and an overly inflated sense of being the most important nation on Earth.

Living here, my attire and tastes have changed. Language, too. Employed by a bank, Robert has necessarily and willingly adopted London fashion. I've gradually acquired a more closely-tailored wardrobe, if still averse to stripes and plaid—*tartan* the check-pattern is often called. My shoes are decidedly less *au courant* than my companion's, however. Garbed as Londoners, with our low-key voices, we don't stand out as Americans, yet outsiders we remain.

Our day trips become the highlight of each weekend. We join the National Trust membership, thus gaining free admission to sites, and with the yearly guidebook in hand, plan explorations farther afield. As spring continues to unfurl in splendor and force, a deepening appreciation for English gardens blossoms in both of us; Robert likes the tailored ones, whereas I prefer the wilder and woolly ones. No surprise, really. On weekends, released from the pressures of work, his banker's phone gladly left at home, we have the leisure to enjoy each other's familiar company. Strolling the manicured grounds of a grand estate or castle, or traipsing through a bluebell woodland, despite the compression on his spine caused by walking, the pain and burdens he carries lightens a bit. Eyes sparkle more brightly blue. A smile lingers at the corners of his mouth. And even under Britain's pouting skies, a ray of sunshine illuminates both our hearts.

WHERE TWO WORLDS TOUCH

Exhausted from the long day and his commute, by dinnertime my companion is running on empty, preferring to listen rather than speak. He says little about his job, regardless that the West End is a rising star irrespective of the bank's unrealistic targets. Many eyes are upon him with surprise, envy, or begrudging approval, as the gay American, back from the edge of death, leads his group to new heights. Robert is more than a bright anomaly; he is a man profoundly changed, and the callous and vapid corporate world no longer suits. His team's accomplishments please him, similarly with a ranking atop the districts and the recognition which comes with that, but his voice and eyes are devoid of emotion and spark.

"I'm beginning to feel like a hamster on the wheel," he sighs morosely, staring into the distance and shaking his head. "Not quite sure how to get off it, as we're both tied to my work permit and dependent on my salary. But I would love to find something different when my contract ends. Maybe a job in the Arts again . . . especially if I can get my citizenship. Wouldn't that be brilliant?"

Robert's father was born in England, first son of an American soldier stationed here during WWII who, along with so many other enlisted Yanks, fell in love with an English girl. Under the changes to UK immigration and citizenship law, Robert can apply for a British passport and potentially obtain dual citizenship. With his father's birth certificate in hand, he recently launched the process, and his extended family in Wales, whom we have visited, enthusiastically support and will sponsor the application.

I earnestly hope Robert's UK passport will manifest, thus allowing him to find employment independent from a foreign work contract, though what exactly that portends for my dependent's visa is unclear. Unfortunately, the dear man doesn't have a smidgen of extra energy or time to look for a new career. He can only place one foot in front of the other and march stoically onwards in stalwart fashion, one grey day at a time, spending his precious hours in the dull banking chambers of central London. Torture for the day complete, after the packed commute, he resuscitates while floating in the warm pool, or walking arm in arm down the narrow, tree-shaded lane following supper and on weekends. He is less and less fond of donning his banker's attire, those dark suits which I drive weekly to Tenterden for cleaning.

"Sometimes tightening my tie, it feels like a noose around my neck."

The unsettling image from the Wimbledon house flashes through my mind.

I admire him. Deeply. We are strong in different ways, yet I doubt I would bear up under the pain and daily grind. Feeling stuck and trapped is anathema; almost assuredly I would snap, but then what? Walk out the door of the office when others financially depend on me? Gauging from the flatness of his eyes and tone when he speaks of the hamster on a wheel, *caged* is exactly how he feels.

The world economy continues to go *arse over tits*, as the Brits say. During the past few weeks, the modest income I draw from a family property and a long-term lease agreement has dried up indefinitely. Never a significant source of funds, certainly not enough to live solely upon, this unforeseen austerity squeezes my already thin pockets. Living in a foreign country without paying work, having no quarterly stipend, I've totally become Robert's dependent.

For the bulk of our previous relating, my mate earned more money than I did. As a healer, nonconformist, and loosely defined *artist*, I've long eschewed work or any path which does not speak to my soul. Nor am I the competitive sort, bothered by not being primary breadwinner in the household. Quite the opposite. Years ago, we realized our life together proved more satisfactory if I worked *less* and tended hearth and home— cooking, cleaning, yard work, grocery shopping, laundry—mundane duties I don't mind overly much. Responsibilities and chores sorted, weekends were basically clear, allowing us to spend our time engaged in things more pleasurable than home-keeping. And my independent income permitted me to maintain a healing arts practice and teaching, and later my chef work, at a moderate level where it didn't consume me.

Now, for the first time, I wrestle with my own independence—or the lack of it. My self-reliant nature prefers greater liberty, but currently I'm dealt a less appealing hand of cards. So be it. We both agree on the awkwardness of Robert paying me for the housework and general assistance. Too rigid and contrived. If we were a couple, I would attend to the household duties regardless. I've willingly chosen the role of comrade who bolsters him through an unexpected death and rebirth; money matters and autonomy aside, we will find a way forward.

Cultural ideals of independence notwithstanding, we are all indebted to each other and nature. Looking deeper than a surface view, *nothing* is separate but inexplicably entwined and mutually beholden. Notions of being insulated or detached from natural law—supposing humans are masters of the web of life rather than interwoven into it—are hubris, ignorance, or both. Yet like Superman or the Lone Ranger, the ego clutches tightly its own story and agenda.

Frankly, I'm unaccustomed to any sort of identity crisis. I've always been a force of *will*, and I never considered my attachments to what unconsciously defined me or the roles I held, until now when they suddenly no longer apply. I'm not even the banker's partner anymore. Beyond *outsider*, my identity has disappeared, leaving me invisible. No convenient label, no business card to hand out. Who would I offer it to, anyway? Farmer Paul on his tractor rolling through the orchards? The sheep bleating in the fields? Without work or money, who am I?

How unanticipated, both the loss of income and existential angst triggered in me.

Struggling for self-sufficiency, some days, I feel like merely the personal assistant or ex-househusband, taking Robert to the station each morning and fetching him in the evening. And sometimes this rubs and chafes. Yet mysterious gifts hide in every situation, so I will surrender and allow myself to receive support in return; like flower and bee, each helping the other in sacred reciprocity.

Yes, I will *lean into* this, observing my own resistance. The familiar heaviness of a burden, or feeling stuck in a rut, I know too well. Attempt to shake off any self-pity or seeing the glass as only half-full. Surely Robert, deeply changed by a life-threatening illness and soul encounter, struggles similarly. No longer who he was, but still bound to a job role now too restrictive for his spirit, and no clear vision or foreseeable path to his next evolution. *Crisis* is unrivaled for unraveling our ego's constructions and persona, allowing a new and more authentic self to emerge—*if* we will surrender and say yes. A deconstruction of self is at hand, for both of us in differing ways. And though I cannot see the outline or even a beginning shape, maybe in this unfamiliar land, a new version of myself will arise in an unlooked-for fashion.

Moreso than residing in London, we are outsiders. Slim chance exists of making friends through Robert's work, not simply because of his management role but our rural distancing. Never mind we prefer more colorful, creative, and free-thinking folk. Who knows when or if we will manage to meet someone to join up with for the occasional day out, or with whom to linger at table over a good meal like we used to do in former days of dinner parties and entertaining. Undefined as our current relationship remains, at least Robert and I have each other.

Confined by the logistics of our countryside existence, my only social point of contact is meaningless interactions in Tenterden when I venture out on errands, and the weekly "veg box" delivery from Abel & Cole. Unarguably, having a shared language is useful; living in Tuscany, Greece, or anywhere I might struggle to communicate, the isolation would undoubtedly feel far more acute. I'm unquestionably alone, but thankfully not lonely.

I have my rituals. Daily walking and writing, puttering in the homey kitchen, crafting bread, a cup of tea and book on the terrace, pulling weeds, the antics of the fluffy lambs bounding through the fields, these all sustain and nurture. Each tethers my authentic self in a foreign land—*yes, this is who I am*—even as my identity dissolves like the proverbial caterpillar in its cocoon.

From time to time, the feral part of me drifts back into slumber, curled contentedly by the warmth of the hearth, lulled and soothed by the scents of tasty things in the kitchen. A bucolic green countryside beyond the walls. Until waking again, restless, hearing a distant call of thunder or Pan pipes. Standing at the window, the wild, solitary creature of myself stares longingly out, pacing by the door, yearning to go and wander far from home on unknown paths. Seeking something more than solace. Sleep beneath the stars. Eat food charred over an open fire. Dance naked beneath the moon.

How deeply I desire to belong to a landscape and place, to know it in my bones and breath, not merely passing through or a temporary vista. A home more discernible and solid than some idea or fanciful sentiment. Yet such belonging eludes me, and perhaps my fate is to keep roaming as a vagabond or gypsy soul. The perpetual outsider.

For now, in a world that has banished "otherness"—shadow, deformity, queerness, myth, and magic—the Shaman broods at the rear of the garden, upholding re-enchantment, and calling me.

Don't go back to sleep.

~

Our familiar scene unfolds nightly: dining in the farmhouse kitchen to the tune of cold rain falling in the darkness outside, Robert wearing his blue Hamburg jumper and seated in the chair closest to the warmth of the Rayburn. Held by a gracious house too large for two, we mostly inhabit the kitchen and secondary, rear reception with its Swedish log burner, desiring warmth and comfort. Sheltered by old bricks and wooden beams, we return to each other after a long day apart, reweaving the silken cords of connection.

Tucking into a just-baked quiche filled with still-warm custard of fresh local asparagus and smoky ham, the flaky golden crust shattering under the tines of his fork, Robert looks at me. Soft and undefended in countenance, tender with vulnerability.

"I've shared this before. When I was in hospital, my repeated thought was how I didn't want to be here, and I didn't want to die in cold, grey England." He pauses for a moment, choosing his words. "I don't wish to stay working for Lloyds or in banking . . . but now that you're with me, I don't really want to go back to the States. I'm more at home *here*."

The sentiment runs deeper than America's current political zeitgeist with its nationalistic, fear-mongering and religious tones, unpalatable to both of us. Given his childhood spent in Germany, much about Europe feels more aligned to his preferences and sensibilities.

With a quiet start, something has shifted.

My previous life has unraveled, leaving me with no income, no tangible career or working identity, and my tiny tribe of wilderness guides all live across the Atlantic. This dear man and I remain outsiders, nascent arrivals in an unfamiliar countryside. Yet even with my intermittent longing for undomesticated places, and the flickering shadows of lingering blue sadness, surprisingly, I don't want to return to America, either. Not even to the cherished *soulscape* of New Mexico. Funny, that.

Reason falters at times, and life looks differently inside the Mystery.

Hearing his words, feeling the truth of my own concurrent inclination and change of heart, a gentle ease fills me. A subtle relaxation from head to toe, eyes softening, and breath expanding in my belly once more with a knowing, trusting *yes*. Time to shove off from shore, sailing toward an unknown, uncharted destination. Only the soul's compass to navigate by, and distant, diamond constellations in the heart.

REVELATION

THE FIRST OF May is Beltane. In Celtic and neo-pagan calendars, the date marks the midpoint between the spring equinox and summer solstice, with ancient traditions of bonfires, fertility rites, dancing, and carnal delight. A celebration of the interpenetration of the Wild God and Goddess, the sacred marriage of masculine and feminine. As with Samhain or All Souls Night six months hence, the veil between worlds hangs gossamer thin and easily pierced, thus a time-honored eventide for ritual and magic in a more enchanted world.

Overcome by exhaustion, Robert does not wish to walk along the lane, so I go alone for a stroll to admire the pearl of moon shining brightly on an auspicious night. A chance to offer prayers and intentions to the firmament, standing at the edge of a shimmering wheat field in the cool, silver-clad night, feeling the whoosh of darkness around me.

Barefoot, returning to the farmhouse along the rustling, dark lane, I meet a large, russet fox and we both stop to regard each other. As if at court and greeting a nobleman or lady, I bow with a mischievous smile. The glistening canid eyes contemplate me for a minute, briefly assessing my relevance. Am I friend, foe, or merely inconsequential? With a twitch of bushy red tail, the creature turns and disappears beneath a hedge along a driveway, its verdict unknown.

In following days, May erupts with unadulterated glory. The colorful, cultivated tulips have withered along with the enchanting bluebells, but a riot of flowers bursts loose everywhere. The gurgling stream in front of the house flows full, dotted overnight with a dozen, yellow fuzzy ducklings zipping across the surface as they paddle briskly after their mother.

Balmy, fair skies and longed-for warmth lure me to sit on the rear terrace—a "sun trap," the estate agent called it—shaded by a newly acquired, red canvas parasol. Typing on my MacBook, a wooden tray beside me with requisite tea and biscuits. A little smile on my face whenever the occasional pheasant emerges furtively from under cover of the tall, clipped hedge to dash across the lawn with neck outstretched, running for the shelter of the box hedge opposite. Birds never cease to entertain me.

Most of the fluffy lambs are gone, quieting the soundscape. One moonless night shortly before Easter, the sheep *bah-bah-bah* loudly in distressed chorus for hours, keeping both of us awake, rousing us each time we finally fall back to sleep.

"What is going on with the sheep tonight?" Robert asks groggily in the dark.

Heavy in heart, certain of the answer, I hesitate to speak its weight aloud. Staring up at the canopy of the bed above us, I find my tired voice.

"I think they probably took the lambs today and the mothers are distraught, calling for their babies."

"What do you mean, *they took the lambs* . . . ? Who took them, the farmers? Why did they take them?"

"Well, Easter is coming."

Silence. In his sleepy state of mind, he has not yet connected the picture.

"I don't understand."

"Lamb is very popular at Easter."

As if the linen roof of the four-posted bed has dropped, a sense of shock smothers Robert when the pieces click, his palate conflicting with his heart. He has always enjoyed eating lamb. I can almost feel the tightening in his chest, his body going weak.

"Oh my god," he whispers hollowly. "You mean, those adorable babies frolicking in the fields, those . . . that is the lamb we eat?"

"Yes, Robert, they are raised primarily for meat. Sad, isn't it? You honestly never made the connection until just now?"

88 ◆ WHERE TWO WORLDS TOUCH

An extended stillness settles, broken only by the plaintive ewes in the moonlit, empty field.

"No," he chokes with emotion. "I am never eating lamb again."

So acutely sensitive these days, if mostly in a good way. I reach over and gingerly drape my arm across his shoulders, feeling the stifled sobs as he buries his face deeper into the pillow.

Bless him, he's come undone. Silently, I bless those little ones taken for killing, as well as the anguished ewes bleating ceaselessly, rending the dark night and our fragile hearts. *Bless us all.*

On my walks the next days, a few fluffy infants remain in a couple of grassy pastures, but most have vanished, shipped off to the slaughterhouse for holiday consumption and Sunday roasts. Previously a vegetarian for more than a dozen years, with subsequent stints as a vegan, rarely do I eat any sort of red meat. Crossing the lamb-less expanses on my ramble, sharing a sentimental solidarity with Robert, I too foreswear eating or cooking the endearing, bouncing yeanlings.

My hours of roaming have lengthened further, the footpath journeys encompassing longer circles afield. Every now and then, I pull the small black Moleskine sketchbook and fountain pen from my rucksack to jot down insights, observations, and flashes of inspiration. Notes for short pieces I've been writing lately, mostly reflections on walking in nature. Without fail, I fall indiscriminately in love a dozen times on every ramble. Besotted by a butterfly. A heron or a water vole. Oak tree. Wildflower. Clouds. *Life.*

Coming and going from the house, whether on foot or in the car, the number of ducklings counted along the stream declines rapidly. One day, ten remained of the former twelve. A few days later only seven. Then five. Three. Eventually just one. Foxes make the most likely culprit, though weasels, stoats, and feral cats are all contenders, and even other birds. Risky fate as a duckling in the countryside, an inviting snack for some creature's gullet.

"Have you noticed the poor little ducklings?"

I have returned in the car from Tenterden, and Sara has pulled in behind me, the top down on her Mini Cooper, and stepped out to open their gate. Clad in a rainbow-striped jumper with an elf-like hood, she wears purple jeans and pink Converse high tops.

"You mean the fact they are disappearing daily? That there aren't any left?" I glance toward the gurgling irrigation channel nearly overflowing its banks.

"Exactly!" She raises both hands in an exasperated gesture. "Don't know where she's keeping them but she's a terrible mother, that one. I've nicknamed her Useless. Let's just hope the last one turns out to be Lucky."

Hopping back in her car, she revs the engine, and drives through the open gate with a wave and a friendly smile.

~

"I want you to know I've been trying for a month to book a table at Petersham Nurseries Cafe, to take you back there on your birthday, but I can't get one. The earliest opening is middle of next month . . . and I've been calling for weeks. I even tried *begging*. My assistant, Julia, tried too. No luck."

What a prince, this man.

During round one of our London residency, Robert and I, with his mum and Stephen, his 20-something cousin from Wales, enjoyed a memorable lunch at the upscale but rustic, outdoor restaurant. I initially learned of the place after browsing the cookery section of Hatchard's Piccadilly, where I picked up Skye Gyngell's just-released, *A Year In My Kitchen*, spotlighting her restaurant located in a garden nursery near Richmond-upon-Thames. The food in her book rang chimes with me—sophisticated without pretentiousness or stuffiness—a tasteful tribute to seasonal bounty. Smitten, I rang the restaurant and booked a table for lunch on my upcoming birthday.

Everything about our dining experience thrilled. The relaxed air and earthy setting, the garden nursery itself; mismatched bistro tables set up in a plant-filled greenhouse with a gravel floor, and waitresses wearing

90   ◆ WHERE TWO WORLDS TOUCH

Wellies. Artful, delicious, and immaculate food. Everything casual *and* elegant. When I rose from our table and went strolling to find the loo, walking down a path, I passed the small hut of a kitchen where Skye was bent intently over a customer's plate, adding a chef's finishing details of perfection. She looked up and smiled.

Within a year, the charming cafe had doubled its number of tables in the greenhouse, yet it was impossible to get a seat without booking well in advance. The cognoscenti, with their silver forks and "foodie" blogs, had spoken and the word was out.

I hadn't given more than a passing thought to my impending solar return, so Robert's gesture and effort touches me.

"I wanted to surprise you on your birthday. I know how much you've wanted to go back there, how you love her food and cookbooks . . . but the earliest table is in June."

He looks crestfallen, a young boy who dropped his ice cream cone. I kiss his cheek with a smile and squeeze his hand, reassuring him.

"No worries, sweet man. We will think of something else, and I'm sure it will be just lovely. Far less expensive, too!"

~

My birthday falls on a Saturday, and for our weekend outing we head to Monk's House in Sussex. Held by the National Trust, the country home of Virginia Woolf is a landmark I desire to visit, having read her notable book-length essay, *A Room of One's Own*, as well as one of her novels, *Mrs Dalloway*, arguably her most famous work. A novel perhaps easily dismissed for its rather boring plot—a day in the life of upper-class Clarissa Dalloway as she prepares for a party at her home that evening—yet extraordinary in its language. And the author's sensitivity to finding delight in the mundane moments of a day, the simple and ordinary, reflects my own guiding philosophy.

Woolf deeply intrigues me: an early modernist, brilliant, cloaked in sadness, in love with both her husband, Leonard, and aristocratic Vita

Sackville-West, creator of the Sissinghurst garden. No stranger to the weight of shadows, she struggled continually from what would now be considered bipolar disorder, until finally weighting down her coat pockets with stones and drowning herself in the River Ouse not far from the house. Her famous farewell note to Leonard is utterly heartbreaking.

Located in the village of Rodmell in the South Downs, Monk's House is an eighteenth century weatherboard cottage modest in size, renovated and expanded upon from smaller, sixteenth century origins, with a large glasshouse conservatory built upon one wall of the dwelling. We've arrived precisely at opening time, and entering the gate, a stampede of color sweeps over me in the informal garden. A jubilee of flowers, trees, small orchard, and miniature pond. My favorite sort of outdoor artistry. Nothing too formal or grand.

Pleasantly uncrowded, roughly a dozen other visitors are present. Given my nonconformist tastes, the residence is one I *should* like with its rustic simplicity, yet from the moment of stepping indoors, a crushing sadness and gloom descends, as if the low ceiling and weight of the house itself presses down. The pea green walls of the main reception are anything but cheery. My chest feels tight, an emotional affect not my own. Even Virginia's bedroom, with its single, narrow bed beside the fireplace and scores of books, feels profoundly melancholic despite the room's brightness thanks to windows. Robert lingers in the house to observe the sights and details, but I must escape the somber air. The dwelling is haunted—not by ghosts of Virginia or Leonard per se, but an overwhelmingly morose presence.

Free of the oppressive residence and grateful for a blue sky, trying to shake the shadow, I meander through the vividly blooming garden, appreciating the May flowers and buzzing honeybees. To the rear of the property is Virginia's writing lodge, originally a toolshed. Scarcely more than a wooden hut, the studio has broad windows and sits sheltered beneath an oak tree. No one else is about, and I peer in through the locked glass doors, admiring her wide desk with its ink well, blotters and paper, as if she just stepped out for a couple of hours. A kerosine wick lamp made of

92   ◆ WHERE TWO WORLDS TOUCH

copper with a dusty glass chimney. Here, Woolf wrote most of her novels, working in quiet seclusion, overlooking the garden and landscape that offered joy and solace even through her sunless, troubled hours.

For an *empath*, sorrow still inhabits this place, and the crepuscular weight—an unexpected broadside collision with my psyche—presses on me. Seated alone on a wooden bench, the impact of Woolf's residence, seeing her room and desk, unlocks a tenderness within me barely short of a tear. Too many years I've struggled with depression, wrestling with my own dark angels, pinned down by their unrelenting might. An unknowing scion in a birth family lineage of psychic gifts, depressive and bipolar disorders, and suicides, a legacy I'm determined to renounce and rewrite.

Robert finds me wrapped in blue. After peering into her studio and reading the informational display, he sits to give his aching back a rest. Until this visit, he was unaware of the Bloomsbury group: the avant-garde set of writers, intellectuals, artists and philosophers, of whom Woolf was a central figure.

"It's all so dark," I mutter, a murkiness in my voice.

"The house? I didn't really notice. I was thinking it was sort of pleasant with its artsy feel. But now that you mention it . . . "

Wooden benches or chairs are soon uncomfortable for my comrade, so we rise to stroll around and explore the cheery garden further.

"Isn't it lovely?" comments an attractive woman with dark but greying hair cut stylishly. A score of silver bangles adorn both wrists, and a lengthy and sizable turquoise necklace dramatically accents her belted black cashmere dress. Robert and I stand near the house, aimlessly gazing toward Virginia's bedroom, the stranger just a few feet away. "And her bedroom, how fascinating to see all her books, the titles of what she read. I wished I could touch them."

Addressed by someone unknown, both of us are briefly caught off-guard at the untypical friendliness, so very *un*-English. Likely she overheard our conversation and realized we are a couple of gay foreigners, non-threatening enough. My counterpart, in his convivial style, begins a discourse with the woman, admitting he didn't know much about Woolf other than what I shared with him on the drive here, and it's my birthday outing.

"Are you enjoying it?" She turns to me with a direct, inquisitive gaze.

"Honestly, I find it a bit gloomy and dark. Not the lighting but the *feel* of it."

Like the fox in the lane on Beltane night, she regards me for a long moment, considering.

"Yes, I can see what you mean. I think Leonard, her husband, lived here with a very deep sadness after she left. They were married a long time, you know. It must have been terribly lonely and depressing to lose her as he did."

My thoughts exactly.

"Have you been to Charleston Farmhouse yet?"

Robert and I glance at each other, shaking heads in unison.

"No? Oh, you simply *must* go! It's just over the hill, really. Not more than five miles, I'm sure. It is utterly wonderful."

Something about this woman I warm to immediately, an aspect beyond her amiability. Possibly it's her clothing, the loads of silver and turquoise à la Santa Fe, but I'm taken by a sudden yearning to be friends somehow.

She tilts her head conspiratorially and smiles.

"Trust me, it's not nearly so depressing as this place. Virginia's sister lived there, along with Duncan Grant and a bunch of other Bloomsbury artists. They're the ones who did most of the art inside the house here. It's much more Bohemian, and every bit of Charleston has been turned into art—doors, walls, ceilings. There's really nothing like it. Do yourself a favour and go. I promise, you won't be disappointed."

Thanking her for the suggestion, we part ways. A cloud of blue grey still drapes my shoulders, but the sunny day and freedom from the house helps lift my mood. Despite the effusive garden, enough of this place. We will go to the nearby market town of Lewes to find a nice birthday lunch, and then, perhaps, go in search of the Bloomsbury farmhouse.

~

Charleston is a seventeenth century brick farmhouse with walls clad

94   ◆ WHERE TWO WORLDS TOUCH

in thick foliage of ivy, decorated further by a latticework of climbing pink roses, and twisted ropes of rowdy wisteria. After browsing the gift shop and purchasing tickets for the next tour, we have twenty minutes before the group entry, so Robert and I stroll over to sit on a bench beside the large pond of liquid jade, watching other visitors mill about. Basking in the sunshine, warming my bones, I'm already lighter, clearer, and glad we've come. A pleasant garden reliably brings me home to myself, and the ambience here feels thankfully livelier than Woolf's house. Sunlight refracts and ripples across the pond in handfuls of sparkling white diamonds. On the far edge, a whimsical statue of a side-lying, levitating woman floats in midair, cleverly held aloft and suspended by her long hair trailing to the water's surface.

"I like this place already," proclaims my companion, adjusting his sunglasses and flashing me a smile, mirroring my unspoken sentiments.

Our tour guide is a middle-aged woman with curly grey hair, wearing glasses too large for her face and amplifying her mirthful eyes. An artist herself, she is well-spoken, knowledgeable, and rich with stories about the unusual group of people who once dwelt at Charleston. In 1916, the artist Vanessa Bell, sibling of Virginia, relocated here to be closer to her sister, bringing along two children from an ended marriage as well as Duncan Grant, a fellow artist who was the love of her life. Duncan, however, was a gay man who brought his lover to reside in the next bedroom. This unconventional household, which later included Vanessa's former-husband, in addition to an ever-revolving cast of the Bloomsbury set, collectively turned the farmhouse into a living work of art; a full-time *atelier* for creativity, liberal thinking, and non-traditional ways.

True to the assurance of the likable woman in the garden at Rodmell, nearly every foot of space available for art has indeed been played upon. Walls, ceilings, and doors are covered with hand-blocked prints, original paintings, or turned into capricious murals. Fireplaces, chimneypieces, and moldings are all painted uniquely. The furniture itself is decorated, upholstered in hand-painted fabrics, or handmade, while custom tiles and ceramics, fired in the farmhouse kiln, greet at every turn. Drawings and works by Picasso, Renoir, Derain, Delacroix and others are tucked about. In sum, the residence radiates an uninhibited celebration of life—complete with painted nudes of both genders, almost everything imbued with a touch of post-Impressionism whimsy and *joie de vivre.*

Here is a place of unorthodox lives and love, I smile to myself. A welcoming of *gayness* in every sense of the word.

Touring the rooms, listening to the anecdotal tales of the farmhouse and its colorfully eccentric inhabitants, my heart wears a secret grin— my favorite story being the Russian ballerina married to a neighbor, who danced naked among the cows, twirling her long shawl as she spun through the ankle-high wet grass. Stodgy old England be damned.

This must be artist's heaven. Such a delightful consent to life. The sheer abundance of creativity on display overwhelms, too much to take in, and my soul flutters gently in quiet joy. Gone from my chest is the darkness of Monk's House; instead, something gracious and bright envelops me. Mostly I want to reach out and take Robert's hand, knowing he feels the benevolent spirit of this place, too.

Like the décor of the house itself, the gardens are punctuated with handmade statuary, displaying a sense of humor and levity. The brick-walled kitchen garden is undergoing restoration, but even with the unfinished stage of construction and replanting, it tempts me to sit for a while, reading or daydreaming. The sunny, enclosed space is precisely the sort of *potager* I dream of having one day, should I ever find my patch of good earth to call home.

On the surface, we have a recipe for madness: a bohemian artist, her gay lover—with whom she later conceived a child—and *his* lover, two children, an ex-husband, and a host of visiting intellectuals, writers, artists, and philosophers. All of them living decidedly out-of-the-box in a time when Victorian thinking and morals held sway in England, and homosexuality was cause for imprisonment. Surely, the household had its fair share of dysfunctionality and heartache, but mostly Charleston was a striking experiment in bold, non-conformist models of living and loving. A haven for free self-expression.

96 ◆ WHERE TWO WORLDS TOUCH

"It will be an odd life, but . . . it ought to be a good one for painting," wrote Vanessa Bell.

Undoubtedly it was.

Driving home to Kent, both of us are happily silent for the first stage of the journey, still digesting the afternoon's tour, content with tea and carrot cake afterwards in the cafe. Warmly in the glow of such a life-affirming experience, as if we have just read a wonderful book aloud or watched a joyous film. Comforted, like holding a round, polished green stone in the hand, worn smooth from years of rubbing and wishing upon it. The springtime landscape of the South Downs passes steadily by the car's windows, a vaguely hypnotic blur, until finally I speak.

"Thank you for a lovely birthday."

"You are welcome, love."

Robert smiles with twinkling blue eyes and reaches over to place a hand on my knee.

"It turned out much better than a lunch at Petersham, I think."

I cover his pale hand with my own, giving it a gentle squeeze.

"Actually, I think the real purpose of the day," he adds thoughtfully, "if you want to call it that, wasn't about Woolf's house at all. That was just the pivot to get us to Charleston."

"Agreed. And I loved the house was such a celebration, a non-tragic depiction of homosexuality. So refreshing."

"Yes, me too."

In a curious way, visiting the Bloomsbury farmstead in Sussex has granted us liberty in our own exploration of a non-defined relating, for in sharing the great canopied bed in the Kent farmhouse, the two of us have eased back into the realm of lovers. Familiar. Tender. Good.

Love is.

We have freedom to create whatever we wish rather than remain limited by traditional models. Countless styles and options for relationship exist, not merely the few which human society upholds, like monogamous or "open." Why must our togetherness even require a label? Can we not simply be sovereign as lovers and best friends? Any relating, conventional or

REVELATION ♦ *97*

not, functions *entirely* upon the consciousness of the individuals involved, reflecting the inner work they have done or haven't, as well as their notions of ownership and fidelity.

We are fashioning something new, this man and I, liberated from the old wounds and binding gravity that held us too long. How serendipitous an unplanned visit to a Bohemian farmhouse from the Victorian Age should end up inspiring a modern interpretation of love. As frequently happens in life, we expectantly went looking for one thing but ended up discovering something else entirely, which far surpassed the original intention.

It will be an odd life, but . . . it ought to be a good one for loving.

Beyond a new relationship, what are we creating? In my expanse of solo hours, the question of our true calling in the world hovers in my mind, unanswered. Both in heart and soul, I know Robert has far more to offer than managing a district for Lloyds. The artist in him feels ready to resurface and sing again, literally or metaphorically. More than once these past months, I suggested to him a gift lies in his wound, that somehow his brush with death might form the work he's *really* meant to do going forward, or at least some portion of it. Challenges always carry a hidden genius, even if we don't discover such until much later—strange bestowals that prompt us to grow and evolve.

My dear man wants desperately to find his new vocation or calling, and I search for my own alongside, if skeptical I'll discover it in England as an outsider, a domesticated wayfarer. Odder things have happened, however. For now, the glimmering golden thread leads onward across Kentish fields. And I remind myself even the incandescent stars are born amid chaos and destruction of what came before.

~

Late May. I am walking a dirt footpath through familiar pastures and orchards, marveling at the exquisite illumination of the evening that coaxes out the utmost splendor of everything it touches. Every whispering field stands forth to become a luminous, Impressionist painting. Each tree, crowned in leafy glory, transforms into a dancer on stage in a golden spotlight. I, lucky soul, sit spellbound in the front row of the audience, dazzled as the spectacle unfurls before me, unsure where to turn my head or look next because *everything* is surreal in its radiance.

At this hour of the evening, wild rabbits in the fields are thick as thieves. Seemingly everywhere, alarmed at my hulking approach, some of them preciously tiny and scarcely larger than my fist, all bounding quickly into the safety of underground warrens and thickly green hedgerows.

Scents of dry earth, heady grass, and sweet flowers intoxicate me. Passing a darkly alluring burrow beneath tree roots, a cozy den for some wild creature, I catch the unmistakable whiff of acrid fox urine.

Hello, clever Fox. It's been a while since I've seen you on my doorstep or in the lane. Are you watching me from a sheltered spot?

Robert has flown to Florida to visit his mum, strong enough to travel on his own, and I am contentedly savoring a week of solitude. Without him to cook for, I'm undertaking one of my yearly cleansing fasts—a conscious abstinence from food as part of a ten-day, internal cleansing program learned years ago in Hawaii from the famous healer and *kahuna* Auntie Margaret Machado.

On the third day of fasting my body feels light as air, my senses keen and unusually sharp. I wander in a split mode of consciousness, like dolphins who sleep and dream in the dark sea while half their brain stays awake to remind them to surface and breathe. Musing on *sleep* and *waking* as a metaphor for awareness in life, enraptured by the sights, sounds, and smells around me, gathering sensual treasures for the temple of my soul. The wind on my face, stirring my mane of greying hair; an audible, textural crunch of earth beneath my shoes; the way my breath feels in the hollows of my legs; how the swaying movement of the trees sends subtle ripples throughout my own body sensation; the flow of vitality through me in a current of aliveness and power.

Irrespective of the evening hour and abstinence from food, my energy soars. I am a chant of muscles, sinews, and bones humming together in harmonious resonance. Walking in nature brings me into a sensory rapture as nothing else does but dancing and making love.

The Technicolor sunset could take your breath away. Even the rabbits sit up to notice. Passing through an apple grove, the leaves' size has increased dramatically since coming this way a week ago, along with swelling polyps adorned with faded remnants of blossoms. How I adore this aged orchard with its orderly rows of gnarled soldiers, soon to bear sweet fruit instead of guns or swords. In the season of dramatic growth, a quickening surges in me too, germinating into some new creation to offer the world.

Alas, I don't yet know what it might be.

Below me, the weald of Kent stretches and rolls away towards the South Downs and the distant English Channel, a vista glinting in the pastel twilight of a spring evening. Halting at a tilted wooden fence post, gazing towards the setting sun, unexpectedly, a silver bell rings out within my chest, scattering my thoughts with its crystalline tone.

For a sublime shining minute, the veil falls away and this lovely facet of the world transcends a picturesque, resplendent landscape of dusky light and shadow. I behold a living miracle defying comprehension. Each blade of grass, every purple clover flower, all the buzzing insects, the noble trees dancing in unseen currents of conscious air, the living soil and microbes— *everything* is sentient and spinning with cosmic intelligence. Each molecule communicates and hums in harmonic relationship with everything around it. Our planet is the ultimate symphony of *consciousness*.

Illuminating the quantum concept, in this rarefied moment across painted fields at sunset, I literally *see* the Unified Field of energy. Regardless of the distinctly unique and seemingly separate objects forming the ecosystem around me, from English oak to ring-neck pheasant to wriggling pond newt, the entirety comprises one seamless conversation. A boundless, mutual co-arising. Each thing co-exists in a sphere of incomprehensible, interdependent relationship and harmony, existing both in form and non-form.

Standing upon the skirt of the hill, my own life pales in significance, as passing as a noisy bumblebee. Yet I, too, am irreducibly the same elemental mind that breathes in blazing stars and sighs in the terrible beauty of

100 ◆ WHERE TWO WORLDS TOUCH

galaxies. With each inhale, I draw in the living intelligence, a suprasomatic sentience, suffusing cells and blood with far more than mere oxygen. *Inspiration*, in a word, permeated with the creative imagination and breath of the Divine.

Through an elongated minute of expansive perception, reality splits wide open and I gaze inside of everything: simultaneous light and shadow, fathomless intelligence, harmonic frequencies, and a mind-shattering complexity of relationship. Visible and invisible. Sound and silence. Structure and energy.

Awesome is far too clunky and meager to describe the moment. *Sublime, revelatory, rapture* . . . all words fail and fall short. How does one capture the Infinite when it reveals itself?

Wordlessly, every atom of my body sings as part of a celestial chorus. Even as I tremble, the bell in my chest again rings out with its clear, high tone across the fields, calling all to exultant celebration like the trees at dawn.

Holy, holy.

⁓

Finally moving on from stunned revelation, an airiness animates me, as if someone has stripped away heavy outer layers; ones I never realized were leaden and dead. Though the mystical union of the higher, transpersonal state has already faded, I drift through the swaying green wheat field in an altered awareness—a heightened acuity I'm unaccustomed to, even as a *sensitive*. Exposed as a tender mollusk with its protective, lacquered shell pried open. Will something vast and dark now snatch me up to swallow me whole?

Yes, I accept. I will not resist but surrender to the Mystery unfolding.

Long ago, I grasped that only by fully embracing our mortality, the sure inevitability of death, can one appreciate the preciousness of existence. Engaging life with sensory awareness and *soul*, choosing to consciously inhabit the vessel of body and breath, our days echo with the voice of the sacred. We are only passing through. How will we live and savor this endless moment of now?

From the hill, descending across the field of emerald, an apple orchard grows to my left. Still in an altered state, woven of light mesh rather than flesh and bone, porous to the pulsing web of life around me, a voice whispers.

Go naked to the gods.

In a flash, a dream surfaces from the previous night, in which I walked naked down a country dirt road alongside an orchard to my left. Seeing a woman approaching, embarrassed for my nudity, I stepped among the trees to hide, hoping she wouldn't see me.

Go naked to the gods.

Potentially more than a mishmash of neural firings, our dreams—both sleeping and waking—often carry important invitations and messages from the subconscious. Recalling last night's enigmatic storyline, with the apple orchard on my left, an upwelling of energy rises in a strong vibration, along with an overcoming desire to remove my clothes and walk naked through the field. Expand in bodymind rather than contract in fearfulness. A tremulous urgency to be essentially and unutterably myself—unclad—to reenact the nightdream, though I'm unclear why.

Fear swirls icily in my gut, whirling and mixing with the rising core of energy. My eyes scan the surrounding fields of rippling green wheat to the edge of the hill hemmed in dusky ribbons of rose-infused light. The nearest farmhouse is more than a half-mile distant. I'm not an exhibitionist, and though I've shed clothes beneath the moon in darkness, doing so in fading daylight seems an entirely different matter.

This is crazy. I'll be arrested in a foreign country for public nudity in a wheat field.

The bioelectric tremor is a scream waiting to explode. My body quivers visibly with both fear and anticipation. In the evening breeze, I battle myself, squeezed by breathless anxiety and shame despite the energy seeking expansion.

Just do it. Take off your clothes.

Slowly I unbutton and remove my shirt, the evening air chilly enough my brown nipples contract and stand up perkily. I pause for a minute, hesitating. Shaking. Then I shed my shoes, slip off socks, and step free of my old, faded jeans.

I will not limit myself in fear . . . I will go naked to the gods.

Stripped bare, my arms outstretched to the periwinkle sky and gentle breeze, the wind moves around me, appraising my offering with soft fingers that measure and murmur.

Carrying clothes in one hand and shoes in the other, I walk gingerly. Bare soles explode with sensation at crunchy soil, prickly grasses, and jagged rock. Manroot hanging freely, bouncing lightly from side to side, I savor being unbound and exposed. Radically free.

Step by tender step, I follow the worn footpath across the field of knee-high wheat, parting a grassy sea like some naked, mad prophet. Quaveringly alive. Every sense heightened. Treading the rough ground, wondering who sees me, chuckling at my self-conscious fears—imagining dialogues between my potential observers, human and otherwise. Only humankind would be fussed.

How tightly shame keeps us bound.

Gradually, fear falls away. Shoulders roll back to widen my chest, and I breathe fully into my entire torso, belly expanding and softening. All senses dilate in communion with the evening sky above, the air dancing round, and earth underfoot.

At the far side of the wide field, a five-minute walk at my barefooted pace, I stop at a fence post and reclothe myself, grateful for warmth. I step back into my shoes, a welcome sheath for tenderized feet, and traverse the two remaining fields stretching between me and the narrow lane leading home.

Unlooked for, I've passed some strange initiation: an opportunity to move past fear and shame, trusting a deeper energy of expansion. A dramatic emergence from the shell versus continued containment in patterns of safety and protection. And suddenly, everything I once knew, or thought I knew—including what I envisioned for my life and work—is *far* too small and restrictive.

When one opens to possibility, possibility opens.

Weightless as a thin cloud, like a wisp of intention and amethyst smoke rising from a smoldering stick of sandalwood incense on the altar of a shrine, I am a humble, trembling prayer. Nothing more.

Back at the farmhouse, stepping inside the heavy front door, a hushed haven greets me with familiar scents of wood, dried sage, and lavender. Under my skin, effervescent energy streams and bubbles, and though I don't generally write in the evenings, I must put words to paper. Right now... *write* now. Epiphany at the fence post notwithstanding, apart from the nearly unbearable lightness, something else is arriving *through* me—whether a grey dove of inspiration or a storm of lightning bolts, I can't yet discern. My awareness is a supernova, exploding outward in rings of a shock wave.

Leaving shoes in the foyer, barefoot on the cool wooden floors, I head to the kitchen and put the kettle on for tea. My ephemeral state demands a delicate and aromatic brew such as jasmine pearls.

A few minutes later, seated at the darkly polished, large dining table with A4 notepad and fountain pen, the Asian-style, celadon porcelain teacup with removable infuser steaming fragrantly beside me, I begin to write. The pen's gold nib glides swiftly across the page with a familiar scratching in the stillness, trailing a jumble of black letters and insights in its wake, the birth of something new.

Don't go back to sleep.

AFTERSHOCKS

THE AFTERSHOCK OF highly expanded awareness and perception endures for days. I move through the house, the garden, and fields with a core of radiant energy streaming outward, as if I am a quantum expansion. My physical shape and energetic boundary have diffused and become nebulous, composed of luminous ether more than flesh. An enduring lightness feels almost disconcerting, impossible to put into words, and the veil between worlds is thin. Nonexistent, possibly.

Paranormal events have punctuated my life since childhood, including a lucid dream *soul directive* in my early twenties; a direct experience of Source as a blazing sun of consciousness, overwhelming with love, and leaving me with tears streaming down my cheeks, even if the actual guidance felt deeply mysterious. *You are here to teach.*

For years, I wondered, but teach *what?*

As an adult, I have wrestled with experiences of non-consensus reality, attempting to verify or dismiss the validity of such occurrences. Sometimes, these manifestations—be they sightings, astral visitors, disembodied voices, psychic knowing or curious presaging—offer mystical guidance or insight; others merely remind me *reality* is much larger, and far more mysterious, than the so-called material world of matter and physics.

The fencepost revelation is different from previous events and utterly profound; not only for the ongoing weightlessness—as if I've been rearranged on a molecular or quantum level—but for obliterating my existing worldview. Large enough to love the world with outstretched arms,

I can embrace its suffering, the totality of joy, and deep mystery, knowing nothing is separate from myself.

In one shining instant, my work these past years with clients, groups, and men's work suddenly feels far too limited, like peering through a keyhole. Apart from hands-on healing, when energy comes directly through my hands and the *high sense perception* activates, I have largely followed other peoples' maps and modalities. I've learned my various crafts as apprentices do, versus such work being *revealed* or organically developing on its own. Now, as if *seeing* some invisible thing on a hilltop, my own expression and offering—something seeking to materialize *through* me—is arriving.

Amid my expanse of hours alone at the farmhouse, again and again I circle back to the initial words penned upon returning from the twilight field; several scribbled pages about the Erotic Warrior, a vague metaphor or emerging archetype. The stream-of-conscious download is unfocused and inchoate, anything but erudite, and I shirk from what I've written, finding it awkward. Embarrassing, almost. "Erotic Warrior" sounds like something from a trashy romance novel or, worse, a cheap porn film. A whispering voice urges me to continue, a book is emerging here, but I don't want to write about *that*, whatever it may be.

I pace the sun-kissed terrace, relishing the warm flagstones under my bare soles; intently considering the garden flowers as if great works of art brought to life, or cryptic messages in need of deciphering. Resistance is worth examining more closely, I know. Shrinking from this idea of the Erotic Warrior—an agent for embodied *eros*—ready to censor it or walk away, what does my reticence divulge about my own sexual and sensual nature, an aspect of my being I thought was relatively uninhibited. What shame do I still carry?

Despite inhabiting a non-consensus reality, and irrespective of my radical expansion, I'm avoiding what seeks recognition. A reluctant mystic, I remain.

Revelation notwithstanding, other unforeseen currents churn and merge in strange confluence. A quickening of springtime, new energies pressing forth. An intriguing man grabs my attention via OUTeverywhere, a UK-based gay online network which emphasizes and promotes events, gatherings, and outings. While aiming to provide more than simply a dating, chat, or hookup site, certainly the online nexus is employed for that, too. During my first round in London, through the website I found the OUT Spirituality group, a monthly gathering at St. James's Church near Piccadilly; a group of thirty or forty men sitting politely in chairs in a drab basement room, with an individual presenting a talk for the evening on some facet of spirituality. I attended a couple of times, thinking feasibly to meet a like-minded friend or two, but the staid assemblage wasn't my cup of tea. OUTeverywhere is also how I discovered a small writer's group meeting monthly at Gay's The Word, a long-established LGBTQ bookshop close to Russell Square; a gathering of amateur wordsmiths I joined twice, and likely would have returned had I not gone back to America.

Stellar is new to OUTeverywhere and has discovered my profile among a few others with a keyword search for *spiritual*. Liking my photo and what I've written as a personal description, he reaches out to me via the site's email. His picture shows a handsome, slender, clean-shaven man in his thirties with thick but short dark hair and smiling eyes. His description of himself as a "spiritual author" immediately piques my interest. Exchanging messages, a mutual curiosity and attraction rising, though he lives an hour away, the next day he drives to the farmhouse so we can meet in person. Robert's absence makes it convenient to connect with the stranger. Nearly serendipitous. In light of my fasting and highly expansive state, feeling delicate and rearranged, I'm disinclined to entertain the company of anyone, yet temptation catches me sideways, and I say yes.

The afternoon shines bright and warm, a paragon of late springtime. Hesitant but excited, dressed in casual jeans and a pale blue linen shirt with sleeves rolled up, standing by the front windows as I wait for his car to appear in the gravel drive, anxious energy churns in my gut.

What am I doing?

With Robert and I lovers again, is this rendezvous off-limits? No. Maybe. Who knows.

Tall, thin-framed and articulate, Stellar is soft-spoken with an accent placing him as an English southerner of good education. A keen intelligence is apparent from the first minutes of our meeting. I make an obligatory pot of tea and we sit in the front reception, a more formal room than the rear salon. His relaxed body posture counters my upright poise and the respectful distance I place between us, even as we meet each other's inquisitive open gaze. Searching the depths, looking and feeling for soul, assessing one another. Our rapport feels easy and instant, a door swinging ajar, an openness in the belly and chest, though our respective spiritual paths are divergent. Decidedly in the New Age camp, he *channels* higher energies and entities, thus the books he writes. For various reasons, I shut the gate on channeling years ago, and now stand at the opposite pole; drawn to ensouled mysteries of earth, soma, and psyche—the embodied and sensate realms versus the disincarnate. Recently separated from his partner of several years, they remain living together as best friends, a situation oddly resembling my own.

"If Robert and I met today at this point in our lives, I don't think we'd be together," I shrug casually, blue and white teacup balanced on the saucer in my hand. "We're very different, and we seem to be on contrasting journeys, as well."

Speaking the words, I wonder if they ring true.

An urge to kiss the handsome visitor pulls like warm gravity, an attraction I've not felt in a long time. At my suggestion, we go for a casual walk up the leafy lane and follow a footpath across a few grassy fields populated with shaggy ewes. Exchanging stories. Glances. Smiles. Clearly, being outside doesn't constitute a direct or important part of Stellar's life; nature is something *out there*, observed or watched on a television or computer monitor. Decidedly not *weatherproof*—comfortable in any sort of weather and able to enjoy it. Regardless, how nice to walk with someone and share an active ramble, as opposed to dear Robert, weak and winded, worn out with even modest effort. Having a vibrant, virile man at my side

108 ◆ WHERE TWO WORLDS TOUCH

electrifies quietly with a pleasing hum.

Returning to the farmhouse, on the green loveseat we lock together, pleasurably snogging, but I send him home without deeper carnal knowledge. Neither prim nor prude, all my senses have heightened with the cleansing fast and expansive state, like I'm some electromagnetic meter, vibrating at a high frequency. Arguably, such acuity makes a fine condition for intimacy, especially sex, but it feels too much with a stranger.

The tremulous intensity of life these past days—light playing upon fields, wind stroking the trees and the dance of shadows, the thrum of life, the touch of a hand—nearly overwhelms. Nothing stops at the surface but penetrates intensely and echoes . . . *echoes.*

Over the next days, slowly I return to more normal sensitivities. The gustatory delight of even the simplest food after one abstains from eating for an extended time bears savoring, and a ripe, juicy strawberry is surely the most luscious thing on earth. Given our immediate and easy connection, Stellar and I meet twice more before Robert's return, quickly tangled up naked, exploring another element of deliciousness.

"You know," I smile, laying a hand on his impressive manroot as we rest, pleasantly spent on the bed, "to be smart, handsome, spiritual *and* endowed like a demigod . . . that's just too many boxes for one man to tick."

He grins playfully, his dark eyes bright, shrugging away the flattery, then traces a single finger across my chest and down my abdomen.

"Well, you are *exactly* what I ordered," he murmurs in a dulcet tone, "as if I designed you. I did, in fact."

"Did what?"

"Designed you. Perfectly."

How unexpected, this. And surprisingly complicated. Irrespective that since the visit to Charleston farmhouse both Robert and I embrace the possibility that infinite models of relationship exist, and despite my repeated emphasis we are *not* reunited as partners, I am essentially his dependent. What repercussions exist with dating a different man?

My love for my former mate runs deep, but am I in *love* with Robert? Certainly, the old version—the corporate, bank management, increasingly soul-less man—did not spark my heart anymore. The nascent configuration, tender and delicately emerged from his shattered shell, is simultaneously familiar and unfamiliar. Perhaps arrogantly, I have long wished for a more spiritually-inclined partner, or one distinctly on a seeker's journey, a side-by-side counterpart versus always being the spiritual pathfinder, and now in Stellar such potential hovers nearby.

A week passes after Robert's return before I convey what has transpired, knowing such news doesn't make the best welcome home. Throughout, my new flame and I exchange texts and occasional clandestine phone calls, easy enough with my housemate gone at work during the day. And Stellar is sympathetic to my need for a bit of space and time before unveiling our intimate connection.

A ship tossed on a stormy sea, conflicted and cowardly, anxiousness whirling perpetually in my gut, cold and dank, I wait for an opportune moment but no easy way exists. When I finally summon the courage to tell Robert, predictably, pain clouds his face, followed by hot bolts of anger. Emotional lightning strikes the house and sets it afire. A personal earthquake topples everything on top of us in a heap of rubble.

"I *so* wanted a second chance," he sobs in the kitchen, turned away from me and staring at the wall. "I hoped so desperately this might work out between us . . . and now you're breaking my heart."

Seeing his drawn, weeping face guts me, as if my viscera were tumbling out onto the cool terracotta floor. I want to point out that I have made no promises, and kept a heart's distance between us, or even say I'm sorry—all of which are true.

Damn the gods. Their divine comedy is really a tragedy of the human heart.

"So now what?" he flashes a cold stare. "You're going to keep living under this roof with me supporting you, while you go off and sleep in his bed, or he comes here? That's hardly fair."

I sigh from depths of bluest grey, heavy on an interstitial level, staring out the window above the kitchen sink, not seeing the terrace or exuberant May garden beyond.

"I don't know, Robert. I don't have any answers yet. It probably isn't fair, you're right. But I need to explore this."

Conciliatory, I offer something concessional about myriad models of relationship, not having to define our relating and we can love more than one person, but he cuts me short with the sweep of his hand wielding an invisible knife, a jagged blade of bleached bone.

"No, I can't handle that—living together but you loving someone else. My heart doesn't work that way. I *need* to feel loved. And I want it to be by you."

He storms from the kitchen and stomps upstairs. The room lingers with frost. Remaining at the wide porcelain sink, staring blankly outside to the low sky, split down the middle, my lips pursed, I silently hate myself for hurting him so.

Storm clouds descend upon the farmhouse, even within its rooms. Our emotional landscape becomes winter, with Robert sullen and withdrawn. A tempestuous week passes slowly. The space between us in the great canopied bed feels wider than the Thames, and a comfortable residence built of old brick and beams has transformed into ice and steel. Driving to and from the rail station constitutes a torture of silence. Everything in our life has grown thorns overnight, each move fraught with uncertainty and tension.

As the Brits say, I've set the cat amongst the pigeons.

Unseen hands continue to pull me in opposite directions. In crushing Robert's hopes and expectations, dating someone won't be possible under present circumstances. I'm unclear whether my UK dependent's visa allows me to get a job, but nonetheless, finding employment while living in the countryside and having only Robert's car, the logistics daunt. If things intensify with Stellar, I will have to create paid work and eventually find a new place to live—yet that wouldn't support my comrade getting fully back on his feet.

He lashes at me from a cold and dark place inside.

"I just can't believe it. We finally move to the countryside to build the life we've always wanted, and now you're falling in love with someone else. What a bitter fucking joke."

I don't wish to fight, and he doesn't want to hear my repeated apologies. Regardless, I no longer care to keep saying *sorry*.

Stellar's ex-partner will be away, so he and I make plans to spend the night together at the renovated barn house they rent close to Gatwick airport. I am crossing a bridge, or possibly burning one behind me. Struggling for what to say to my companion, in the end, I prevaricate and tell him only I am going to pass the evening with my new friend, but will be home later tonight, thinking in some muddled reasoning this lie is easier on Robert than bare honesty.

I take a cab to the station and then the train to Godstone, such a curious name for a town, where my date picks me up in his little black Kia. In the earnest way of new lovers, gladness and hunger swirl heatedly in my core and loins, eager for our tryst. Yet guilt wracks and troubles me for withholding the full truth, and my innards are a dozen glistening snakes curling over each other, hissing.

This man and I are very different, our perspectives on the spiritual journey being the least of it. He doesn't cook or have much interest in doing so, but knowing my culinary background, purchased some meals from a local company called COOK, which specializes in "freshly made" frozen entrees. He heats our dinner using the oven rather than the microwave, knowing my aversion to such contraptions—not simply on principle but as a *sensitive*, feeling a distinct, uncomfortable buzz when in proximity to one in active operation. A sweet gesture, yet the food is chunky, dull, and uninspired. Frankly, I steer clear of anything frozen or prepared in bulk by anonymous hands, for it lacks an essential spirit of life, to say nothing of flavor.

"I don't care what food tastes like so long as it's *hot*," he says, taking a bite of the Indian-flavored casserole.

Seated in the small, unfamiliar kitchen, I'm politely trying to find a

112 ◆ WHERE TWO WORLDS TOUCH

lukewarm adjective for the meal, observing his sleek black cat devour a dish of miniature prawns by the fridge. Stellar sees through me.

"You're going to be a lot of work, aren't you?"

My exact thoughts about him. Mirroring my two, brief dating episodes in New Mexico during the year previous, suddenly I face another poignant reminder of how much Robert and I share after all the years together—everything from an agreement on furnishings and house décor, unperfumed soaps and toiletries, to a certain appreciation of food and life's niceties. Such a huge step to start over. A murky river of grief courses down through my abdomen, dragging me into its current and sucking the oxygen from my lungs. I want to break free and enjoy the evening, but a dark tide sweeps me out to sea.

So much depth and history between us. Gone.

Later in the evening, I step outside to phone Robert, saying Stellar invited me to smoke some cannabis, something I've not done in at least a dozen years but decided to partake, that I'm in an altered state and won't be returning to the station tonight.

His response is brusque and clipped.

"I saw your toothbrush was missing. I know you're not coming home."

"I'll be back tomorrow and will take a cab home from the station," I concede with a sigh, watching an orange-painted EasyJet on final approach to Gatwick, its cylindrical belly stuffed with bargain holidaymakers returning to the UK.

Why does my own heart feel like it's breaking?

Sex with Stellar is deliriously intense. Entwined in a hazy heat of passion, perception warped and stretched by an illicit substance, for a while I almost forget my troubles. Yet I lie awake most of the night in the foreign bed, wandering a desolate place within myself, blazingly sad and empty. Hunting for what I've lost. Somewhere near midnight, forever my witching hour, staring at the clouded moon through the large skylight overhead, a distinct voice speaks in my mind.

Instead of seeking love elsewhere, discover the barriers you have built against it within you.

Dear old Rumi, once again delivering a dash of wisdom and mystic guidance.

What am I doing here?

Against all expectation, my former partner is on the journey I long hoped—selfishly—he would undertake in a conscious way, finding a path back to his soul. Do I now turn from him, choosing the novelty of an alluring man? Or will I risk my own broken heart that Robert might really join me in an uncharted circle of love? My once-again-companion, previously guarded like a fortress, stands open and undefended for possibly the first genuine time.

Stellar's soft, dark hair is tousled, his face contentedly peaceful while he sleeps. Lightly, I touch the smooth muscles of his bare upper arm, pulling away from this lovely spiritual dreamer, ending our relating before we have even begun.

$\sim$

"So, how was your night?"

Robert's voice is flat, his posture rigid as iron. A cold-shouldered soldier. He left the car at the station when he drove himself in the morning due to my absence, has arrived home, marched upstairs to change his clothes, and entered the kitchen.

"Difficult."

Carving the roast chicken recently removed from the oven, I sever a juicy drumstick and thigh, placing the pieces upon waiting plates. Alongside, a salad of freshly podded broad beans and English peas, French ewes' feta, aromatic mint with caramelized red onions, all dressed in a lemon vinaigrette.

"I'm not sure I'll see him again . . . and I'm truly sorry I've hurt you."

Glowering in a chair beside the Rayburn, his energetic armor softens a bit. My response is something other than what he expected or prepared for. Downcast and heavy with thoughts scattered, I endeavor to set emotions aside, at least while preparing dinner, lest we end up unwell and weeping at

114 ◆ WHERE TWO WORLDS TOUCH

our meal from sad energy.

The bifurcated door is slightly open, inviting twilight to drift in with a reviving, cool breath. I set the dinner plates on the kitchen trolley, already laid with our everyday navy-blue linens and cutlery, retrieve my glass of Provençal rosé from beside the sink, and then sit to eat.

Silence reigns. The meal disappears. A dark sea lies between us. Perhaps just a river and not uncrossable but, still, what to say? All day, I have navigated inner tides, contemplating the Rumi-esque voice in the middle of the night, gauging its merit as rudder, oar, or sail for traversing unknown waters.

⌒

Late morning in the rear garden on a sunny day. Shirtless, luxuriating in warmth and blue skies, the colorful chorus of flowers accompanied by birdsong and the occasional two-note dirge of a distant cuckoo. In my peripheral vision, I spy our familiar furtive pheasant scramming across the lawn for the perceived safety of the yew border past the pool. Yet I am elsewhere in mind and spirit, facing a crossroads and unclear which direction to go. Unsure where either path leads.

The therapist in me knows initial wounds form in early relationship with one's family of origin, becoming the underpinnings of our character and persona. In a developmental psychology model, every child draws a subconscious map of their family reality—how to earn love, be recognized, say no, get needs met, or simply survive. A construct that remains in place for much, if not all, of one's life, guiding our choices and largely determining one's perception and outcome of situations, especially in relationship. The unconscious map reveals itself in time through our interactions with the world, in responses both emotional and somatic.

The rub is our patterns—the core wounds and strategies—formed in relationship. Because such habits and defenses are only triggered in relating, *only in relationship* do we shift them. With awareness, one can complete the missed developmental steps, or discover the "missing resource," and gradually rewrite the map. In a conscious and mindful relationship, intimate relating isn't merely about happiness or feeling fulfilled by someone, but rather the opportunity for *transformation*. The potential for it, at least. Committed partnership or marriage is the fiery cauldron wherein we melt down. And just possibly, with willingness, vulnerability, and a bit of grace, a reforging takes place—or like the ancient pursuit of alchemy, a transubstantiation from base elements into gold.

Perched at the weathered picnic table, shaded beneath the red canvas parasol, with wooden tray holding a pot of tea and plate of shortbread rounds, I contemplate what I'm still learning in relationship. The wounds and the gifts, whatever they may be, will sooner or later come forth, whether my intimate relating is with Robert, Stellar, or someone else. One cannot escape archetypes and character strategies, at least not until recognizing them. Am I stepping away from—or back toward—Robert simply from my own grief at starting over?

Crunching toothily into a sweet, crumbly biscuit and sipping the tepid black tea, I stare upwards at the hurtling puffy clouds, as if following their shifting shapes will lead me to some resolution. My internal pieces refuse to fit together in a coherent picture, leaving me disjointed and scattered.

I've written for much of the morning, my hand and trusty fountain pen pulled across the notebook by a creative tow. Alas, I'm still ambivalent over the initial outpouring on the evening of the fencepost epiphany—the metaphor of an Erotic Warrior—unable to see how it aligns with the early pages of manuscript now emerging.

Enough. The sunny afternoon is impossible to resist, I must go for a walk. Rather than anguish or ponder the way ahead, better to move my body and spirit by walking an actual footpath—where the choice I should make at this crucial relationship juncture will become apparent.

⟨⟩

Our patchwork quilt lays folded on the bench of the picnic table, and I've set a cushion out for Robert so he will be more comfortable while he

116 ◆ WHERE TWO WORLDS TOUCH

sits and eats. Today is the warmest of the year to date, a perfect evening to dine *al fresco*. He wears his perpetual, navy blue Hamburg jumper, and regardless of the evening's summery feel, the air between us weighs heavy and tense, laced with wisps of fog. The man withholds his heart, the door to me mostly closed. I top up my requisite glass of dry, southern French rosé, and we settle in to dine beneath the generous parasol. Lifting fork and knife, cutting into the harissa-marinated, grilled chicken with its slightly charred skin, I drag a bite through the garlicky yoghurt and olive oil sauce. The taste briefly makes me swoon. So good, it forbids restraint.

I toss some surface conversation—the food, his day and work, my walk—into the air, but monosyllabic answers and silence reveal Robert has no interest in small talk. Let's get down to the roots, then.

"I'm not going to pursue anything further with Stellar."

A brief pause in his eating, a slowing of fork to mouth as his blue-grey eyes glance up at me. I meet them only briefly. Tilting my head in a familiar gesture, I reach to swirl the salmon-hued wine in its shapely glass and launch into what must be said.

"Fourteen years ago, after our first two years together, when I went off to New Mexico to find myself—feeling you and I were done—in those months living alone on the mesa, it dawned on me I had a lot of learning to do in relationship. And I wanted to do such learning *with you*. Enough so, I abandoned that wild, soul place and the shaman's tower, left Taos of my heart, and came back to Boulder to build a life together.

Spending the night with Stellar, lying awake and hearing the message in my head—*instead of seeking love elsewhere, discover the barriers you have built against it within you*—I've realized in the past couple of days I *still* have learning to do in relationship. I don't think the process ever ends. And once again, I've come to the conclusion I want to do my ongoing learning with *you*."

Searching for his eyes. His heart.

"You've been hurt, and I'm genuinely sorry for that. On my walks, I've considered whether some part of me needed to push you away, or to wound you in return for breaking my heart in London. Conceivably, that's lurking under the surface somewhere, but I really doubt my subconscious was being punitive. That's not who I am, anymore. Yes, I'll admit a piece of me wishes for a mate who doesn't seem fractured, one who wants to go wandering across fields with me and get roughed up a bit in sex. Right now, you still feel a little broken . . . maybe even a lot broken. But the hidden truth of being cracked apart, shattered even, is only then can we become something else—that person who is *meant* to be.

A lot of shifts are going on right now . . . for both of us. I'm still trying to integrate what occurred at the fencepost when the Universe unveiled its symphony of consciousness. Personally, I think Stellar is actually just a *catalyst*—one of those intersections of fate and destiny where suddenly our course is altered by the choice we make."

A pause. I swirl my wine again and lift the glass to inhale notes of wild herbs, grapefruit, and a whisper of strawberry. Sip. Swallow.

"I can't define exactly how our relationship would look but I want to identify formally as *partners* again, not simply linger in a vague, convenient nonconformity . . . "

Pushing another morsel of spicy chicken through its bath of creamy sauce and raising it to my mouth, I chew silently for a minute. The rear garden feels hushed, the birds already settled and the sky fading into violet. Only the clink of cutlery on crockery punctuates the air.

"There has always been so much that's genuinely *good* about us as a couple, despite our differences," I resume, eyeing him directly. "We're both deeply changed now after our separate year . . . altered in the right ways. And I believe we can be even better as a pair than before. Much better."

My outpouring of words finishes. A placid breeze trails past us, stirring the display of flowers by the covered pool and the trees along the lane opposite the box hedge, setting them to dance and whisper. Robert's eyes have shifted and softened, reflecting the changing sky, his rigid posture easing slightly. Laying aside his fork and knife, he reaches for my hand. Squeezes it tightly.

"You have no idea how much I love you. My life has such incredible richness when you are in it, because of what *you* bring to it. That's what I

118 ◆ WHERE TWO WORLDS TOUCH

want. I've already told you of my agonizing grief in the hospital, when all I wished for was to not die alone in cold, grey England but to have another chance at life together."

I smile briefly, an upwelling of emotion bringing a warm tear to my eye.

"And I *too* believe we can be even better as a couple than we were before, especially because you're always the one who calls me back to my *soul*. I still dream we will create some sort of work together as a team, building a life which supports us by using the combined talents we bring to the table."

"That would be lovely. We do make a very good team."

Even as evening fades towards dusk, everything has lightened. The thicket of brambles has vanished, supplanted by a cautiously optimistic moment—an injured bird gingerly opening a tightly-held wing, testing its readiness for flight. Something new has coalesced and ignited, even if its ultimate shape is yet unformed.

We will go on together.

⌒

Another twilight. Out walking, roaming through orchards of apple and pear with their swelling fruit, tracing the hem of a hill and gazing out over the Weald, passing near to the fencepost where revelation struck. Tapestries of apricot clouds are draped across the frescoed expanse of fading sky, decorating an exquisite palace for the soul. A fair wind stirs the silvery elms along the lane in a lulling susurration, layered with *cooing* of wood pigeons returning to roost. Reaching the farmhouse drive, I open the wide timbered gate, step through, and swing it shut behind me.

With a click of the latch, human realms draw me back. The closing or opening of a gate always seems a symbolic gesture; the crossing into, or emerging from, different spheres. For me, returning from my ramble of earthly reverie, at the portal comes an accompanying shift in energy and consciousness, a subtle change in bodily sensation. Gradually, my expansiveness wanes, becoming denser and not so porous, as the peculiar heaviness of the manmade world exerts its effects on me.

Walking sandals dangling in left hand, my bare feet crunch tenderly along the river of pale gravel forming the driveway, a conversation of unclad sole and shifting stones. I step onto the broad green lawn, embellished gaily with purple clover blossoms and tiny yellow flowers, enjoying the soft springiness underfoot. Crossing towards the front door of the farmhouse, I come up short. On the grass lies a crumpled grey snakeskin, last sign of some former occupant who wriggled free and slithered gracefully on. Like a child on Christmas morning unwrapping presents, I am thrilled.

Bending down, I tenderly lift the paper-like tube. One end is crumpled tightly—an opaque, scaled accordion—while the rest of the length is elongated and flat. Pulling gingerly at the bunched end, curious whether the skin will lengthen without tearing, it gives only modestly and then begins to rip. Roughly a foot and a half long, the dull silver sheath probably belonged to a grass snake, common in this part of England. A uniformly ribbed underside, a translucent ladder of evenly spaced rungs, contrasts the top of neatly honeycombed triangular scales. The casing feels damp and cool, almost clammy in my hands, as if its previous wearer left only moments ago and vanished in the evening breeze. Raising the skin to my nose, a scent somewhere between fishy and grassy wafts up from its hollow length.

How odd I didn't see this when setting out on my walk, and strange to find it here at all, knowing snakes don't molt without effort; they must rub against something like a stone or branch to initially break free. The sloughing process begins at the head, and once the skin around mouth and nose is loosened and dislodged, the serpent makes use of a rough object to trap and hold the outer covering while deliberately emerging. The entire ordeal feels richly symbolic. A perfect metaphor.

I carry my find gingerly indoors, opening the cast-iron latch of the oak front door with one hand, and stepping across the threshold into the cool, welcoming sanctuary. In my outdoor wanderings and occasional encounters with snakes—like the four-foot long greenish-gold rattlesnake I met up the hill from my jewel box casita in Taos, sunning itself in early spring warmth—I've long hoped to come across such a thing to add to my collection of bones and feathers. This one has appeared practically on the doorstep, a timely and tactile representation of transformation.

Quel mystère.

Upstairs, I lay the wrinkled, grey-silver skin upon my altar of cherished objects: an elk-hide rattle, a moose jawbone, an owl's intact brown wing, a golden beeswax taper, a smoky quartz crystal, along with an array of other worthless treasures picked up on ramblings, both on and off the trail. Each a talisman or charm for a poet, shaman, or fool. Like blue Celtic dragons or wings tattooed around my forearms, such objects belie me as the heathen I am. A man with a gentle wildness of spirit and sensual appreciation for life and nature. A Soul Artist.

One finger trailing along the opaque parchment, I muse on *shedding one's skin*—escaping the confines of our own making. What obstacles must we rub against to loosen the calcified shell of one's persona? Maybe the opinions and expectations of others; or personal limitations, fears, and self-doubt. My guarded solitude, perhaps. And seldom do we realize *friction* is the grist or spark for growth and eventual freedom.

Beyond the crisscross of old leaded glass, daylight fades and darkness gathers its velvet robes. A magical hour, opposite spoke of the cosmic wheel from dawn, when otherworldly powers and spirits once again draw close. Familiar shapes begin to retreat, shedding their color and dayworld disguises, slipping from rigid form, becoming *other* and free again. The snake, too. In a mythic and magical point of view, perchance the pale sheath's former occupant tired of being a serpent and transformed into a raven or some other creature, after realizing its true identity, destined for a different expression in life.

Eyeing the lilac sky and lengthening shadows, an impression overcomes me, as at other times, of hovering at the threshold where realms overlap, joining as lovers. A mandorla, of sorts. The non-physical place where I am most at home and fully myself—a wild soul tending the hearth fire at the vestibule between worlds. The *Mundus Imaginalis* flutters near, the "imaginal realm," so termed by Islamic scholar Henry Corbin; a domain of archetypes where human psyche meets the mythical, wherein we encounter the soul of the world. A dimension, when accessed, which inspires profound creativity—the precious gift of humanity.

This brief aperture at dusk, when the tension of opposites is elegantly held and balanced, when a door is "round and open" in Rumi's words, calls to me. As with dawn, here is a perfect opportunity to give my attention to a larger and more mysterious reality; to wonder, as my nameless longing reaches out and is wordlessly met in return.

Holy, holy.

Standing at the window, for several long, wordless minutes, I weigh my desire, ache, and hunger, pondering what their deeper, hidden value may be. Surely *eros* as a cosmic force pulls us toward our destiny. In all myths and stories, a choice must be made with a corresponding price to pay. What will the would-be hero gain from the decision he faces—even in choosing to delay and *not* make the choice? What will we find, and potentially lose, should we plunge into the depths of our longing?

At the rear of the garden, the otherworldly Shaman stands draped in indigo, sovereign like some forgotten god of an ancient grove. Much as I yearn for untamed, solitary places where magic endures, unexpectedly I'm heeding something else, another voice: my desire for a true, slow-burning love in the heart and soul. Inexplicably, such a *pas de deux* is still Robert and our two different worlds that touch.

I have cast my lot. Now the Fates will decide where we go and what happens next.

CONNEMARA

A SOFT, LAVENDER summer light falls upon the seaside town of Clifden. Our first trip to Ireland brings us to Connemara, a relatively hale region on the westerly coast, the very edge of Europe.

A rugged landscape of green and brown, studded with a few trees and modest, square white houses, welcomes us with a wholly different energy than southern England. The robust, marine air reminds me curiously of Scotland. Something powerful and untamed still exists here, if only in spirit. Observing an unfamiliar world through the passenger window of a rental car, I grasp for words that give shape to my impressions, but they elude me. Mostly it feels like I've stepped free of a stuffy room at a boring cocktail party into the fresh cool breeze.

Already it's clear Connemara constitutes a domain of the elements, a threshold of stark earth, the cold grey sea, and a burdened sky. Merino sheep with thick, shaggy coats and great curled horns wander the low hillsides, freely crossing the winding road, keeping drivers at attention, especially as daylight wanes.

"Connemara road hazards," smiles the friendly lad at the front desk of the bed and breakfast where we will spend the next several nights, when I mention the sheep. Ginger hair, freckles, and a singsong accent, he seems nonplussed by the two American men from London who will be sharing a bed. Handing us a classic key on a chain with a heavy brass ball, he points down the well-worn carpeted hallway.

The countryside inn is a grand dame edging steadily into decline,

CONNEMARA ◆ *123*

clinging to the weathered charm of a bygone era. The out-of-date, solid wood furnishings of the rooms are accompanied by clunky bath fixtures, outmoded tile, tattered carpets and faded, thick draperies, too frayed and stained to be elegant. Cracks fissure the walls like dark spider webs, the patterned paper peeling away at the edges, the ceilings mottled by leaks over the years.

From guestrooms to the bar, at every turn the house shows its long-standing duel with nature. Our room has no Internet connection, no coffee maker, no electric hairdryer in the bathroom, and the television is a hefty square box weighing sixty pounds. A relic. She clings to her ways, this country lady. A character reminiscent of a woman wearing a beaded dress and flapper-era headband with feather. Stories live here, slowing slipping from memory into mist, trailing a decrepit charm. How unexpectedly pleasing to step backward in time, an oddly agreeable change from sterile modernity and sleekly anonymous hotels.

Coming here is a bold leap, the result of Robert enrolling in a workshop led by two of my former mentors from the States. The five-day gathering promises an experiential plunge into the depths of soul: extended time on the open land, working with dreams and personal process in an intimate group, all while exposed to and enfolded by the forms and forces of nature. Removed from the comforts and distractions of home, the retreat offers an opportunity to pause—a dive into one's inner mysteries in search of clarity, guidance, and a renewed sense of self. The intensive is co-sponsored by a group in Ireland but facilitated by the organization in the States that, until just recently, I apprenticed with—guiding participants into wilderness and nature-based personal discovery. Depth-oriented ecotherapy, one might call such work.

Learning of the Ireland retreat with Peter and Annie in the guide roles, I pitched it to my mate, knowing his thirst for something soulful to help quench his listlessness at Lloyds. To my surprise and delight, he grabbed at the idea immediately.

"I need something like this right now," he nodded, reading the program description. "Something to help me get back to what's *real*, to find a

124 ◆ WHERE TWO WORLDS TOUCH

different path, especially since I'm still stuck in banker's world."

"Wanker's world . . . "

"It's wally world, for sure."

Now in Connemara, wearing a wool tweed derby cap and clothes for an outdoor ramble, the banker has been left behind in England or somewhere along the road, and the blue-eyed troubadour of Robert's younger days reappears. A sizable step from his usual, well-insulated comfort zone, being outdoors for five days in the cool of an Irish summer will push his limits. He'll have no comfortable place to sit for extended periods when the group gathers in a circle, and he must keep sufficiently warm to minimize his pain.

I've outfitted him as adeptly as possible after rummaging through my own kit and backpacking gear, and he purchased additional outdoors clothing. The guides and other participants will be camping in individual tents on the open land, but Robert sleeping on the ground simply isn't feasible, even with a cushion, nor on a cot in the stone hut the group will be using to cook meals and occasionally warm up by a peat fire. His nightly hot soak is a necessary ritual, the only way paraspinal muscles loosen and ease their restrictive gauntlet, especially after a long day of sitting or standing. In light of the circumstances, Annie and Peter have made a special exception despite that doing so breaks the container of the group, allowing him to stay in town each night to have a decent bed and bath.

"I feel a little awkward about it," Robert admits as we prepare to depart our dilapidated room, packing his small blue rucksack for the day. "I hate calling attention to my condition. I don't want anyone's sympathy or special consideration."

A hand on his shoulder, I grin conspiratorially.

"Trust me, after the first day or two outdoors in the cold and rain, sleeping in a tent, what the other participants will feel is *envy*. Speaking from experience, I assure you, they're all going to be longing for a hot shower and comfortable bed, and you're the lucky sod holding the winning lottery ticket for that. You get warm breakfast and coffee each morning, too. People will barter their soul for such things after a few days of camping, I swear."

CONNEMARA ◆ *125*

A twenty-minute drive takes us to the group gathering beyond the end of an unpaved track near Glenbrickeen Lough. Here and there, a scattering of nylon domes and tents of various colors dot the empty landscape, and as Robert turns the Volkswagen around, he shimmers with nervous excitement for his gamble.

The crisp Connemara air intoxicates with brine and unrestrained vigor. *Elemental* is the word surfacing repeatedly in my awareness. Away from town, man's impact upon the land feels minimal and fleeting, only the lightest touch. The guides and locals call it a *bog*, which for me conjures a marshy image, but the craggy green swells and wide expanse are not what I envisioned at all. Much as I enjoy being outside, the thought of this seaside realm in the icy grip of winter makes my bones shiver. Protectively, I'm relieved Robert will come back to the inn each evening; the warmth and comfort will bolster a richly rewarding experience versus one where he suffers substantially.

Approximately a year has passed since I last saw Peter at a retreat in Colorado, and longer from the time when I laid eyes upon Annie. With a brief, smiling reunion and firm hugs exchanged, I introduce them to Robert, the man they have heard about in my stories but never met, the sole American participant besides them. Innately convivial, at ease with groups, a person who makes friends quickly, his taut nervousness is not for any social reluctance but rather the uncertainty of how his body will respond in the unsheltered outdoors. Standing next to him, scanning his rigid stance, I squeeze his hand once tightly in an affirming signal, knowing his back hurts and he has a pocket stuffed with pain medication, yet his brave soul puts up a good front.

Bless his wool socks.

My hours are free until I return to fetch my comrade this evening, and I spend the first day wandering the shops of town. Apart from food, and occasionally for clothes, I've generally relinquished shopping as a pastime. Little do I truly need. Moreover, this wandering gypsy feels loath to accumulate more *stuff*, foreseeing stacks of cartons for moving house again, and I find more pleasure lately in getting rid of things than bringing home new ones. Today, on holiday of sorts, I browse aimlessly through Clifden, tempted by a few trinkets here and there—a ring encircled with a Celtic knot, a silver cuff depicting the Tree of Life—but I pass them by, eventually settling in for lunch at a cheery pub.

Dining alone doesn't fuss me a bit. To the contrary, absorbing the congenial atmosphere and lilting Irish voices stokes a mild happiness, a new experience in an unfamiliar country. Seated near the front windows, looking out at the street and passersby, I dine on *moules & frites*, surprised and delighted at their deliciousness, some of the best I've tasted. The mussels are bathed in a savory white wine and garlic broth, the French fries golden and appealingly crisp on the outside, tender in the middle. Perfection. Every bite.

My thoughts repeatedly drift to Robert. Wondering how he's faring, whether all goes okay with his folding camp chair and sitting, hoping he feels warm enough. On some level, I wish we were puttering around town and exploring together, but I trust he's having a worthwhile adventure of a different sort.

Ambling down a narrow, grey street, passing a window, an unusual object behind the glass catches my eye. An oblong rock, seven inches long, carved with the words, *Imagination is evidence of the Divine.* I halt in my tracks. Why yes, I smile. The stone's inscription lingers with me throughout the afternoon, as if carrying it, and I jot the phrase down in my small black notebook. Any distinct thread eludes me, but some inscrutable connection exists to the book I have begun writing.

Evening arrives in periwinkle and silver over the land and sea to the west, as I return for my counterpart after his supper with the group. The sky glimmers clear and the first heavenly diamonds of stars sparkle brightly. Standing alongside the rental car in the profound quiet of the panorama, feeling expansive, some faint magic endures in the soul of the land itself, never forgotten. An abiding world for faerie folk and the Sidhe. Beyond doubt, this land still sings for those who listen. Closing my eyes, I strain to hear something akin to the trees at dawn along our lane.

Only silence woven with wind song.

Observing my partner approach along the dirt track from the locked gate, the stiffness of his step reveals a man who is tired, chilled, and in pain. Yet when he reaches the car, a grin lifts his face, and even in the dim light his eyes glint jewel-like. Bumping along the rough road back towards Clifden, in a fatigued voice he shares his immediate liking and mild awe of Peter and Annie, such a formidable, well-balanced duo.

I know firsthand the gift of sitting with wise teachers in a wild, undisturbed place, how landscape transforms a person in subtle and profound ways. My heart smiles, recognizing his genuine welcome by these two former mentors of mine who have guided hundreds of individuals into the richly evocative, occasionally terrifying depths of soul.

Not so long ago, an invitation might have come to assist Peter and Annie on this intensive, especially living in Europe with easy access to Ireland. In the days following my fencepost revelation, however, I departed the organization they remain connected to. Institute politics and etiquette aside, this is Robert's exploration. He doesn't need me sitting across the circle in a guide role, listening to his stories and observing his personal process. No, he must have absolute freedom to share whatever arises during this time of seeking.

Back in our weather-stained room, a weary but soulful adventurer regales me with his impressions of others in the group, the ones who merit his regard and those he finds challenging. Already, an affinity for Maria, a Swedish woman in the long-term apprenticeship program I recently abandoned. Animatedly, he relays how, as they sat in the open air in a circle of folding camp chairs, some Connemara ponies came by, apparently wild and free roaming on the windy bog, calmly interested in the little band of humans. Curious enough to approach but not too near.

"There is a beautiful grey one who came very close to where I sat alone for a while. I reached out to him, offering my hand, wishing I had a carrot or a sugar cube or something to offer. Reminded me of being with my parent's horses, Cagney and Juno. They call them 'ponies' but they're really

128 ◆ WHERE TWO WORLDS TOUCH

good-sized. Apparently, they form part of the local history around here, descended from Viking horses."

My mate's effusive elation transcends what I have seen in him in ages, a glimpse of the bright spirit I fell in love with so many years ago. Brilliant. What unforeseen grace this soul quest at the edge of the world.

Each morning we have breakfast together at the inn, Robert eating scrambled eggs and sausage, or blueberry pancakes. Muesli and yoghurt satisfy me. Then we get in the car and head out to the lake where, past the final open gate, we halt short of the parked vehicles of the other participants, wanting our arrival to not intrude, even from a distance. The *soulwork* intensive marks a deliberate disconnect from phones, Internet, television, and the distractions and addictions of the modern world, thus we come and go unobtrusively.

Exchanging places at the wheel, I sit and watch my companion walk away, clad in multiple layers and coat with a scarf tightly around his neck, wool cap, and the blue Osprey daypack I bought him strapped to his back. When he reaches the far gate and climbs over, I wave goodbye as he glances back with a smile, a sharp ache of love in my chest, a swelling of admiration for his brave journey and this new phase of inner searching.

Admittedly, I envy Robert his days out on the bog. The green countryside and moist air of the ocean couldn't be farther from the arid world of New Mexico, but its rugged remoteness resonates on a primal level of my being, a slightly melancholic chord plucked by unseen hands. I yearn to strike out on foot and walk for hours, encountering no other human, as in Taos and roaming the fragrant, dusty mesa. Gathering windswept stories and sun-bleached bones, as I did. Returning from such rambles with my senses, heart, and soul ablaze, a creature of another realm with a strange light in my eyes and instinctual ease in my gait. Slightly feral. Touched by an enchantment. Here, at the shore of a darkly flashing sea, something undomesticated and essential stirs in me, as if I am inexplicably fully *human* once more.

I will go walking, probably in Connemara National Park nearby. My soul *needs* to intimately encounter this rough, alluring land; human bones roving across the rocky grey ones, speaking to each other and sharing breath like lovers. Gracefully alive. Yet I equally desire to sit by the window in our tattered room and write, for when the soul arises so too does creativity and the deep imagination, one and the same. Like a little bird, inspiration to work on the fledgling book manuscript has alighted, a readiness to welcome whatever wants to surface from the subterranean wellspring of words.

Briefly, I flash on the works of John O'Donohue, Irish poet and author of the bestselling *Anam Cara*. Connemara was his home. Recalling his books, now that I've felt the land here, inviting and harsh in an exposed way, his lyrical words brush my soul. The confluence of elements—an ancient alchemy of earth, sea and sky—lulls me into an unspoken conversation. Unquestionably, standing circles of upright stones belong in this place; ageless, monolithic storytellers that evoke the songs of earth and stars, even if silent to our ears. And wild mystery remains a currency of the realm.

Regardless of July and technically being summertime, the cool days almost entice me to buy an Irish wool sweater and wear it everywhere. The omnipresent wind is formidable, a commanding entity in its own right. Staring at the cold grey ocean one afternoon, imagining the lives of fishermen in boats offshore, hauling in nets as their ancestors did for ages, humility takes me down. What do I know of real strength, fortitude, or hardship? Would my soul thrive in such a place or simply be blown about and deranged? Probably I would morph into a crazy-haired madman, a reluctant mystic turned seer. A shaman and holy fool, or, at the very least, an aspiring Earth poet. Worse things could transpire, I suppose.

"I think living here, even visiting," I say to Robert as we drive back from the campsite one evening, "one cannot help but understand something about the elemental nature of the soul. And you don't have to be out on the bog to *feel* it."

Timeless power of the region aside, wherever I go in town, whether into the shops or a pub for lunch, the Irish are much friendlier than the

130 ◆ WHERE TWO WORLDS TOUCH

English. Less contained. More willing to offer a stranger a smile. Likely to burst into a song or a jig at any moment. Even in this relatively unforgiving land alongside the frigid sea, the general sense is a welcoming one. A warm humanness. Perhaps if I returned in the deep gloom of winter I might detect a different mood, but surely then we would all be tucked indoors in a toasty pub with pints of good ale while listening to fiddle, flute, folk harp and cheerful voices. Difficult to imagine *that* as anything but jovial, no matter the weather outside. Music seems woven into the fabric of life here.

Never a locale I felt drawn to or wished to explore, Ireland has surprised me. Whilst I don't feel an immediate somatic recognition or memory as on my first visit to Italy—an overbearing sense of arriving at an ancestral, genetic place of origination though I know nothing of my blood lineage or DNA—my body buzzes softly with life force and a forgotten chant of the world. Possibly, I wouldn't detect the wordless evensong amid the noisy, glistening streets of Dublin, but on this unsheltered and formidable coast, it rattles my bones, calling the wild soul home.

⌒

The room with its stained carpet, worn floral curtains and ivy print wallpaper, smells faintly of mildew. My steamy morning shower was hours ago yet the glass remains frosted with condensation. Furry traces of green and black mold discreetly border all the windowpanes. Embraced by the empty quietude of the inn, within the hush of the refuge where I sit observing the torrential downpour outside, I am expansive as the undulating lands surrounding this timeworn house. Relaxed and open like tender hands held forth in offering. The essence of tranquility in the storm.

Silence rumbles within. Deep stillness and spaciousness fill me, as between heartbeats and bridging the luminous stars. Each breath mirrors the tide, rolling in and out, cycling in a slow and easy rhythm. My body feels loosely unwound from a tightly constricted knot; a shawl of raw silk draped over a chair. An entirely pleasant change.

Through the slightly ajar window comes the steady, murmuring *whoosh* of a squall, compelling the trees to bend and dance against a misty backdrop indistinguishable from sea and sky. The windswept, green-clad sentinels sway beside a jigsaw puzzle wall of stones with a rusted iron gate, framing a patch of lawn bordered with dusky hydrangeas. Beyond, a pasture slopes down to the leaden bay lost in swirling silver clouds of fog. Emerald and grey are the entirety of world in my view. Nothing else exists. And a sideways rain fiercely lashes all. Is it like this out on the bog where my beloved sits with a small band of intrepid souls?

As I write, the gale rattles the window on old brass hinges with an invisible cat's paw, seeking entry. Perhaps merely attention.

I am elemental. Bow to me. Sing to me.

My plan was to walk the hills in Connemara National Park, but even with rain gear, the weather is fouler than I care to roam in. Thus, I sit with a pot of afternoon tea and disappointingly dry scones, listening to the eternal voices of the elements. Savoring solitude as I do.

Tomorrow, hopefully, I will go hill climbing, nourishing my bodysoul with active movement and exercise in the coastal air. For now, contentedness fills me on a corpuscular level, enchanted by the rural spell of Ireland. My trusty fountain pen threads across the notebook, gradually building a chapter for the emerging manuscript, guided by some Muse or spirits of the tempest.

Imagination is evidence of the Divine.

Robert sinks stiffly and slowly into the nearly scalding bath I have prepared for him. As if the bathroom were a private spa, the drops of juniper, cypress, high-altitude lavender and sweet orange distributed into the water scent the vapors with a therapeutic effect, holistic aromatherapy in action.

"They sent us out for a solo walk on the land. We had two hours on our own. I wandered around for a while, sort of unsure where go, wanting to be a good way apart from the others but not wanting to walk too far. It's hard

132 ◆ WHERE TWO WORLDS TOUCH

to walk on the bog, very uneven, and you know how that hurts my spine. I found myself drawn to a spot with some rocks and a small tree. For some reason, I wanted to be close to that tree, not that it would offer any shelter if the rain came again. Which it did, of course."

He laughs briefly and inches down into the steaming water, closing his eyes, skin already turning pink from the warmth of the soak. Closing the lid on the toilet, I sit upon it as a chair beside him.

"Actually, the rain didn't last long, and it wasn't that intense. I just pulled my hood close and sat there, blessing you for the waterproof 'kit', until I noticed this little red bug on the rock next to me. I sat there for a long time looking at it. I swear, it stared back at me, like I was the biggest thing it had ever seen. It had absolutely huge eyes. I don't know how long we stared at each other. I must be the first human it has encountered, some giant who suddenly appeared in its world and rearranged his view of the universe.

The ponies came by again, and that grey one I bonded with the other day walked right up, sniffing me, just out of reach. They are definitely wild because they stay a little bit away. Maybe they belong to someone, they seem comfortable around people, but obviously no one rides them.

Mostly I just sat there, bundled up, feeling cold and my spine hurting, but decided I would simply *feel* it—not only the pain but also this incredible landscape, admiring the beauty of it, feeling very wide open. Peaceful, really. It's like you said when we arrived and then again the other day, one can't be here and *not* understand something of the soul."

I smile both inside and out. Listening. No words need speaking. Gratification exists simply in hearing the details of Robert's day on the land and with the group.

"Something about the tree spoke to me. It has red berries. I can't really explain it, what it *felt* like, I mean. You want to hear something crazy? Well, you won't think it's crazy at all, and I love that about you. I felt like it was watching over me."

Slipping down fully into the water, he glances briefly at me, scanning for my reaction. Confirmation, possibly, I don't think he's gone round the bend, but I do not raise an eyebrow at his confession.

"Later, when we told our stories in the circle, I was recounting my time under the tree, describing it, and Paul says to me, 'That's a rowan tree. In Celtic legend and local lore, they have the energy of protection. It's a tree often associated with the Goddess, as well.'"

He grins with satisfaction, closing his eyes, inhaling the fragrant steam. "How cool is that?"

Continuing to smile at this dear man, naked and pink in the tub of hot, aromatic water, I'm pleased for his out-of-the box escape from the vapid world of banking. Removed from everything superficial and mundane, immersed in the visceral and authentic. Something shifts for him here at this earthly, remote threshold. Or like a seed lying dormant, waiting for the right conditions, a kernel inside finally begins to germinate, split, and sprout with new life.

In the old, tiled bathroom, my heart pushes against its cage of ribs, now unlocked and open. What a gift, our simple, ordinary moment together, words of Rumi riding a coastal wind, ever encouraging me to wake up.

The minute I heard my first love story
I started looking for you, not knowing
how blind that was.
Lovers don't finally meet somewhere.
They're in each other all along.

~

The workshop draws to its close on a cool blue, blustery day. The weather-weary participants and guides finally emerge from their isolation, knitted tightly together in a circle of friendship: Irish, north and south, English, and American. Via Robert as messenger, Annie and Peter have invited me to join the final lunch, and with gladness I accept.

Bouncing along the now familiar track, movement to the left turns my head, and I see five large, red deer bound across the uneven terrain. Four females accompany a stag with an impressive rack of horns. Instantly,

134 ◆ WHERE TWO WORLDS TOUCH

a joyous tumult of invisible hooves and wings rises inside me. I stop the car and watch them move swiftly away towards the shimmering loch, the very image of beauty and grace. Once these creatures were nearly extinct from hunting, and visitors do not frequently spy them, so I acknowledge the sighting as a special blessing.

Annie sits beside me at a battered, time-worn picnic table near the stone cottage, our flimsy paper plates holding vegetable quiche and a heap of nondescript, pasta-laden casserole. Warmly layered to fend off the bullying wind, the knitted wool cap over her blonde hair is rolled down past her ears. Irrespective of the marine gusts, a new Donegal flecked-tweed sweater purchased in Clifden keeps me comfortably warm, the charcoal grey wool unsurpassed in softness and luster. And my essential cashmere scarf further helps defy the chill.

"In my twenty years of guiding, this is some of the most powerful land I have ever encountered."

"I believe you. Even coming and going with Robert, I feel its wildness in my own bones."

Like me, my former mentor was a bodyworker for decades. Both of us share a heightened sensitivity to the *feeling* of things—the emotion and energy in bodies or nature, especially those we touch.

The participants mull about with their plates and plastic cutlery, looking for a place to sit, the camaraderie of a shared meal hovering in the air but tinged with *denouement*. Robert stands nearby, talking with Peter and another member of the group. I catch Annie's gaze wander over to him and rest, as if placing a hand in the center of his back.

"There is a lot of soulful depth in that man," she says approvingly, taking a bite of soggy quiche and flashing me a pearly smile.

"I wouldn't be with anyone other than that."

"I know this to be very true."

"Personally, I think he's really a druid, but he doesn't realize it yet. His Celtic roots intrigue him, and he wants to explore them further. He will in some way, I suspect. I'm just happy we're on a renewed adventure together . . . apprenticing to soulful romance."

"And that, my dear River, is the only sort of romance *really* worth having. Where each understands the deep mystery of the other brings forward something essential in ourselves. For healing. For learning. For transformation."

Sage woman. I lean up against her to gently butt with my shoulder in friendly acknowledgement. I'm cherishing our brief reunion, wondering when or if I will see her in the future, hoping the thread between us is strong enough to stitch our paths together again one day, even across an ocean. Soul tribe is precious and rare—always discovered and chosen rather than born into. As my connection with the States wanes, my tribe dwindles, and the diminishing circle serves to remind me that, even in relationship, we face our struggles mostly alone.

~

As Robert drives us back to Shannon for our flight, watching the Irish landscape pass by, I rouse from quiet ruminating and offer a proclamation.

"I would like to return here. I have a weakness for wild and lonely places in the world, you know. I can envision coming back to write. Maybe I will find a cottage right beside the sea, where I hear its chanting voice all day and night, and then hunker down for a month, scribbling away by the peat-burning fireplace while the spirits moan around the chimney and door."

Wool derby cap set jauntily atop his head, my partner's eyes gleam clear as the aquamarine sky.

"Yes, knowing you all these years, I'm sure the spirits will show up *wherever* you go . . . but especially in a land like this. Can I come and visit?"

Tilting my head and looking out the car window as we round a curve, I feign a pause to consider.

"Yes, mon chéri. Give me a week or so alone on each end, and you may come for a stretch in the middle."

"Just make sure the cottage is warm. And there's a decent bathtub. I don't fancy going camping."

"Which for you means any place that doesn't have a hotel spa, I know."

136 ◆ WHERE TWO WORLDS TOUCH

"Exactly. My days of roughing it are behind me. You can go off and sleep in the dirt, eating granola and twigs, but I need my comforts, thank you. And a decent bed. God, I can't wait to get home to our own bed!"

Our little escape is over. Connemara has touched us, stirring the spirit like music. In a way that defies laying a finger upon or description, some sort of necessary healing has happened for my dear man. Perhaps not on the physical level; the time outdoors has pushed his body to the limit, leaving him locked up and rigid, but nothing is merely physical. Something within him has shifted a few degrees closer to the soul's magnetic pole, mysterious and indefinable as that is. A recalibration of the heart's compass. And his gaze still shines glassy as a falcon's.

The competent chauffeur, he reaches over and places a hand on my knee in a familiar gesture, though he must let go routinely to shift gears with the car's manual transmission. "Love, I cannot thank you enough for supporting me on this. I probably wouldn't have done it without you."

"On a journey together, each supports the other. We're a team."

"Very true. After these days with such incredible people who are so *real* and in touch with what life is really about, I can barely think about going back to the bank." A dark wing or trailing cloud passes briefly over, shadowing his countenance. "At least we're not returning to London, I wouldn't be able to handle it. The city is just too intense given how sensitive I am nowadays. I'm so glad we get to go home to our little farm in Kent, instead."

How precious he calls it "the farm." I chuckle inwardly, feeling the lightness of mirth.

"It's hardly a farm. Once upon a time, but not now."

"Well, with the ducks and wildlife and neighbor's sheep fields, and Paul and Sara's orchards, it *feels* like a farm. I wish it were ours. I've always wanted to be a gentleman farmer."

"Yes, I know. You've mentioned it a hundred times over the years."

"Maybe we could buy it! I can get financing through Lloyds." His voice raises slightly with excitement as he looks to me for a reaction.

"You can't be a gentleman farmer with simply a house and garden in the countryside but no *acreage*, dear," I shake my head.

"I suppose that's true. But I hope we'll find our little farm someday. I've always wanted to have alpacas, you know."

"Yes, love, you've mentioned that a few times, too," I roll my eyes playfully, adding a drawn out sigh for melodramatic effect, "and yours truly will likely be the one who takes care of them."

"Because you do it so well!" He laughs aloud and flashes me a smile. "Mostly I'm just glad to be there with you . . . Mr. Wild Soul roaming the fields, chasing clouds and wild geese or whatever."

"And here all this time I thought I was stalking my elusive happiness and wild plums. Baking bread as a consolation . . . or soulful nourishment."

"Oh, I can't wait to go home and have dinner, there's nothing better than your food in our lovely kitchen."

⌒‿

Goodness, indeed, life at the farmhouse together. England feels utterly domesticated after the west coast of Ireland. Everything kempt, groomed, and rigid. Less than friendly. Thank the gods we've not returned to Wimbledon or the city but instead to pastoral Kent.

Outdoors in the garden next to the pool, a pair of secateurs in hand, bare soles kissing earth and grey stone, I tremble slightly. Energy hums in my core, a fusion of nervousness and anticipation. I inhale a full breath, sensing the bottoms of my feet, *earthing* myself. The moment I've waited for has arrived.

Bending to cut a handful of yellow and purple blossoms, I retrace my steps through the open bifurcated door. Robert sits beside the kitchen trolley where I've placed our Sunday afternoon tea and biscuits, reading an email on his smartphone. Crossing the room, I kneel upon the terracotta tile floor in front of him and hold out the garden-fresh flowers, pulse racing.

"Will you marry me?"

For an instant, his face is blank with non-comprehension.

"I love you. Marry me."

138 ◆ WHERE TWO WORLDS TOUCH

Like the sun rising over a mountain, its first rays warming and illuminating everything touched, the man's face transforms, blue eyes widening.

"I love you and want to move deeper into a conscious, transforming relationship, growing old together. No one else but *you.*"

Laying the phone aside, he reaches out to place his hands on the pale blue linen sleeves of my shirt and pulls me close. The flowers between us don't interfere with a kiss, a tender response answering before words do.

"Yes, River Heartsong. I will marry you."

Quivering, I am sunlight upon moving water, rippling joy that dances and sings. Emotion cracks his voice as we kiss again. Familiar. Good. The salty taste of his happy tears.

"You know it's what I've always wanted."

I nod, rising to stand as my dodgy knee groans and creaks, still holding the garden blooms and offer them to him. Teapot sits abandoned on the trolley and steeping too long, its brew turning dark and tannic.

"I wasn't ready before—wasn't sure you were really going to come around to the soul's authentic journey—but Ireland proved it to me. I'm ready now . . . and I love you so."

Another gentle kiss leaning in, then I lift his hand and pull him from the chair to his feet.

"Let's go upstairs," I grin with an eyebrow raised in suggestive innuendo.

He smiles, nodding, wiping crystalline droplets from his cheek with one hand, holding the garden flowers in the other.

"Just as soon as I put these blooms in some water," I add, taking the modest bouquet back from him and then catching sight of the neglected teapot. "Bugger, the tea!"

"Ah, now *that's* marriage. 'Oh, baby, let's have sex!' 'Yes, dear, let me finish this task first . . .'"

At the sink, I fill a cobalt blue glass vase with water and place the flower stems within, both of us chuckling at the orders of domesticity overruling a sexual escapade.

"You're right. To hell with the tea. I'd rather have you instead . . . and tea later."

"Are you going to tell your family we're engaged?"

A singular look his direction, shaking my head, one hand on my hip, then reaching out for his hand.

"Don't ruin our moment of fearless affection, Robert. Let's get naked."

HIGHFIELD

THE OPEN KITCHEN door invites the fading light and cool breeze of evening as we eat supper. Earlier today, I purchased a couple of fresh red mullets from Barry the fishmonger, their eyes glassy and still sparkling, and after pan-searing, have topped them with a piquant green sauce of fresh herbs, capers, anchovies, and lemon. Some courgette fritters rest on our plates to accompany, mandated by the large and flavorless zucchini which arrived in this week's veg box delivery.

Robert has no love for non-filleted fish, finding it tedious to dissect and eat. Too much work for too little pleasure, and invariably he ends up choking on some small, hidden shard of osseous matter. Anything cooked on the bone tastes better, however, and while I always consider what my companion would prefer to eat, tonight is a cook's prerogative dinner.

"So, I met with Peter today, the regional manager. You know, the one who hired me from America."

I have never met the man or anyone at Lloyds other than Robert's assistant and a few people at the Covent Garden branch, but I certainly know of Peter in the upper circle of dark suits. I nod obligingly, appreciating the fritters' taste and crispy, fried crunch.

"He rang and asked if I could come to his office. When my morning meetings were over, I went, and after complimenting me for the latest district rankings—we're once again on top—he said, 'I have a big ask of you. I'm aware you and your partner have just relocated to Kent, but I wonder if you would consider taking the reins of a much larger, troubled district southwest of London. It has been underperforming for years. Perhaps as the clever outsider, *you* are the one to finally get it on its feet. It's quite a large project and rather a lot that I'm asking, I realize. It won't be easy . . . but if you succeed like you have in the West End, it will really make your mark with Lloyds.'"

Robert pauses, pushing at a morsel of fish on his plate, nudging it left and then right. I set down my own fork with a soft clink of metal on ceramic, a sudden twisting in my innards, a chill upon me but not from the open door.

"What did you answer?"

"That I'd have to consult with you about it, naturally. The last thing either one of us wants to do is move house, I know."

At the thought of leaving this farmhouse with its pool and generous kitchen, for a moment the room spins. The terracotta floor has dropped away. Winds of change begin to blow, and within my heart, the doves quietly roosting all launch into flight with a distressed commotion. Robert eats silently, cutting into one of his courgette fritters and waiting for me to respond, and a lengthy, drawn-out minute slips by before I can articulate amid the internal turmoil.

"I will be terribly sad to move from this lovely house . . . this kitchen . . . the pool. What about your back? The warm water is *so* good for you . . . I hate to leave it, expensive a venture as it is."

"I know, me too. Believe me, love, it isn't an easy decision. I'm not even sure exactly where the new district is. I mean, I have the names of the bank branches and their towns. Maybe we can map it out. Peter says it's a really lovely area, one of the most desirable in England. I think it's down near Southampton where my grandparents lived. We might even be able to find another house like this one, with a good kitchen and a pool."

"What about the lease?"

"Because the bank is moving me, Lloyds will cover the rent on this house until the agency lets it to another tenant."

Mutely eyeing the half-eaten mullet on my plate, hunger evaporates. A swirl of the pale gold Albariño in its glass, a disinterested sniff, a sip and

142 ◆ WHERE TWO WORLDS TOUCH

a swish round the mouth; not really contemplating the northern Spanish wine but rather this unforeseen turn of events. Working in London has become increasingly difficult for my newly sensitive mate, not so much for the actual challenges of his job but the overwhelming energy of the city, along with the daily commute on a packed train. The constant buzz and hum of the metropolis. Once he thrived on the energy, but now it wearies and wears him down, and my role is to support as best I may.

"It isn't up to me, Robert, it's ultimately your decision. If it helps and boosts you at work, then that's what we'll do. Full stop. There's nothing holding me here. The few Watsu clients who have ventured down from London don't even cover the cost of heating the pool, we both realize that. They mostly just help me pretend I'm not totally invisible in life . . . but maybe my real work now is actually the emerging book manuscript. I know you're ready to get away from the crush of going into the city every day."

Still staring at my plate and its half-exposed fish skeleton, a familiar heaviness places unseen hands upon my shoulders, pulling me down. Things change in a flash. Robert proposes we think it over, mapping out the new district and weighing the options. Much as I would love to be disabused of future sight, I know we will be going. Our painted gypsy caravan will soon roll on to another campsite somewhere amid England's green hills.

～

For the next two days, life feels upended. I recall a passage in one of Marlena de Blasi's memoirs wherein, preparing to move from Tuscany to Umbria, the house in which she and Fernando reside becomes just *a place they are waiting to leave.*

Yes, that's exactly how things stand.

Déraciné. Encore.

Whether at the kitchen sink or pulling weeds, repeatedly a gloomy inner dialogue ensnares me. Telling myself that departing the glorious kitchen with ducks and flowers outside, the otherworldly Shaman in the garden, and all the things I love about this gracious house, hardly is it the end of the world. Life moves in mysterious ways and shifting currents. Surely, something else good will present itself. An escape from working in Central London will be better for Robert. I hope as much, yet I cannot shake the despondency on me like a wayfarer's cloak of blue.

My mate brings home a large map. With a yellow highlighter, he circles the towns with Lloyds branches and loosely outlines the South Downs district. This schematic tells me little however, for it charts nothing of the landscape, whether the towns and villages possess any charm or are merely industrial and bleak. What does it *feel* like? The tactile, empathic, nature-loving sensualist of me wants to know.

"I'll need your help with finding us a house," Robert entreats, his blue eyes cautiously searching my face. "You always do that for us and somehow find just the right place."

"Actually, *you* found the Wimbledon house."

"I know, it was terrible. We lost our dog and essentially got divorced. Obviously, things go much better when *you* choose the house . . . hopefully it will be something like this one."

He smiles and I try to meet his gaze with something other than sadness, biting my lower lip, my spirit lost in a summer fog.

So be it. But where to begin? The area soon under Robert's leadership is large, and other than mapping out the rail stations, I've no real clue where to commence the house hunting process.

"My office will be in Farnham, and unless we live very close to there, I'll have to drive to work each day. Wait, strike that; I basically need the car every day because I'll be traveling all over the district for branch visits."

"Okay, we need a nice town where I can get what we require for our daily life. And ideally a direct line into London. I guess that's where to start."

A day or two later, washing earth-crusted potatoes at the wide kitchen sink, staring out the windows at the lanky purple flowers on the terrace as they bend and nod softly in the breeze, I remain sketched in indigo. Still slightly overwhelmed by the task of locating a good house, packing and moving again, leaving this haven and heading into the unknown ahead.

Waitrose.

I blink. Hands halt their scrubbing. Narrow the search by locating the Waitrose locations in the new district and then look for houses in the immediate vicinity of each. I can live without a car, but as a cook I will not manage without a decent grocery store.

Three Waitrose stores are in the wide patch; thus, the field shrinks distinctly. Further, only two in towns with a direct train to London. Just four months after finding this country haven, once again I begin scouring property agency websites, the yellow highlighted map open beside me on the table and a requisite cup of tea, debating whether it's too early in the day for a glass of wine instead. A more potent sip of solace.

In the targeted areas of Sussex and Surrey, properties cost considerably more than pastoral Kent. I find nothing with a pool and little to spark my interest. Every single house pictured sits under a dull grey sky. How dejecting to leave lovely Babylon Lane and settle in a droll neighborhood or cookie-cutter subdivision, dwellings pressed up close. My stomach clutches and inhalation goes shallow and tight.

No, no, no.

Gradually, I whittle the uninspired list down to three properties, which gauging from the photos look promising but I'm not holding my already-restricted breath. Too often, pictures are selectively snapped to omit the garage immediately next door or the busy road, and seldom give indication of what surrounds. One of the options, however, is a brick cottage with a high, steeply gabled roof set among some mature trees. Possibly it backs against a large park or green field, offering at least a modicum of distance from any house in that direction. Whatever the case, the environment doesn't appear like a typical suburban neighborhood.

Accordingly, I schedule with various agencies for Robert and me to view the contending properties on the weekend. The trip is roughly eighty miles by motorway, an hour and forty minutes west to the Sussex Downs. A region appealingly clad with deciduous trees, vaguely it reminds of areas of the Pacific Northwest but with English brick and timber villages thrown in for picturesque effect.

The first house we visit is clearly not for us, apparent from the moment we pull into the drive, before even setting foot in the door. Built in a nondescript, pleasant enough neighborhood that does not warm my heart, the dwellings on either side have children's toys and bicycles strewn about. Regardless of a pretty garden—selectively photographed for maximum allure on the website—it smacks of English suburbia, and the prospect of families with kids on either side sends me fleeing.

The second property, ten minutes from the first and shown by the same agent, could be occupied in a desperate pinch. Situated in a quiet, spacious development on a hill, the residence boasts a lovely terrace and garden with a pleasing view, but the house is badly butchered and renovated inside. The chrome nightmare of a kitchen glows with horrid fluorescent lights and blue accent lighting, lacking a single window. My hopes are sinking. I'm tired, depressed about the relocation, and quite ready for a proper cup of tea. A fat slice of cake, alongside.

"Third time is the charm," says Robert, as we motor towards Haslemere, a small town with a newly opened Waitrose.

"Let's hope. That's much better than 'three strikes and you're out.'"

Upstairs at the estate agency, confusion erupts. Though we have booked an appointment to view the house, the cleaning woman, who went to the residence earlier, has not returned with the keys. Maybe she is still there, offers the assistant, attempting to ring the cleaner's mobile phone but no one answers.

"It's just over the hill, five minutes away. We'll simply go to the house and meet her," suggests the agent, a slender woman with blonde hair, wearing a necklace and bracelet of exceptionally large, lacquered grey nuggets, nearly the size of golf balls. They must be hollow and lightweight, else she would be unable to raise her hand, and the rocks around her neck would pull her forward to the floor.

Following the agent's oxidized black BMW, we wind through the

146 ◆ WHERE TWO WORLDS TOUCH

historic town, cresting a wooded hill, eventually turning at a crossroads to enter a small village, passing a few houses with tidy gardens, an old stone church, a central cricket green, and a classic-style pub. We trail her into a shady dell and along a narrow, oak-lined lane where the cottage sits at the end of the road, and from the photos, I recognize its steep gabled roof. As we approach and pull through the open gate into a wide gravel motor court, no sign of the cleaning lady.

Parked alongside the agent's vehicle, we step out into the cool of an afternoon rapidly clouding over. Legs feel cramped, and my lower back hurts; Robert's must feel even worse. My companion and I have spent too much time in the car today, traveling circuitous roads, and we still face a long drive back to Kent.

All seems placid and serene. A soft breeze carries fragrances of fields, greenery, and distant rain. The grounds of the cottage resemble a small park, sprinkled randomly with trees, shrubs, and flowers. What I had struggled to discern in the online picture is now revealed as a large, open field at the edge of the garden, with nothing but trees in the far distance. Momentarily, a thrum of wings inside my heart. A glimmer of hope, perhaps. A lightening of limbs, and an involuntary inhale.

The glowering grey sky descends swiftly, threatening to rain at any minute. The cleaning lady has gone, the cottage is locked, and we cannot get inside. Flustered, Anne of the oversize jewelry phones the office and discovers the keys have just arrived back at the agency. While she arranges for someone to bring them to us, Robert and I wander round the dwelling, peering in the windows.

Through the glass, a monochrome environment of neutral tones: cream-colored walls and doors, cream curtains, and uninspiring, pale beige wall-to-wall carpet. In an unfortunate modernization, someone plastered the original wood beams and filled the spaces between them, making the ceiling low, flat and white. The main reception has a giant inglenook brick fireplace, thankfully *not* whitewashed, with wide French doors and a large bay window, making a room of abundant light. Cheery, almost.

Circling around the backside, I peek into the kitchen window and

HIGHFIELD ◆ *147*

my spirit plummets. The small space is outfitted with white laminate countertops, an electric hob, and a soulless, cheap metal sink. If the room has a fridge, I can't see it. The most appealing element seems to be the broad window I dejectedly gaze through. Robert, beside me, immediately reads my thoughts and feelings.

"It's not *that* bad . . . I mean, it's bigger and better than Wimbledon! The space is kind of light and airy in a sterile way. And the window has a nice view . . . "

He turns around to consider the brick garage and oak-canopied lane behind us.

Bless him, he's clutching at straws and desperately seeking redemption. I do appreciate the gesture. We both know what we're giving up in this relocation but unsure what, if anything, either of us will gain.

Apart from one immediate neighbor next to the drive, the cottage sits pleasantly apart, bordered by a tree-lined private lane leading around a bend and over a hill. The south side of the property abuts a wheat field, beyond which the downs lie in the distance but no other dwellings. Roughly a half-acre, possibly larger, the grassy plot is mostly laid to lawn and unimaginative landscaping, studded here and there with various fruit trees—plum, apple, pear. Near the center, a tall, unfamiliar tree rises fifty to sixty feet high, with a pleasing shape and thickly furrowed bark. Robert heads in its direction while I meander to the fence line along the southerly field.

Gazing out into the clouded distance, I could be standing on the shore of a mirror-like lake in rosy dawn light. The setting feels utterly peaceful, more so than Babylon Lane. Rather than domesticated fields of sheep and tidy orchards, a mainly wooded vista with green trees stretches away like a vast, green ribbon. The tightness in my belly relaxes. I exhale softly. Always a good sign.

The clouds begin falling to earth. On the stone terrace outside the locked front door, Robert and I contemplate a little fishpond—its surface totally choked with lurid green moss and floating vegetation, seemingly solid enough to stand upon—when a roar and screech of gravel announces another agent pulling into the drive, arriving with keys. We gain access to

148 ◆ WHERE TWO WORLDS TOUCH

the cottage just as the heavens let loose with downward might.

The low ceilings are not overly oppressive, but the modernization throughout feels tragic. Whoever renovated the house had no eye for charm or personality, and the neutral tone of everything is bland as paste. Irrespective of fresh paint, the entire dwelling cries out for a decorator's warming touch. White metal, conical sconces affixed to the wall in each room remind me of an industrial-style desk lamp I had in the 1980's. Dreadful.

Surveying the empty rooms as I follow Robert on the tour, I try to visualize the space with our furnishings inside, art hung on the walls, and a splash of color from a nice carpet or two thrown down. New curtains, for a start.

"Once upon a time, this cottage must have oozed charm," I comment, leaving the rest of my sentiment unspoken.

"The landlords like to keep their properties very clean and light. They own two other cottages on the lane, and they don't allow painting of the walls."

Two moderately sized bedrooms sit upstairs at opposite ends of the central hallway, both with a large picture window, overlooking the field and lane, respectively. Each has a separate, small bathroom, one with a shower and the other with a modest tub, yet significantly larger than the hobbit bath Robert squishes into currently.

"The best part of this house is the loft," says Anne, gesturing to the nearly vertical wooden staircase that ascends between the two bathrooms. Robert leads the way, followed by me, and then the agent.

On the uppermost floor, due to the steeply pitched, A-frame ceiling and roofline, an adult can only stand fully upright in the middle of the space. The length of the loft is divided into two zones; a child's bedroom with a great skylight and a narrow window, and, at the other end, ducking under a low beam and miniature doorway fit for a halfling, a sizeable bathroom laid with dusky rose carpet. Against the window, a full-sized pink tub, bestowing an unsurpassed panorama of the wheatfield and far, wooded downs.

"Oh my god," Robert exclaims, his face illuminated by something close to joy. "A proper tub . . . with a view. This is fabulous!"

"How curious to find this rose-pink carpet here but nowhere else in the house," I shake my head, puzzled. "And how on earth did they get this tub up here?"

My partner already envisions soaking under the sloped ceiling, gazing out and watching the moonrise. Admittedly, the cozy loft bedroom seems an alluring option for a writing nest of sorts, with a small desk beside the clerestory window, looking over the drive and oaks. The agent is correct; the best part of the cottage is tucked under the peaked roof.

Alas, the woefully sterile kitchen strikes a distinct counterpose. My critical gaze takes in the white linoleum floor, the white Formica counters, plain white laminate cabinets, and the metal sink under the large but singular window. The sole element of character is an untreated pine door with a decorative cast-iron latch, which opens to a narrow utility room where I encounter another metal sink, a water heater, a standard washing machine but no dryer, and the back door.

"There isn't a microwave," the agent points out, "but hopefully you have your own you could place on the counter."

"I don't use a microwave," I mumble dismissingly, staring at the miniscule fridge, no taller than the dishwasher tucked under one of the counters, small even by European standards and something of a poor jest. Did a cook never inhabit this house?

"The previous tenants bought a large refrigerator and placed it in the laundry room, in front of the rear door," explains Anne, pointing.

If we take the cottage, we will have to do the same. The current fridge can hold only some beverages and ingredients for a single night's supper. Given I won't have a car, that simply won't suffice.

My body sags with disappointment, and I chew my lip in unconscious habit, arms crossed loosely over each other. So much for our options. Robert and Anne chat amicably while I weigh the various factors, my hopes dashed by this uninspired kitchen.

150 ◆ WHERE TWO WORLDS TOUCH

Only a soft drizzle persists of the deluge. The agent locks the front door with an old brass key and discusses with Robert the details of an application, the landlords, and the gardener. Pulling up the hood of my rain jacket, I stroll across the soggy lawn to stand once more at the tall deer fence and look out, needing to feel the expansiveness again in my bodysoul to offset the lackluster interior of the residence. Then I turn back toward the little brick house with its steeply peaked roof, closing my eyes and imagining how it might be to live here at Highfield Cottage. Appreciating the tranquil, sheltered location of a shady lane with only a wheat field and rolling downs beyond.

Enfolded by nature and unpretentious, maybe we're suited for each other after all. Undoubtedly, I can wield my decorating mojo to make things inviting. Under a grey sky, a sizable border of English lavender outside the main reception appears oddly luminous, as if illuminated from within. Wherever I live, *Lavandula angustifolia* always grows in a pot or the garden. A well-established bush thrives under the kitchen window of the farmhouse next to the large rosemary shrub, adorned daily with a cadre of loving, buzzing honeybees. Is the vibrant, living hedge of lavender beautifying the cottage terrace a sign or affirmation?

Driving over the hill to Haslemere, Robert and I consider the possibilities. The small bedroom in the loft would be an ideal writing room, though my folding campaign desk likely won't navigate the ladder-like stairs and narrow entry. The Spa, as we dub the top floor's bath with its inexplicable mauve carpet and full-sized pink bathtub overlooking the fields, could compel Robert to sign a lease immediately. While the cottage is less than half the size of the Kent farmhouse, its Sussex price tag costs £400 more monthly.

"Can you live with that kitchen?"

"Hospital surgery rooms have more charm," I sigh, staring blankly at the unfamiliar town passing as we navigate back to the central car park near the agency, "but if we get a decent fridge, I'll make do. Like you said, at least

HIGHFIELD ◆ *151*

it's better than Wimbledon."

"Wimbledon was a joke."

"Help me out, mate, we're looking for the silver lining here."

"Right, sorry. This cottage has a very nice view from the kitchen, don't you agree?"

Obtaining the full application from the estate agent's office, we walk a few hundred yards to the High Street, stopping in at a Costa coffeeshop to fill out the forms and caffeinate ourselves. Double macchiato for me. A *flat white* for Robert, who opts for a slice of carrot cake as well, unable to resist such things, ever. Perched side by side on tall chairs inside the front window, both of us tired, we contemplate the town's main thoroughfare. Some of the buildings are half-timbered, the rest are brick, and everything has a quintessential English charm, replete with baskets of colorful flowers suspended from the Victorian lampposts.

In our short stroll from the agency, we've passed an attractive fishmonger shop, and two doors down, a cheese and wine shop holds promise. Along with Waitrose, albeit a smaller-sized store newly opened after conversion from an old lackluster supermarket chain, my basic requirements as a cook are nicely represented. I won't generally have a car, but regular bus service connects from the crossroads over the hill, manageable enough. Indeed, Haslemere offers more than either the villages of Chart Sutton or Headcorn nearest the Kent farmhouse. The train station lies within easy reach when either of us need to venture into London, and studying the scene from Costa, eyeing the local bookshop and a kitchen shop across the street, everything appears to line up.

Yes, it's sorted really. We've crossed out all the other options, and the clock ticks down rapidly.

"Of course you've found us another charming house, my love," says Robert, affectionately draping his arm around my shoulder when he has finished reading through the rental application. "I'm so truly sorry we have to leave your dream kitchen and the pool. Someday I'll find a way to make it up to you. You'll work some River magic as always, and the place will feel like home within a week. You always create a beautiful space for us."

152 ◆ WHERE TWO WORLDS TOUCH

"It's one of my superpowers, homemaking," I shrug, but my tone is deflated, lodged between resignation and despondency.

"For sure."

"Maybe I should wear a cape instead of my French cook's apron. I've secretly fancied having a cape . . . "

My heart aches with leaving the Kent farmhouse, but this corner of Surrey and West Sussex feels good in my bones, belly, and breath. The wooded hills around the cottage already call me to wander and explore on foot. I will purchase a local Ordinance Survey map and head out among the whispering trees to rediscover myself once more. Probably deer and foxes, too. With some luck, a wee bit of enchantment.

Here we go again. The painted gypsy caravan rolls onward.

⌒⌣

The fetid little fishpond and I deepen our acquaintance thanks to a rake. Mere steps away from the cottage front door, I pass the lurid tangle multiple times a day, consequently a rehabilitation is in order. Among the unkempt flowers and bushes next to the pond's easterly edge, I discovered the submersible air pump that once circulated the water, its black cord neatly severed, most probably by a lawn mower blade.

New pump notwithstanding, the first step in restoring the pond to health requires removing the choking vegetation and thickly floating carpet of algae. Unable to reach the center from the water's rim, and reluctant to wade into the unknown jade depths, a garden rake found in the garage becomes my arm extension.

Thus, a sunny afternoon finds me pulling great tangles of waterweeds and scum onto the lawn. With each pass over the matted surface, I twist the rake handle to scoop into the green soup, and then heave the soaking, heavy contents over my shoulder. Hundreds of glistening black, aquatic snails are being unexpectedly evicted from their murky home and I suffer a twinge of remorse. Perhaps a saint would remove them all from the wet, exposed mass and throw them back in, but I'm not so exalted or Buddhist.

HIGHFIELD ◆ *153*

Robert goes to work, facing his first few days at the new office and making initial visits to the closer bank branches, driving around the South Downs. In my typical manner, within the first seventy-two hours of stepping in the door, all the cartons are unpacked, and our new place set promptly in order. I require my house to be a refuge, a sanctuary for body and soul, not stacks of boxes or clutter piled around.

Delectably warm days have blessed us since arriving, and I carry the tea tray outdoors to sit at our round bistro table with its wooden chairs. The half-acre property still seems park-like, and seated on the terrace, whether with a cup of tea or a glass of wine, I'm at some quaint Café du Parc, listening to birdsong and catching various scents upon the breeze. A confessed tree hugger, I miss the otherworldly Shaman, reminding me of the mythopoetic story and enchanted reality, but the elegant, unfamiliar tree at the center of the garden has a commanding presence. Whenever a breeze dances through its boughs, the entirety shimmers and whispers akin to gentle rain falling on a rooftop. Lovely. Energetically, something like a twinkle ripples through me in response. Certainly, this place isn't wild like Connemara, not even close, but our new setting feels expansive, and I'm grateful for the buoyancy of spirit.

Cleaning, sorting, tidying. Pulling weeds. Such are my chosen tasks each time I arrive at a new place, getting to know its corners, attempting to feel at home. Painting, sometimes. Although we have only recently moved in, and despite my mourning for the farmhouse kitchen, the charms of a homely cottage at the terminus of an oak-shaded lane swiftly seduce me. The bland, monotone interior feels warmed and softened by the addition of our solid wood furniture and antiques, a few colorful silk runners draped across end tables and dressers, some woven and tufted wool rugs laid down. Nomads we may be, but for better or worse our belongings don't comply sensibly. Already Highfield is surprisingly hospitable, reinforcing my impression on our first visit that somehow the place suited us. The Kent farmhouse was a tailor-made linen shirt, casually stylish, sported loose and untucked; this modest house is a worker's green corduroy, with worn patches at the elbows. Different but equally comfortable to wear.

154 ◆ WHERE TWO WORLDS TOUCH

A message on my mobile phone from our new landlord invites us to their house on Saturday. "Come at midday," he instructs, "and we'll have drinks and get to know each other a bit. Just follow the drive and go past the barn." The invitation, delivered in a boisterous English baritone, relays a summons more than suggestion.

The agency in Haslemere handles our tenancy, so we've not met the cottage owners, but, unquestionably, they know we are two gay Americans and Robert works for Lloyds. On the application, I listed my occupation as *writer*, the first time I've done so. The landlords own a five-hundred-acre farm, at the edge of which sits Highfield, along with some other rentals in their portfolio. According to Anne the agent, they host a yearly Christmas holiday party to which we may be invited if we're "very lucky." Their annual soiree doesn't interest me in the least, but we shall see what plays out. More immediately pressing, I ponder what *midday* means in England. Is it *exactly* noon? Drinks at twelve seems slightly odd to me if lunch isn't served, but what do I understand as an uncultured outsider.

⌒〰

Saturday morning arrives in a sundress of robin's egg blue, dancing outside the windows. I've arisen early as usual while Robert sleeps late, exhausted from work and details of his new post. Having decided I cannot show up empty-handed at the landlords' house, I'm assembling a raspberry tart, one of my favorite confections. A simple and enticing Provençal recipe I've made for years. The crust can hardly be called proper pastry; rather a sweet dough pressed with fingertips into the edges of the tart tin and then pre-baked until golden, but it tastes divine. Honey and almond-infused custard, rich with free-range eggs and thick yellow cream, is poured in after the shell has cooked, and then placed back in the oven until barely set. A bowl of fragrant, ripe raspberries beside me, I arrange the delicate jewels atop the cooled base, spiraling them from the center outwards, when Robert shuffles into the kitchen, ready for morning coffee and breakfast.

"I woke up because the house smells delicious, and I was dreaming of

HIGHFIELD ◆ *155*

good things to eat." He eyes the tart with still sleepy eyes and a little boy's face, rubbing his stomach. "Oh, you made that tart I love!"

"It's to take to the landlords today," I say apologetically, shaking my head.

"You didn't make one for us . . . ?"

He glances around the small white kitchen, an expression caught somewhere between disbelief and dismay.

"Non, *mon petit*," I shrug, continuing to place the velvet, garnet berries in their circular design.

Crestfallen, his shoulders slump slightly in defeat.

"But I *love* this tart. I was hoping to eat it for my breakfast."

"Well, perhaps the Brookhursts will share at midday. But if they don't, I'll make us another one tomorrow."

"Are there scones at least?"

"Yes, two from yesterday. You can warm them up with some jam and they'll be perfectly fine."

"Are you making tea?"

His second sweeping glance of the kitchen towards the hob prompts me to chuckle, knowing the translation of his query is, *will you make me some tea . . . ?*

"Yes, love. I was just putting the kettle on. It's time for another cup, I'm sure."

A couple of hours later, ready to depart, I dust the raspberries with a faint snowfall of icing sugar, more for presentation than added sweetness, and place the tart in a cake tote to carry it. Stepping out from the door, we pass through the narrow gap in the hedge beneath the tall oaks and, arm in arm, walk along the landlords' long private drive, me carrying our offering. The sky shines cerulean blue, embellished with cotton clouds, a day warm enough to manage without a light jacket, though we each wear one. England means rain, after all, and the heavens may be pissing down thirty minutes from now.

A half-mile walk, twice we step aside for a car passing us, probably locals who board their horses at the landlords' stable. The open expanse of wheat

156 ◆ WHERE TWO WORLDS TOUCH

bordering Highfield adjoins a similar one of green grain, hemmed from the narrow lane by a split rail fence, and a narrow rectangular field beyond. The midsummer air smells fresh and moist, not yet baked and dry as in months ahead. Strolling alongside my mate here in the Sussex countryside, hearing only the twitter of birds and murmuring of trees, a couple of wanderers beginning yet another new chapter in our ongoing story, a felt benevolence envelops us. A kinesthetic lightness of being—like the inspiration of breath itself. Somehow, in the upheaval of leaving Kent and the dear farmhouse, stepping into uncertainty, an unlooked-for grace has found us anew.

Surrendering. Relinquishing fear. Embracing uncertainty and unknowing. Rather than wanting everything to work out perfectly, letting go of expectation and attachment instead. My ongoing lessons, indubitably.

Again and again, without fail, grace manifests in my life in some curious fashion or other. Yet a jump into the unknown is still required—crossing a chasm with no bridge in sight, merely a rope. Or nothing at all to hold to.

Leap and the net will appear, people say. If only it were so easy.

What if, at this point in humanity's saga, our individual lives are meant to embody *personal* evolution—to transform and grow past limiting patterns and beliefs? And what if the opportunity and invitation for that process always requires us to risk and expand in yes, rather than contract in familiar containment, the "no" of staying small and seemingly safe.

Safety is largely an illusion. A notion we cling to almost desperately, believing it can somehow be achieved and secured, and life will finally be all right.

Here, now, arms linked as we walk, as if the summer-clad countryside recites the great poet's words, a snippet of Walt Whitman floats through my mind.

Happiness, not in another place but this place . . . not for another hour, but this hour.

Yes, indeed. Let me treasure the moment, appreciating the goodness and beauty all around. Trusting a larger, inexplicable force or mysterious plan unfolding beyond my limited perceptions. Much as I yearn for a home where we might finally settle, to find our place in the world—sensing the place *itself* has called us—the familiar ache feels lessened somehow. Just possibly, life will one day lead us to an optimal locale for rewilding heart and soul, where nature summons forth a deep authenticity, a resonant harmony in one's very being.

Equally plausible, like the mystical Tarot deck, perhaps this existence is really the Fool's journey—traipsing through life's lessons, karmic influences, and archetypal themes, as represented by the characters of the Major Arcana, from the Magician to the World, until ultimately reaching his destination. Who can say.

Fool and reluctant mystic, repeatedly letting go and starting over, I will gather the myriad gifts of this day. And as if my heart were a handcrafted bowl held outstretched, I welcome the unknown blessings already on their way.

Just say *yes*.

EDGEWALKERS

At the end of a shady lane, we settle in once more, establishing our routines and rituals. Robert takes the car daily to reach his Farnham office, yet unexpectedly I feel less isolated in our new location than in Kent. On any given day, I can reach Haslemere by setting out on foot to the village crossroads, roughly a mile and a half, and catching the bus. Freed from driving to the train station each morning and returning to fetch my mate in the evening strangely affords me greater liberty, loosening the uncomfortable harness of househusband. Despite not having an auto at my disposal, already I'm *more* independent.

Upon reaching the High Street, I disembark near the bookshop with its blue awning, and Pizza Express next door with tables and green chairs set out front, from whence I trot around the corner to Waitrose. Recently, I learned one may shop in-store and have their purchases delivered by a van driver, a vastly superior option to the disappointing online service I tried previously. Now I can do a substantial weekly shopping without requiring the car, and even a modest haul of provisions no longer must be carted home in heavy bags or bulging backpack.

Groceries purchased and delivery booked, I stop at the fishmonger to browse the fresh catch, all of them with clear glassy eyes as if just hauled from the waters and resting on piled ice. The reserved, spectacle-wearing fellow behind the counter is less cheery and talkative than Barry in Kent, but no matter. When he has cleaned and then sealed my selection in vacuum-lock foil and placed the fish in a plastic carry bag, I slip the purchase into my rucksack and exit the shop with a jingle of brass bells on the glass door.

A few steps down the street, past the hardware shop, I stop in at the Haslemere Cellar and Cheesebox, where predictably I'll choose some plump, garlicky olives in addition to a fat wedge of Berkswell, the sublime raw ewe's milk cheese from Warwickshire, vaguely reminiscent of a Tuscan Pecorino or a good Manchego but *better.* One day, browsing the wines, a sexy, dark-haired man in his mid-thirties catches my eye. Slender and dressed in a well-fitting tailored shirt with French cuffs, expensive trousers nicely accentuating a firmly sculpted bum, his stylishly pointed black leather shoes scream London. He contemplates the Bordeaux section with his young daughter in tow, a blonde and pretty girl wearing a frilly pink dress, her head a mass of unruly ringlets.

"Daddy, why do you buy so much wine?" she asks in a small, high voice, following him patiently.

Without missing a beat or turning to glance at her while considering the mid-range bottle he holds, his response sounds tired but kind.

"Because Daddy has children, darling."

I turn away to hide my amusement, suppressing a laugh.

Basic errands complete, weighted down with a bottle of something or other, olives, cheese, and a fish or two, depending on how long I've spent at my various stops, I have roughly twenty minutes before the bus is due. If I miss it, the next one arrives in an hour. Time permitting, Costa lures me in for a cappuccino. Having tried the local coffee shop a couple doors down and found it abysmal, despite my preference for independent businesses, the national chain wins my money. Cup and saucer in hand, I perch on a high seat in the front window, observing the weekday scene. Knowing no one, my outing delivers a short, weekly respite from an otherwise solitary, invisible existence; immersed in a social milieu of noisy espresso grinders, the clink of cutlery on plates, and a range of genteel, southern English accents. The intonation is how English *should* sound, I think.

Hearing Americans when out and about in London, or watching a Hollywood movie with Robert, our use of language strikes me as brassy. Clipped. Harsh, almost. Certainly, we speak American at home, but our

160 ◆ WHERE TWO WORLDS TOUCH

dialect continues to shift steadily, adopting local parlance. My musically inclined ear has a penchant for accents, and whenever talking to someone who speaks with a foreign tilt, inevitably I reply similarly, mimicking their tone. Presumably, an abundance of mirror neurons in my brain elicits this response, but, whatever the case, deliberate focus must be summoned to resist. Robert finds my reflexive mirroring humorous. While neither trying nor wanting to be English, my speech pattern adjusts when in public, softening the hard consonants and morphing into a subtly British, southerly inflection.

I've long delighted in well-written books, ones with slightly formal or old-fashioned prose like the classics, but only since coming to England have I discovered how much I also enjoy *hearing* words spoken well. Our language can be beautiful, it deserves elegance and elocution, with nuances of expression. What a pleasure words such as *dulcet, cosseting,* and *detritus*—terms most Americans don't even know—are sprinkled through everyday conversation in England. I speak more deliberately now, closer attention paid to my vocabulary. Partly because I hear well-spoken language surrounding me in this well-heeled region, situated close enough to London for husbands to commute to high-paying jobs, earning our area of Surrey and Sussex its moniker "the stockbroker belt." The handsome, well-dressed daddy in the wine shop isn't a bit out of place here.

Time to go. Finishing the last bit of milky foam at the bottom of the ceramic cup, I don my light jacket, lift a loaded rucksack from the floor beside my chair, and step out onto the High Street, rain or shine. Earbuds wired to the iPhone in a pocket, I push them securely in my ears, then count out the required fare in coinage as the bus approaches.

Keeping it real, I smile bemusedly, riding the countryside coach carrying groceries in my backpack.

Onward, wayfarer. Rolling over the hill to the crossroads and beyond on foot. The mundane interwoven with magic, the warp and weft on the loom of a life, in a tapestry of ordinary days.

EDGEWALKERS ◆ *161*

September arrives wearing a windy, grey dress, commanding everyone's attention as she twirls into the room, unannounced and dramatic. The air feels cool and weighty. A low sky glints dully with the flatness of hammered tin, and trees wave uncountable slender green hands skywards, feeling the change.

Only last week I perspired in humid sunshine while ascending the lane, carrying globe artichokes, broad beans, fragrant basil, French apricots and juicy pluots, returning from the greengrocer near the crossroads. Summer has vanished. Unpacking the weekly veg box delivery, I colorfully decorate the kitchen's white Formica countertop with autumnal bounty; potatoes still crusted in dark earth, plump and phallic carrots, pungent leeks, flat green beans, a round gem squash of darkest green burnished with gold, fleshy portobello mushrooms, and terracotta-hued sweet yams. I pile the less perishable items into the willow *bannetons* and a handcrafted earthenware bowl, creating a display of nature's artful offerings, warming the sterile workspace with garden-style goodness.

A weekend. Late morning, pleasantly at home in our usual way. Robert is tired, stiff, and moving slowly. To brighten his mood, I have made him a breakfast of scrambled eggs, heritage pork link sausages, English muffins with jam, and coffee alongside. Robust Assam tea for me to help kickstart the grey autumn day.

June hovers nine months in the future, but the vague outline of our wedding becomes a discussion. Exactly *where* it will occur remains unclear, other than somewhere nearby in southern England. We would prefer to marry outdoors, but in Britain, even in the laughingly brief window of summer, one must be prepared for rain. The only thing we've distinguished is our ceremony won't be a conventional one, and we will not wear tuxedos, preferring Italian linen suits instead. Casually elegant. Perfectly rumpled. Robert, in his typically excited and inclusive fashion, informed his family of our engagement long before I even considered uttering a word to mine.

"You are *going* to tell them, aren't you?" he enquires, buttering the

162 ◆ WHERE TWO WORLDS TOUCH

English muffin on his plate and spreading it thickly with sweet strawberry preserves.

"Of course, I am. But I'm in my usual need-to-know-basis-only mode, dragging my heels a bit."

A sip of tea, contemplating the sky outside and falling leaves, the kerfuffle of little garden birds at the feeder beyond the stone terrace.

"Well, if they're going to travel to England, they probably need to know sooner rather than later."

"I was thinking of writing them this weekend."

"You could pick up the phone and ring them, you know. It wouldn't kill you, and they'd love to hear your voice. It's not expensive to call the States on our mobile plan."

"Don't get pushy, dear."

"I wouldn't dream of it. These eggs are delicious, by the way. Simply perfect. You put Parmesan in them, didn't you?"

Interlocking logistics tend to overwhelm me, and I don't feel any hurry to start juggling the details of our wedding or the arrival of family. If it were entirely my decision, the event would merely be the two of us with an officiant we've chosen, but I accept the relevance of such a ceremony lies partly in making a public stance, witnessed by friends and family, particularly as a same-sex couple.

Our pockets don't feel very deep. Robert's salary adequately provides for the two of us but is hardly extravagant, and my income remains nonexistent. Planning a wedding and its costs, my stomach tightens, let alone the thought of extended houseguests. Inwardly, I lament the complications of an overseas event. Many of the people dearest to us will be deterred by flying to England *and* paying for their lodging. A couple of bed and breakfasts are close by, along with a decent inn or two near Haslemere, but none of them are inexpensive. Anyone traveling from the West Coast of the States for our celebration will be staying a minimum of five days, it's too far to come otherwise, and who wouldn't want to see a bit of Britain once they have arrived? For our friends in Hawaii, where we lived several years, joining us requires a ticket halfway around the globe. Add to this the currency conversion rate is not in Americans' favor.

Alongside my adoptive father and stepmom, I have brothers with wives, or girlfriends, as well as a nephew. Robert, an only child, simply has his divorced parents and their tense dynamics with each other.

Over the course of multiple discussions—at the table, driving in the car, coffee and cake in Haslemere—we ultimately agree: out of fairness, finances, and logistics, we will limit the gathering to our parents. Included in the small circle will be Stephen who, having spent the summer with Robert in London while I was in New Mexico, has become more a younger brother than a cousin. My mate decides we must also invite Stephen's girlfriend because you cannot invite half a couple, overruling my stance. Unsurprisingly, his decision triggers a mild uproar amid the rest of his northern family, the Welsh clan who all want to attend, and as he relates the latest drama to me, my response is simply an I-told-you-so look. Hopefully, the dust will settle soon.

We concur the wedding officiant can only be my dear soul-sister in the States, an extraordinarily talented, multilingual singer-songwriter. The most lucent human being I've had the grace and privilege to know. A brilliant woman who reads quantum physics in French at bedtime, a person who has taught me kindness and the power of intent. A kindred celebrant of beauty. A woman who, were I not a gay man and she not a lesbian, could be the love of my life. In light of Stephen's girlfriend attending, we will invite Erika's new partner, a woman we've not met but whether she will come time will tell.

The intimate group seems manageable and mostly sorted at minimal cost and impact. Still, as a solitary creature, my anxiety rises with the prospect of seven guests loitering around the house for several days. Repeatedly, I find myself fiddling with my silver Navajo cuff, twisting it aimlessly on my wrist, or holding the curvaceous Māori whalebone pendant around my neck, rubbing it between thumb and forefinger, its smooth surface like aged ivory. Thinking about the details, I pull at my bottom lip, pensively. We live in a cottage, and the kitchen with its minuscule fridge is something of a bad joke. Having people in my dwelling for an extended time feels stressful, not

164 ◆ WHERE TWO WORLDS TOUCH

enjoyable, and while many things in life I share generously, personal space isn't one of them.

My current plan involves preparing a fabulous dinner the night before the ceremony, assisted by Erika, with whom creating meals always brings delight. My cherished stepmother, a genuine-issue Woodstock hippie, a shoot-from-the-hip kind of woman, is more than capable in the kitchen and possesses a knack for hearty, simple food. Yet given the modest space, only Erika will be my sous-chef, a pleasant, convivial change from doing the work all alone.

I never miss my days of cooking professionally for the rich and famous, the Hollywood and political crowd. The stakes were high and the work was intense, loaded with stress and unpredicted glitches—like my primary client adjourning their party between dinner courses to wander out to the pool, dismissing my objection the next course was coming out of the oven, ready for serving. Dashing to avert disaster. After every long night of juggling logistics, plates, and personalities, I returned home to collapse and recuperate on a quiet morning the next day. Alas, with our houseguests next June, there will be no tranquil, lazy mornings until the wedding week completes. The pot in my belly simmers, and I breathe into my gut to turn down the flame, reminding myself we have months yet in which to plan and prepare. I push the noisy thoughts away and inhale another deep, visceral breath, whispering silently, *everything will work out.*

Painlessly, I hope.

⁓

Robert spends much of his workday driving the South Downs, making branch visits and establishing an on-site presence with his new team. Several of the low-performing managers are retired-in-place, having little or zero interest in making changes to the business or their scorecard. They realized long ago that district managers come and go as corporate pawns on a chessboard, and with taciturn, stubborn refusal they will outlast any dark suits who arrive with updated schemes to put in place. The labour unions stand firmly entrenched, and slim danger exists of losing one's job for underperformance. Instead, the resistant ones will dig in their heels, hunker down, and prepare for a long and gloomy siege. In my partner's view, a couple of them have singlehandedly redefined *sullen*, though some good apples exist in the basket too. Lloyds' new customer service model holds no appeal for them; why change anything or try something different? Here in England, things should roll along just as they always have, even if the process is convoluted and interminable. With burdened professionalism, they tepidly greet the overly enthusiastic, gay American, and Robert swiftly comprehends the district's troubles have deep roots. To reach even lukewarm success, he faces a long, uphill climb.

On the home front, Alan, the elderly gardener, tends to Highfield as he has for forty years. Nothing changes here. No bright annuals are planted, nothing new is begun, and nothing old is removed unless it has died. He mows the large lawn and trims bushes and hedges exactly as he has always done, his pace unhurried as a mule turning a grindstone. Cut from the same cloth as some of Robert's bank managers, if wearing stained grey coveralls rather than a business suit. On regular, lengthy breaks for tea in his battered red van, he sits with the door ajar, drinking from a sizeable thermos. Maybe it's brandy, I don't know. Friendly enough, he's willing to chat, but with his thick cockney accent and slang, regardless of my well-tuned ear, I only decipher roughly a third of what he says. Mostly I avoid him by staying indoors when he's on the property, or if coming or going on foot, I dash into the cottage to avoid another unintelligible conversation.

Bless us all.

<hr>

Though the footpaths constitute public byways, taking the landlord's magisterial offer in hand, five days a week I amble across their swath of land, a patchwork of young woodlots, grassy pastures, and wheat fields. Walking here brings more enjoyment than agrarian Kent, with a gentle enchantment from the whispering woods hemming the fields, as well as the

166 ◆ WHERE TWO WORLDS TOUCH

semi-wild heath studded with prickly gorse and heather atop Blackdown above our cottage.

Today, passing the unusually quiet stables of the farm, catching the scents of manure, fresh hay, and horses, I'm following the muddy track along the uppermost of the large ponds fringed with tall reeds and grassy banks. Inundated by recent storms, the brownish water is higher than I have yet seen it. Even the giant lily pads float under the surface, transformed into large and flatly round ingredients in a murky soup.

Walking, I ruminate on *path* as a metaphor—looking for one's track in life. By its very nature, any trail only leads to where others have gone, and it strikes me, what if a path doesn't exist to where I'm going because I must blaze one myself?

Heeding some inner whisper, I leave the footpath as it cuts across the lower edge of a pasture where a handful of graceful Arabians graze, and veer left to walk along the field's border of nearly nude trees. Towards the upper reaches of the expanse, another trail ascends the forested hill, and I head for that. Passing the narrow band of woods cloaking a shallow ravine, a faint semblance of track, likely left by deer, leads beguilingly down into the hollow. For a moment I pause, unsure about changing my trajectory, but then follow my intuition and plunge down the slippery slope into the basin of trees. Going rogue, in my fashion.

Half a dozen times I've passed this woodlot of oak, birch, chestnut, and holly, but fixedly kept to the field and path as I headed up or down the hill. Now I discover a wet and moss-grown glade, alive with the polyphonic laughter of water splashing in two small streams joining together at the foot of a mighty tree. Personifying a pagan spirit, a strange and mythic face from another world peers out from the massive base, bearded with moss, and four separate, mature trunks rising from his head resembling antlers or a crown, each twisted round with brown coils of vines and leafy ivy. The forest king.

Boots sinking into a bed of autumn leaves and mud, I stand calmly transfixed by the mystical face, simultaneously absorbing the sights, sounds, and smells around me. Mostly stripped of leaves after a week of fierce rain and wind, the trees' naked forms stand starkly picturesque and shapely. The air carries a crisp flintiness of fresh precipitation layered with aromatic bass notes, the earthy muskiness of decomposing compost, mushrooms, and soil. A vegetal odor, oddly reminiscent of green tea, clings within the damp dell. To a perfunctory pass of the eyes, this sheltered glade is an ordinary patch of woods, but somehow the two gurgling streams and the mighty grandfather tree cast a unique spell. An almost tactile magic radiates—as if I've stumbled into a secret wonderland or a different world. My core expands. Primary senses feel elevated and sharpened. I'm tingling softly as if drawn outwards by gossamer strands, signaling a shift into an altered mode of awareness, as the veil thins between worlds. Too, a familiar sensation at the top of my head, which I experience from time to time, as if an unseen hand applies pressure or miniature horns grow. Everything vibrates with a faint charge, and in concert with other energies or entities— the realm of *invisibles* I know to be real— the presence of the trees feels palpable.

The Green Man is an ancient pagan archetype of masculine connection to nature. Depicted in image and stone with his beard and hair growing or formed of leaves, vines, and boughs, he stewards the forests and land— husbanding the plants and trees, animals, and the Divine Feminine. Existing in conscious relationship and harmony with the living energies of a greater cosmology, he embodies a silent, gentle wisdom through his respect of all living things and their interpenetration. Inherently masculine, his visage offers a compassionate model of manhood and strength: one based on relationship, caring, and stewardship.

Everything is relationship.

Far older than Christianity, the Green Man reemerged powerfully in the twelfth century alongside the Goddess as she became the Holy Mother, Mary. His bearded countenance is carved into stone pillars in cathedrals throughout Europe. At the sacred site of Chartres, France, he can be found at least seventy-two times within the great cathedral, and reputedly over a hundred of his faces decorate Rosslyn Chapel in Scotland.

Though aware of the archetype, I've never personally connected to the

168 ◆ WHERE TWO WORLDS TOUCH

Green Man in any sort of meaningful way. Moving to England, passingly I wondered if his energy might still be present in these verdant isles where he is embedded in local folklore. Possibly, he endures energetically in the still-untamed places less encroached upon by humanity, in a different dimension.

Here, for the first time, I dimly detect his presence. A benevolent sense of interconnected relationship, a vague feeling of *goodness* and something akin to protection; an openness in heart and chest, accompanied by the swirling sensation atop my head. Led intuitively to a mossy dell, inadvertently I'm at the threshold between realms, half expecting a man-like form of glimmering leaves and diaphanous light to step from behind one of the trees, revealed—like the time a luminous, angelic being walked into the room where I sat, facing an uncertain moment in a group circle, and stood behind me with its ethereal hand in the center of my back, filling me with courage and a stream of words.

While I observe nothing out of the day world ordinary, my expanded perception and heightened state persists—lightheaded, spacey, almost gauzy. I have not seen him but, for the first time, understand in a *felt* way the ancient archetype is an authentic force.

I hear the sound first, a delicate tapping of rain on the few remaining leaves high above. An onerous grey sky has materialized from nothing. On the flowing ribbons of water, crystalline rings expand on the surface as droplets complete their gravitational plunge to earth.

The day was sunny and fair when I set out from the cottage twenty minutes ago; now the ceiling of dull pewter falls rapidly. In an unusual twist for this time of year, I've left my raincoat at home, and I have no umbrella, just a lightweight scarf coddling my neck. My eyes sweep the glade for someplace to take shelter, but the bare trees provide no adequate protection or haven. The faint hiss crescendos to a dull roar. An unanticipated deluge is about to drench me. So be it. I haven't spent the time I wish to linger in this special hollow, but I'll soon be back, hoping to detect the Green Man once more. A magic here whispers with a softly mesmerizing voice—many voices—calling my wild soul by a secret name.

As I emerge from the dell, striding across the sodden green field, the phantom clouds let loose with zeal and vigor. Rain crashes down with driving, diagonal force and the near-distant horses lower their noble heads and turn away. I squint into curtains of liquid silver sweeping across the landscape, water streaming from my unruly hair into my eyes, and laugh out loud. *How crazy!* No point running for home or trying to find refuge, I surrender to the celestial baptism. Walking in a downpour and laughing like a madman.

The unforeseen squall lasts only ten minutes. Soaked to the bone, I've transformed into a two-legged, wet muskrat. Entwine some ivy in my hair and brown beard, I might be a soggy Green Man. Only my feet remain dry, tucked snugly into rubber Wellies. Traversing the last flooded field to open the high deer gate, stepping into our park-like garden, the sky gleams a dazzling Wedgwood blue. Everywhere shines the same golden light that graced the world when I set out on today's jaunt, a sparkling iridescence bestowed upon everything. Not a single cloud obscures the heavens except over the distant downs, miles away. A stunning autumn day of radiant splendor enfolds me. Almost impossible. *Almost.*

Drenched and chilled, I'm also fully, gratefully alive, my body coursing with a subtle current of bioelectricity. The torrential cloudburst has washed me clean, and conferred inspiration to sit and engage the manuscript I was avoiding. As always, time spent amid the forms and forces of nature has brought me home to myself, drawing me out of the confines of mind into the larger web of communion.

A brush of mystery. Perchance a trace of magic. A storm out of the blue, and a curious, energetic encounter. Unlooked for, once again the soul of the world has touched me for an unfathomable reason or fate.

Don't go back to sleep.

⌒

"Sometimes I think I married Thoreau, always out wandering in nature," Robert smiles as I recount the day's ramble, my altered awareness in the

170 ◆ WHERE TWO WORLDS TOUCH

mystical glen, and the intriguing recognition of the Green Man's presence.

"I'm sure you mean that as a fine compliment. He is practically the patron saint of environmentalists, after all, but personally I find Thoreau a bit of a 'downer.' He's really quite negative at times. As Mr. Wild Soul Singing the Body Electric, I'm more aligned to Whitman, probably. Except I'm not a poet."

"You *are* a poet, my love. I think poetry is part of your soul. You've written me beautiful poems. I have every one of them saved in my special box next to the bed. Along with every card and letter."

I know he does. Similarly, I have his cards too.

"You're overdue for a new poem or love letter. If working on this stupid book manuscript—whatever it turns out to be—doesn't kill me, kindly remind me and I'll write you something lovely."

Our supper tonight is a roasted beetroot risotto, earthy and rich, the creamy Italian rice turned a vivid magenta hue, dusted with fine shavings of pecorino Romano. A requisite salad of wild rocket alongside for something fresh and green.

"How is the writing going?"

"Horrid. Each day more comes to me that needs saying . . . the scope keeps growing. I'm probably attempting the impossible. *Herculean* feels like the most appropriate word. Or maybe I'm in one of the circles of Hell in Dante's inferno, where aspiring writers are chained, and this is all part of the Divine Comedy."

Exhaling a dramatic sigh, my shoulders slump forward. Briefly, I contemplate the mound of steaming crimson in a wide, shallow bowl before me.

"When I first began this little folly, I was essentially writing what I knew, or thought I did, from years as a bodyworker and healer, as well as the whole eco-depth psychotherapy thing. But somehow, it's shifting, and the deeper I drop into my own embodiment—breath, movement, walking, immersion in nature—everything changes. A lot of what's coming through feels new. I honestly can't say exactly where it originates other than somewhere beyond. Mostly, it feels like I'm catapulting into an evolutionary process. As if the fencepost revelation wasn't enough."

I smile at my betrothed half-heartedly, noting the tiredness in his face from another long day, yet he genuinely, actively listens to my ramble. Bless him.

"It's rather like building a mountain when the only tool I have is a teaspoon, and I'm carrying a smidgen of dirt—one word—at a time. Uphill. Better than Sisyphus endlessly pushing his damned boulder, I suppose."

"It can't be easy to write a book, not a good one anyway. I'd never have the discipline, even if I had inspiration. It makes me glad that you're more content here than in Kent, like the woods and Blackdown seem to have called you home. I can always tell when you are happy and in tune with your soul because the whites of your eyes get bright and clear."

"Well, I wouldn't describe myself as *happy* writing this book manuscript. *Non, je ne m'amuse pas.* But somehow, I'm being *called* to do it. All the curious dreams occurring regularly, where an archetypal, divine feminine figure invites me to do something I'm resistant to. Usually it's a pop star, like Madonna—she's become a regular, insisting I'll dance in her new video despite my objections."

"You do like to hang out with celebrities in your dreams. Weren't you just with Oprah in one of them?"

"Yes, she's repeatedly showing up. Along with Stevie Nicks and Barbra Streisand, both of whom want me to sing on stage with them. Oh, and Céline Dion. It's more than *gay* . . . I'm trafficking in archetypes! Crazy as it might sound, these summonses are related to writing this book that I'm overwhelmed by, feeling it's too big, exceeding my reach and skill."

"Nothing you say sounds crazy to me, love. And what I know about artists, in general, is that they create because somehow, they *must*."

"Well, it does feel that way . . . a strange doom, if I want to be melodramatic about it."

He smiles wearily at me, then his face changes with a moment of reflection or wandering in memory.

"I can't tell you how lonely it was here without you. Not simply because you were gone and a gaping hole opened in my life, that the house became

172 ◆ WHERE TWO WORLDS TOUCH

dead and empty, of course there was that. Maybe it's partly because I'm in banking but England is so . . . unfriendly. I love coming home to a nice dinner and someone to talk with about things that are *real*, which matter in a larger picture. I just hope we can make some friends eventually."

Spoon in hand, I smile and reach for my racy, sleek Sancerre, twirling the glass for a sniff and another swallow like a self-confessed wine geek.

"I agree, it would be lovely to have a sense of community one day, with friends gathered round this table again."

Irrespective of Robert's struggle at work, a blue note of itinerant wistfulness for both of us, we are nourished here; largely through the necessary and sustaining ritual of togetherness over supper, sharing a deliberate, hand-built life. Outsiders. Threshold dwellers. *Edgewalkers*, a foot in two worlds. One struggling to find his soul in a realm where no welcome or place exists for it; the other following his soul across fields, through shady dells and across a scrubby heath, chasing clouds and searching for meaningful words. Both alone in our own way, coming home to each other in the tranquil evening of the countryside for the enduring solace of meaningful companionship.

Grace, indeed.

〜

We have a garden visitor, a little fox who appears at dusk. I first spied him a fortnight ago from the bedroom as he stealthily navigated the border of lavender outside the reception's bay window. Hardly more than a foot tall, gingery red except for grey paws and a white-tipped tail. Lean as bones. Naturally adorable like any young animal, but the dark eyes glinted hungrily.

Initially, I saw only one. A week later, I noticed a second, drinking from the cleaned fishpond on the terrace while its sibling dug at the lawn under the bird table, scavenging the birdseed scattered for the ground feeders—the ones too ungainly, unable, or unwilling to alight on the tall post.

In the early evening, both kits have just appeared, one larger than the other and braver. Is he the male, or simply more assertive and better fed? I stand motionless in the dining room to observe, soft paws padding fondly through my heart.

"Hello, lovelies," I whisper with a smile, a warm glow spreading through me.

Foxes are not strangers to our garden. I find their tracks in the muddy earth and their rank scat in various places, but normally they visit under cover of darkness, silently eyeing us through the illuminated windows or circling around once we extinguish the lights. These diminutive ones have burrowed their way directly into my affection; Robert's too, after I brought him unobtrusively to the window and pointed. Lately, we both watch for them.

"Did you see the pups today?" he asks when seated at the dinner table, glancing toward the darkening garden, as if they might appear on summons.

In the fading daylight, waiting for Robert to come home, my thoughts turn to the feral juveniles. Seated on the Balinese teak bench by the French doors in the reception, reading a book, truthfully, I'm merely marking time and repeatedly looking outside. Hoping. I've even taken to leaving food scraps on the lawn, tossing out chicken bones and other victuals which might appeal, knowing their hunger. Cook that I am, routinely offering comfort and nourishment, now I feed little foxes, too.

Wouldn't the Green Man, keeper and protector of fields and woods, wish me to be kind? A perfect and convenient justification, I'm happy to oblige, as with the host of garden birds we buy seeds for. Taking care of things is what I do.

Yesterday afternoon, seated at the bistro table on the terrace, relishing the weakening autumn sunshine with a linen scarf coiled around my neck in perpetual fashion, fountain pen in hand while I wrote in a notebook, one of the kits arrived in broad daylight. Trotting around the lavender, they stopped in their tracks, as startled to meet me as I was to see them. We held each other's gaze for a moment; the foxy eyes glistening, and large, triangular ears cocked forward on alert. Then the visitor turned and fled back through the tall hedge along the lane, white-tipped tail bouncing, and didn't return until nearly sunset.

Our lives right now seem counterpoised. I am at home and tending the hearth; roaming about on foot, immersed in the living, breathing world, and wading deeper into a creative but challenging work. Robert's hours pass under fluorescent lights in the bleary realms of banking management, his soul sucked dry daily by stultifying details such as outlining performance standards for employees.

The dark suits in the high towers of the City want the South Downs district turned around and profitable, but the local managers have scant interest in the agenda. Robert's group forms part of a larger region with its own new boss, a short man recently promoted to his supervisory role from a different division in the bank. He lacks experience with retail banking, and a hammer is the only tool he possesses. Deficient in interpersonal and coaching skills, his solution to every problem or underperforming manager is to treat it like a nail and pound harder.

Robert's success in London with the West End group arose from his team's weekly meetings, his effective and inspiring coaching of reluctant managers, and true leadership ability. Skills resulting in employee retention and loyalty, along with low turnover numbers, and, in no small part, a key factor why Lloyds recruited him from the States. A skillset which far outstrips his new supervisor, and a situation that doesn't bode well for the portly, balding, and insecure man with pressure on him from higher ranks. Inflamed by the low numbers, weekly he interrogates Robert as to why the changes aren't happening faster. Why hasn't the district gained traction?

My mate's honest assessment is unwelcome: considering the deep-rooted problems and patterns, along with English labour laws, they will have to prepare for a long haul. They must set measurable, enforceable standards and put managers on performance plans, so eventually when targets fail to be met, the individuals can be moved into a different role—unrelated to sales, which is what banking has become. His accurate, realistic view is received poorly by the Small Man.

My companion's heart no longer aligns with his work, and he does not respond favorably to beating down. Few people do. Really an artist at the core, his dark night of the soul in a London hospital—projections crumbling as he confronted his mortality—set him back on course. The Lloyds barge chugs sluggishly in a different direction than he wishes to go, if it's even moving at all. The trip to Connemara, seated in a circle of seekers on the windy bog, simply confirmed finance is dead for him.

As more entangled problems come to light, Robert has also learned a long string of district managers have attempted to resuscitate the troubled South Downs, each of them failing to budge the region from the bottom of the rankings. On paper, the area and demographic are affluent, and London wants more earnings by focusing on sales, insurance, and loans. They don't grasp that in rural banking, the same small business customers and pensioners coming through the door since World War II, their market doesn't wish to be *sold* anything.

The soullessness of finance, his unsupportive and overbearing boss, the systemic issues and faults of the district, all weigh upon Robert's body and spirit like a suit of iron. Meanwhile, the Small Man demands an action plan for the coming week from his managers on a call each Sunday evening.

"I didn't know the background," my mate says dejectedly at dinner, stabbing at the smoked salmon soufflé before him. His eyes are flat grey these days, dull as stones, like when I arrived back in Wimbledon. "I wish someone had told me. Now I understand why a couple of the London managers rang me up and asked, *are you sure you want to do this?* Honestly, I did it because Peter asked me, and I respect him. And I wanted to get out of London . . . but I'm afraid I've made a huge mistake."

The dejection in his voice sounds heavier than a long day of cold rain, and a pang of empathy echoes in my chest. The rising star at Lloyds, once so eager and full of aspiration, has unknowingly booked a First-Class cabin on the Titanic.

LIGHT & SHADOW

I CALL IT the *lookout*. Standing at the high deer fence separating our garden from the southerly wheat field, I gaze toward the rolling, wooded downs. At any hour of the day, often when facing an impasse or perilously slow trickle of words from my pen, I step outdoors and let bare feet carry me across the lawn. The cool grass underfoot swiftly brings me from my head to my soles as I move towards the perimeter of the property. Listening. Observing. A draught of fresh air to clear my mind. Free of masonry walls, connected to the natural world through open senses, my writing finds its wings. My untamed soul, equally so.

Barefoot at the fence line. Flirtatious gusts dance about beneath a pale blue sky laced with wispy clouds, and a perfume of wood smoke drifts from somewhere, tingling my nose like fragrant incense. The campfire scent seems quintessentially autumnal, triggering the impulse to pull on bulky sweaters and cozy scarves, to embark on long, introspective walks, shuffling through ankle-deep drifts of colored parchment leaves. Returning to a toasty house and fragrantly steaming cider mulled with pungent, warming spices.

Autumn always unlocks a benign madness, draping my soul in crimson and gold hues of gentle melancholy. The resplendent foliage and changing moods of weather spur me to set something simmering at the back of the stove, such as a humble bean stew in an earthenware pot. *Au coin de feu*, the French would say. Surely nothing instills a feeling of homey goodness as a meal bubbling softly for hours over a low fire, its alluring aroma enticing to all.

If a single dessert exists that pleases everyone, it's a French apple tart. For me, the pastry must be appealingly golden, buttery, and flaky—shattering beneath the tines of a fork or knife blade. Given the season's fresh apple crop, and a score of unfamiliar British varieties to try, tarts and rustic galettes routinely appear in our house. I'm often at the sink, looking out at the scalloped tin sky and whirling, bronzed leaves, using a favorite culinary tool from E. Dehillerin in Paris. The worn, wooden handle of the peeler feels comfortable in my palm as I draw the notched blade toward me, simultaneously turning the apple in my other hand, playing a little game whether I can strip the waxy, red and green mottled skin entirely in a single, long, curling ribbon.

Contentedly in cook's mode, I undertake my seasonal ritual of *confit de canard*: two days of curing the duck legs in salt and herbs, then submerging them in duck or goose fat to cook over a whisper of flame for two hours, followed by "curing" further in the strained, reserved fat for up to another week. A dish that asks for time and patience rather than trouble yet rewards as little else. When warmed through, the skin crisped in a hot pan or under a broiler, the rich taste makes the slow process worthwhile. A refreshing salad of bitter leaves and citrus alongside, followed by a slice of apple tart with a dollop of crème fraîche, every bite delivers autumnal bliss. A glass of well-crafted Pinot Noir to accompany, I've tipped over into gustatory heaven.

Spiky hulled chestnuts litter the footpaths, and only this year have I finally learned two types exist. The larger ones, recognizable from growing up in the western States, encased in a tough green shell with a host of spears protruding from the exterior, are *horse chestnuts*. I never comprehended why, gathering them on walks, stuffing my pockets with the burnished orbs and bringing them home with anticipation, they were so bitter when roasted. Even blanching them did not help. They tasted nothing at all like the divine morsels from street vendors in Paris, bundled and huddled over their charcoal burners, wearing fingerless wool gloves. The fragrant, nutty scent of those *châtaignes* lingers with me still, as if strolling the Tuileries or Jardin de Luxembourg on a weekend walk, a hand-woven silk scarf wrapped

178 ◆ WHERE TWO WORLDS TOUCH

snugly around my neck.

Conkers, Brits call the horse chestnuts, versus the smaller orbs of a different varietal guardedly enrobed in a more densely spiked, almost furry shell—the ones for eating. Epiphany. Collecting these edibles on my rambles, or when coming home from the crossroads bus stop, an entirely different taste experience graces me here at Highfield. After cutting an 'x' in the flatter side and blanching them in boiling water, I peel away the outer hulls and disrobe the pale-yellow nuts from their slightly fuzzy inner coats. Toasted in a cast-iron pan until slightly charred, the toothy morsels taste slightly sweet. Admittedly, my undertaking constitutes more work than buying the charcoal-roasted nuggets from a street vendor, were I back in France, yet possibly they taste better for the effort and having gathered them myself. An edible story of which I know all the parts, from tree to hand to mouth, an intimately connected and conscious way of eating.

My new, autumn ritual would only be improved, maybe, by owning a long-handled, copper chestnut warmer like I came across in an antique shop in Rye. Then I could roast the nuts over the coals of our fireplace, seated in front of the large hearth in the main salon, a glass of something agreeable at my side, my do-it-by-hand soul blithely blissed out. Despite lacking such a fine, old-time contraption, as the days slip by, I find no shortage of opportunity to revel in the season's bounty, beauty, and delight.

Provence still hovers in my thoughts. Robert and I recently spent a handful of days in the Vaucluse and Luberon, a brief escape, hurtling there and back on high-speed trains. Among the dusty pines in an Old World landscape drenched with Mediterranean light, the air scented by resinous scrubland the French call *garrigue*, even were I not a Francophile, the gypsy in me felt sweetly at home. Back in Sussex, the spice cupboard is freshly stocked with genuine, aromatic *herbes de Provence*, as well as jars of *confiture de figue* and *miel de lavande*, and simply dipping into their sweet contents with a miniature spoon transports me instantly back to sunshine in the Land of the Midi. Yet even while the south of France croons romantically in my heart, autumn in England gracefully seduces me, and I allow the warmth of the Med to slip slowly back into memory.

Have I said it before? I am learning to see. Yes, I am beginning. It still goes badly. But I intend to make the most of my time.

Treasured Rilke and his soulful poetry. Inspired by example, on my wanderings through the landlords' woods and up Blackdown, where I roam the gorse and heather-strewn heath, I learn to see. Little details. Interconnected relationships. The astounding complexity of life in a single inch of soil staggers my mind.

To what will we give the gift of our attention?

Much as I relish walking outdoors, marveling at the picturesque display changing daily, the gradual turning inward of autumn lends itself to writing. Incrementally, the manuscript grows, never mind the initial draft feels clunky and workmanlike. At moments—entire days, even—the task at hand overwhelms, and I grapple with despondency, dissuaded to the core. Until I step outside barefoot, cross the lawn, and stand at the lookout, or go for a suitable, restorative walk in the brisk air, senses cast wide. Within the hushed solitude of the cottage, the only noise other than birds twittering outside is the occasional *cloppity cloppity* of shod hooves passing along the lane. I lay my Parisian fountain pen aside and listen, a smile on my face.

I'm a long way from Pasadena.

Seated cross-legged on a cushion on the floor, the salon's glass-topped coffee table as my desk, hour after hour, I string words into sentences like beads forming a necklace. Interwoven with this process and rumination, if less for the book's actual material than merely my own personal evolution, thoughts orbit around the idea of *sacred reciprocity*—considering what such a notion means in my life, and the ways I embody mutuality, or don't.

What if saying an unequivocal *yes*—whatever life brings, no matter how difficult—is partly what sacred reciprocity entails? If every situation and interaction bring an invitation to *evolve*, can we move through our resistance and trust the greater mystery?

I've spent decades going round in my limitations, walking in shoes too small. In saying yes to writing, this attempt to bring something

180 ◆ WHERE TWO WORLDS TOUCH

ineffable *through* me that feels far beyond my reach, each day I face my resistance. Wrestling with dark angels. Ultimately surrendering. Answering the ongoing dream summonses, a sentence at a time. Somehow, sacred reciprocity exists in this: offering something from my soul—or the greater soul of nature—to the more-than-human world. A mentor of mine once said, *create simply to give it away as an offering to the holy.*

If only I can rise to the challenge and bring the book to life.

⌒

In an unanticipated move, rainbow-clad Sara from Kent comes for a visit. Living next door our few months at the farmhouse, my exchanges with her primarily consisted of brief comings and goings at the gate, occasionally a longer chat, but an easy relating sprang up.

The rental contract commits us to maintaining the Kent property until Savills secures a new tenant, which has not yet occurred. Knowing we face a drive of nearly two hours, to help with the logistics, Sara generously offered to keep an eye on things. Via email, she relays bits of news about the house, garden maintenance, and cleaning, all of which she helped arrange, and through our correspondence, has shared slightly more about herself, including the art degree in-progress. In a characteristically reserved English manner, she doesn't reveal much, but I detect her marriage has troubles, some phantoms rattling the converted barn house and their life.

Our location in West Sussex is not far from West Dean, an arts and crafts college formerly a grand, private estate. Students and visitors attend for residential weekends to study painting, pottery, jewelry making, and a wide array of artistries. Sara's recent note indicated she has some business there, where every so often she enrolls in an art course, and enquired whether she might stop by for a visit.

"I thought perhaps, since you've offered and because I will be quite near to you, that I could stop by for that cup of tea you've suggested. I'm not much of a tea drinker, as you know, but I can bring my own hob-top espresso maker . . . "

The autumn day swirls with leaves and gusts of wind, Robert is at work, and the gate stands open for her arrival. From the kitchen window, I spy the familiar convertible Mini Cooper, top down, as it zooms into the gravel drive, rock-and-roll blaring loud enough to blast out the speakers.

Sunglasses on, our former neighbor steps from her car as I walk out to greet her. The shoulder-length blonde hair is cut in the same style as last I saw her, and true to form she wears a rainbow-striped jumper and purple jeans, with high-top Converse trainers tied by neon pink laces.

Nervous and clearly unsettled, she clutches a large purple purse. Unsure what to do with her hands, stuffs them into pockets as a last resort. The cheerful grin is a polite cover. I know this visit involves a distinct step out of her comfort zone, calling on the two queer Americans.

"What a lovely little spot you've found," she smiles, glancing around the garden. "This is a really charming, quiet lane. It's quite idyllic, isn't it, what with only just one neighbour . . . "

"Well, the cottage is rather plain inside, not nearly as nice as the Kent farmhouse, but I quite enjoy the setting here."

Passing the fishpond on our approach to the front door, she peers into the clean, circulating water.

"No fish?"

"No, not yet. I've been told the herons will come and eat them."

"Indeed, they will. And they'll poke holes in the liner with their sharp beaks and then you'll have a slow leak. Although you can put a bit of nylon netting over the water to keep them out."

"That's exactly what the man at the garden nursery and pond shop in Haslemere told me, but I'm not keen on covering it with mesh, so . . . maybe I'll just keep to the newts and salamanders living at the bottom."

Inside the house, from the depths of her sizable aubergine bag, she withdraws an Italian stovetop espresso maker, along with a tin of Illy decaffeinated espresso. I offered my *cafètiere* when I replied to her self-inviting email, but apparently a French coffee press doesn't suit. This woman takes her java seriously.

"I used to come to Haslemere quite a lot as a child. My maternal grandmother lived here. I remember going to a bookshop . . . it had a wide

182 ◆ WHERE TWO WORLDS TOUCH

blue awning, I think. Isn't it funny the things we recall?"

"There is a nice bookshop on the High Street. And it does have a blue awning."

"Does it? Well, it must be the same one, though I'd be surprised if it was still in business after so many years. Bookshops are suffering these days."

"Not as badly here as they are in America, I'm sure. At least you English still read books."

I take the coffee maker and tin of Italian espresso into the kitchen, the space now slightly less reminiscent of a hospital surgical room since laying down rugs and hanging an art print on the primary wall free of cupboards.

"Do you know how to use one of those? They're quite brilliant. You just unscrew the bottom and put water in it, and the ground espresso gets packed in the little receptacle."

"I had an identical one in Paris."

Setting about the necessary steps of water and coffee, I screw the espresso pot back together and put it on the hob, placing my cobalt blue kettle on another burner to boil for tea. While respective vessels heat, I lead my visitor on a quick tour of the cottage ground floor, though the layout is cozy enough to be self-evident.

"How terribly unfortunate that they covered the old wooden beams and made this flat ceiling. It's very odd."

"Tragic, I think." I shake my head, looking up at the white flatness just a foot above us.

"Well, thank goodness they didn't paint this white too," she remarks, admiring the wide brick hearth in the front reception. "Really lovely. You don't find many of these anymore."

"I light a fire most every night."

Coffee and tea ready, rather than in the main salon, we sit across from each other at the darkly polished rectangle of our well-traveled dining table. A more casual arrangement. Friendlier.

"Paul doesn't approve of my visit," she confides, two hands holding the hand-painted Deruta cup of strong coffee, turning sideways towards the window and garden.

"What, he doesn't want you hanging around with a couple of American poofs?"

Slightly taken aback, her eyes flutter for a second, but I grin and wink disarmingly. She softens energetically, pushing the blonde fringe back from her forehead.

"I'm not sure exactly what it's about, really. He's very controlling of what I do, and, well, it is somewhat unlike me to just go off on my own against his wishes . . . even though I'm actually quite a strong and independent sort of person."

She peers at me earnestly, as if needing to emphasize this point. I sense an undercurrent of things she wants to say, but I simply wait. She plays her cards carefully. Everything will come out eventually.

When we confirmed her stopping by Highfield after the errand at West Dean, in light that we live in a lovely area for walking amid woods and fields, I suggested we could go for a ramble should weather allow. Enquiring now whether she might enjoy a walk, my guest nods enthusiastically, stating she's brought along her boots, and upon finishing our coffee and tea, goes to her car to change footgear.

As I slip into my own boots parked inside the entryway, Sara promptly reappears in shockingly pink Wellies.

"Wow, those are *very* bright."

"Aren't they?" She beams like a happy child, looking down, turning one foot out in display and then the other. "I found them at a garden shop and simply had to have them. I adore pink. Bright colours in general. I refuse to wear black. It's so depressing. Life is serious enough already, who needs black?"

The early afternoon shivers cool and grey, bordering on blustery and temperamental. Stepping around to the cottage rear, we slip through the gap in the hedge and then stroll casually up the long drive leading to the landlord's house and stables, exchanging small talk. How pleasant to walk with someone, to engage in dialogue instead of my usual silent musing and observation.

We pass the mossy dell of the Green Man and then bisect the upper

184 ◆ WHERE TWO WORLDS TOUCH

field where, yesterday, I met Mr. Fox, each of us surprised by the other. Not twelve feet apart, close enough to observe the filtered sunlight glinting in his amber eyes, we stared nearly nose to muzzle. My breath stopped for a second or two, held shallow in my chest, not from any fear but the unexpected magic. A dash of wonder and awe. He twitched his black whiskers, turned abruptly, and loped off towards the line of gilded trees at the top of the field, whereupon he stopped and looked back at me, then disappeared.

At the far boundary of the landlords' farm, climbing over the metal gate, we cross onto the large estate owning the entire, wide hill, continuing with the forty-minute loop I'm leading us on. Up past the Jacobean manor house with its sixteen tall chimneys and stunning view over the far downs, its grandly walled garden with magnificent, centuries old trees, and finally down through a hillside of young woods and back to Highfield Cottage.

Ambling across green pastures, Sara divulges some challenges with art college in Canterbury. Her new series of large, mystical paintings—each one featuring a textured, dripping moon and a dreamlike animal—have drawn sharp criticism from the instructor, who gives her low marks. In front of the class, the teacher made snide comments which were hurtful, demeaning, and terribly inappropriate. In our email exchange, she sent a few photos of her latest works. Each in differing shades of blue night, all possess a magical, moody, and mysterious vibe. In the same message to me, compelled to explain her paintings, she confessed to being a pagan, as well as a solitary *hedgewitch*, though she doesn't follow any dogma or doctrine. I'm unclear exactly what a hedgewitch is, but I don't press for explanation or definition. All things in time.

Like the blowy breeze buffeting us while we thread the hem of the mansion's hill, emotion charges her voice as she relates the ongoing drama.

"Maybe you can consider that your business is to *create*," I offer, "not to get wrapped up in whether your instructor praises the finished product or not. Yes, he's judging you harshly for whatever reason . . . possibly a blocked or frustrated artist himself, who knows. Regardless, you're expressing something from your soul, and *that* is always our true calling. This moon series isn't neat and pretty and proper like English watercolors of a cottage garden, but you've already been-there-and-done-that, as we say. Now, to your credit, you dare to be totally authentic, to surrender to the creative flow, and trust what emerges, without censoring or limiting yourself to a rigid, predictable style."

She considers my words silently as we ascend the grassy slope, following the footpath, two solo ramblers amid a windy, green landscape.

"I know I'm just *moaning*, and I really shouldn't grumble . . . but it's terribly hard. These other students making nice, safe, timid little works— absolutely *nothing* original or interesting about them—getting top marks, while I am ridiculed publicly and graded down by the Prat in the Hat."

"I assure you, beyond art college, no one—*no one*—is going to ask what sort of marks you earned. People will buy your artwork simply because they like it. Full stop. It's incredibly brave to heed what surfaces from the depths of your soul, giving voice to it in a unique expression. I'm struggling to do it with a book manuscript, and the process may just kill me. I have to regularly remind myself of the saying, 'speak your truth, even if your voice shakes.'"

Still climbing the hill, I pause for a minute, catching my own breath, looking up at the high, stray clouds hurtling past overhead. Hands in the pockets of her rainbow hoodie, my once-neighbor smiles brightly. The earlier scowl has vanished. How good to have cheered her, bolstering in a modest way the creative process of becoming authentic as an artist. As a *human*.

We continue up the broad pasture directly below the walled gardens of the imposing brick mansion, where a dozen dark bay and sable mares graze unperturbed by our passing and conversation.

"These are some very expensive horses. Definitely not your average farm animals. Very Sussex. You do realize this is quite a posh little pocket of England you've landed in . . . ?"

She turns around, admiring the vista of wooded countryside, a painted panorama spread below us.

"Really lovely."

"Yes. It's rather a curious twist of fate. I felt so depressed to leave Babylon

186 ◆ WHERE TWO WORLDS TOUCH

Lane, that fabulous kitchen, the pool, the ducks . . . even the quirky artist neighbour who rescues chickens and occasionally left organic apple juice, eggs, or asparagus on our doorstep."

At a low stone wall with a wooden stile for crossing it, I gesture for her to go ahead and wait until she crosses over.

"And yet I adore where we've landed, this lovely countryside to wander through just beyond the garden. I walk almost every day, usually along this same route up to the heath on the summit, but other directions too. The ramble feeds my soul and inspires my writing, and when I get back to the cottage, I put pen to paper. *One cannot fathom the mystery*, is something I often say, but lately, I think maybe The Beatles had it right, and life is the Magical Mystery Tour."

Closing our loop, descending the slopes of Blackdown, following a muddy track through a mixed woodlot, on the ground lie a pair of men's leather work gloves. WARRIOR emblazoned largely in red on each cuff. Halting, I bend to pick them up, whereupon examination, find them in good shape. What a strange find.

"Warrior gloves. Hmm . . . exactly what you need for art college right now. Here, put them on."

"No, I couldn't," she protests, eyes wide and waving her hands as if I have offered her a dead squirrel.

"Yes, you can."

After some cajoling, she slips the gloves reluctantly on and holds them up.

"They're much too large for me."

"Never mind that. Imagine wearing these the next time you have to defend your work in class, perhaps even giving the Prat in the Hat a good knockabout with them."

"It does seem very odd to find them here, just now."

I point at deep ruts in the mud left by large tires.

"Most likely they fell off the handyman's tractor. Talk about a 'prat in the hat', he's a grouchy old bastard. Lives alone at the top of the farm in a dilapidated, stone cottage and has worked for the landlords for years.

Delivered us a cart of fire logs and was thoroughly unpleasant ... called me a 'wanker' as he drove off."

"He didn't! How incredibly rude."

Raising my eyebrows, I shrug. Sara still wears the large gloves, contemplating them fixedly.

"I was rather more imagining something more like Wonder Woman and her magic bracelets ... "

"Alright then," I grin with another shrug of shoulders, "but in the meantime, you've got Warrior gloves."

"Brilliant."

She slides them off and I extend an open palm.

"I'll carry them for you."

Back at the cottage, muddy boots removed and set by the door, the two of us comfortably settle in for another *cuppa*. Illy decaf espresso for the hedgewitch and a preferred cup of russet, malty Assam for me. On a small plate, a pile of rosemary pine nut shortbread rounds, baked earlier in the day. My visitor smiles, her countenance cheery and illuminated, a buttery confection in hand.

"Thank you for this."

"They're quite good, aren't they? The ground pine nuts in the dough, the fresh rosemary ... a sophisticated little biscuit. Rustic but elegant. A grown up's cookie. I'm rather proud of them. They're divine with fresh thyme, too."

"They're utterly delicious, I could eat a tin of them, but I meant *this,*" she sweeps the room and space between us with a gesture. "The day, the walk. Listening to me whinge and moan about art college."

A friendly warmth spreads through my chest and a grin turns up the corners of my mouth.

"You are most welcome. And I am equally in need of a friend. It isn't easy as an outsider in a foreign country, trying to find people you connect with and who want to connect with *you*, in return. Let alone being a *creative*, and matters of soul and whatnot. And never mind I'm essentially a recluse living in the countryside."

"It's a bit awkward, I'll admit, pouring my heart out to you like this. We barely know each other, really."

"That's what friends do."

"Not in England, we don't," she shakes her blonde head emphatically. "I feel slightly embarrassed."

"Well, I suggest it's time to get over that. Being with an American automatically gives you a bit of liberty to defy old rules and stodgy British conventions."

"Do you think so? That might be nice . . . "

"And even apart from queerness, if we spend more time together, you'll find there's little conventional about me, even by American standards."

Herbaceous shortbread held in fingertips, sipping my unsweetened tea, I stare briefly through the windows toward the great tree at the center of the garden. Still clad in autumn gold despite the recent storms. Almost luminous. The Wishing Tree, I've begun to call it, though I can't say why.

"A funny thing we ended up as neighbors. Just when I had been thinking it might be nice to find a friend, maybe a female artist . . . *voilà*! A pagan hedgewitch, no less. Genius, really."

She beams like earlier on our walk, pushing her cropped fringe back from her face, eyes fluttering briefly as if seeing a spirit or on the edge of trance. The peculiar gesture intrigues me as a body-centered therapist. Suddenly, she sighs and looks down at her hands, a cloud settling over her pretty face once more.

"I suppose I should get back on the road. It's rather a long drive, you know. I do hope Paul won't be foul."

"Yes, I hope that, too. I salute you for striking out on your own and coming here."

"Well, I was just in the neighbourhood. It would have been silly not to."

"Maybe, but we both know it's more than that. Truly, I commend you. It was very pleasant to walk and talk with someone. I hope you'll come back again. We can go to the bookshop in Haslemere and have a cappuccino on the High Street."

"That would be lovely."

"Next time, come for lunch. I'm a respectable cook."

"I will do. I'd like that very much."

The little espresso pot cleaned and stashed back in her purple bag, together we walk out to the car, and as she retracts the top of the Mini Cooper, I hand over the Warrior gloves, picked up from the porch.

"You're going to need these. Either when you get home or in the classroom."

She accepts them with a grin and quickly puts on her sunglasses, hiding the spark of glistening emotion in her eye. Turning up the music volume, heavy bass thumping from the speakers, she revs the engine, and tossing a friendly wave my direction, exits the gravel drive. A cloud of dust trails behind as her car rockets down the oak-lined lane. I shut the gate and walk slowly back to the cottage. Gravelly stones and dirt beneath my bare feet. Thinking about supper and what I'll cook this evening. Wondering how Robert's day has played out.

Dallying a minute or two on the terrace, soaking in the tranquility of the garden, a faint breeze shimmers in the Wishing Tree, a soft voice whispering. I'm knackered from two hours of talking and coaching, but surprisingly glad for the day's visit. Unlooked for, the gregarious recluse has made a new friend—a rainbow-wearing hedgewitch, no less.

The Magical Mystery Tour, indeed.

⁓

The tension of Robert's new role grows more acute. My companion focuses upon establishing good interpersonal relationships with staff and building a team in a way the English typically do not, will not, or cannot. Beyond his leadership skills, the very qualities Lloyds recruited him for, as an American he steps free of the well-entrenched divisions of social class, working hierarchy, and accent. His initial supervisor in London, a woman with lean features and a deep chip on her shoulder, who climbed the ranks in male-dominated finance partly due to her fierceness, admonished him early on, "You are too fraternal with your employees. They work for you, not the other way around."

His new boss, the Small Man, says the same thing.

"I believe in encouraging people," Robert counters, blue eyes stern, holding his ground, "not beating them down or treating them like my inferiors. It's a different model than yours, I realize, but I find it more effective."

He stands outside the circle, drawing on a core strength of character; the courage to endure loneliness and separation, day in and day out, when a basic human desire is to *belong*. The same *soul courage* required for full integrity as an individual, free of societal norms and expectations.

Something else keeps my mate in an outsider position, however, an invisible factor growing stronger and more substantial each passing week. Since returning to the bank, he makes a concerted effort to leave the office on time and come home. His shift in priorities was initially mandated by a post-hospital low-energy level and crushing weakness at the end of a day, but he has a newly found acceptance that more work exists than can be accomplished in business hours. And Robert hasn't forgotten putting career ahead of family cost him dearly once before. No longer seeing his job as his life or identity, he endeavors to unshackle from his desk. Yet his declining mood and bleak state of mind weigh upon both of us.

He dresses sluggishly each morning with grim resignation, face devoid of emotion. Stepping into any of his dark wool suits only makes him darker, as if all the light in him is extinguished except in some inner, guarded and secret place no one has access to, perhaps not even himself. He slips steadily into a shadowed malaise, descending once more into the Underworld.

I yearn for a magical talisman to give him, like an amulet of protection or an angelic sword of light. Anything. Something more powerful than nourishing meals and heartfelt companionship.

He struggles with pain and a spine mending at a snail's pace, while the pressure at work mounts steadily and the Small Man fumes with umbrage and pounds harder for results not forthcoming. One needn't to be a healer to know stress is detrimental on myriad levels, from physiological to psychological. In my perspective, *soul sickness* is a real matter when our lives are unbalanced, and healing seldom happens until we make fundamental changes which steer us into integrity.

Ever more frequently in the evenings, Robert has few words at dinner, preferring not to talk about his day. A blank stare and sagging posture accompany his non-responsiveness. He counts the hours since he last took a pain pill, and how long until he can take another. Dismal weather and cold challenge on their own, but the darkness of English winter has come early and descended upon Highfield, shadows gathering round.

I can't save him though I dearly wish to.

Years ago, we came to an understanding and agreement: as with manning a small craft, only one person gets to be off duty on any given stretch. At the time, I was riding the emotional rollercoaster of looking for my birthmother, sinking into despair. Robert steadily kept the watch, a figurative candle shining in the window so I might find my way home through the obscuring gloom. His care and concern were appreciated more than could be articulated, closed-down as I was, like some broken creature turned inward upon itself, but I recognized his protectiveness as a gift of grace and love.

Now is my turn to keep vigil, carrying the lantern. A night passage across stormy waters lies ahead. Time to batten down the hatches. Other than his weekly session on the massage table, not much else can I do besides make a pleasing supper he'll enjoy. Food that comforts and consoles—even if we dine mostly in silence.

"I just want to watch a movie tonight," he announces in a flat, weary tone. "Something mindless. I need an escape."

My counterpart is swimming upstream or being swept out to sea. Either way, his vitality ebbs and he slips away from me. To keep our two-man vessel upright in the waves, I will tend to house and hearth. Love my mate kind-heartedly and supportively. Ask for little, instead be the one who *gives*. Keep the torches burning in this darkness, trusting eventually the tide will shift and possibly our roles too. Who can say, someday it may be my turn to fall back into the abyss.

Faced with Robert's silence and withdrawal, I retreat to my room in

192 ◆ WHERE TWO WORLDS TOUCH

the loft and compose an email or two to the few friends who keep engaged with e-correspondence. Afterwards, I curl up and read until he takes his bath and both of us retire to bed for story time, as white votives flicker at the foot of our canopied bed in the window, casting spheres of light against the blackness outside.

Reading aloud, from time to time I pause, listening. His slow breathing informs me sleep has taken him. Laying aside the book, then rising to blow out the candles, the room plunges into silvery moonlight.

Night after night, an owl calls repeatedly from the oaks flanking the cottage, a haunting voice I adore and listen for.

Whooo . . . whooo . . . whoo are you?

Over and over, blessings manifest in my life. Yet, as with nature, the grace is both abundant *and* measured at the same time—just enough to carry me through, not more than that. Or so it seems. Irrespective of intentions, prayers, and affirmations, I wonder if we unknowingly limit the magic in our lives; subconsciously disbelieving ourselves worthy of more, too wedded to limitations and doubt.

In differing ways, the stories we've inherited or taken on hold us hostage, consciously or not. And we all have parts of ourselves—patterns, strategies, beliefs, lies and shame—which need to die in order that something new may finally be born. Moreover, like the proverbial caterpillar in its chrysalis, for metamorphosis to occur, we must dissolve into a sticky matrix of goo. A soul crisis. Existential angst. The despair of deep self-loathing at the root of internal suffering. The loss of our roles and identity.

Whooo . . . whooo . . . whoo are you?

Autumn slips away and the last painted leaves spiral down from the trees like beautiful, copper butterflies. How many days do any of us have left? Or what measure of grace? There isn't much time, really. Life is fleeting and precious, and we are all merely passing through the world. *Love.* Love now. We mustn't wait for tomorrow or Valentine's Day. I will kiss my beloved tenderly on the nape of his neck and whisper he is beautiful, how I truly appreciate him. This life, the priceless gift of embodiment on a human journey, is ultimately a blessing. Shadows and all.

Rilke rises again in my mind, reminding and guiding me, *Love consists in this, that two solitudes protect and touch and greet each other.*

Whether crossing dark waters or walking a difficult road, a rough passage lies before us. If the gods are kind, we will not only endure but also be transformed, this man and me. May it be so.

The Magical Mystery Tour rolls on.

WINTERSCAPE

In the American Southwest, dating from the pre-Puebloan cultures onward, a *kiva* is a ceremonial chamber built partially or entirely underground. A vertical ladder allows access to the cave-like structure. At Highfield, the loft stairs are nearly as steep as a ladder, and because my writing room on the uppermost floor is also a meditation area, housing my altar of precious objects, a Tibetan prayer rug, and a pile of decorative pillows, I have dubbed it the Sky Kiva. A counter pose, of sorts, to the traditional earthen version, and the space is well lit thanks to the large skylight in the sloping ceiling, as well as a narrow clerestory window in the southerly wall overlooking the lane.

We acquired a petite desk after searching multiple shops around Haslemere. Small and sufficiently lightweight to be maneuvered up the ladder-like stairwell, the tiny table has an angled writing surface that opens to reveal a compartment. My mini-escritoire sits beside the window, where just beyond the leaded panes of glass the upper branches of a rowan tree fan wide, an array of delicate hands crusted with pale, sage-colored lichen, and bejeweled with red, currant-like fruits. As the few remaining leaves fall away in swiftly cooling weather, the silvery-green wooden fingers are often adorned with little black and white-banded Coal Tits. Now and then, joining the party, a large, red-breasted woodpecker, clad in stylish ebony and ivory stripes and spots, with a vibrant cranberry tail and breast. A strapping fellow. What a treat to be so close to him. Childlike glee brims up inside me whenever he alights outside.

Most days, Blue Tits are part of the rowan tree crowd, sporting their soft yellow underbelly with pale blue and white hooded heads. Their twittering capers deliver a delightful distraction from typing on my laptop, as they cling upside down to the branches or sometimes the window hinges. Precious. Even before setting up my sanctuary in the loft, when seated and writing at our dining table, these tiny, colorful characters on the stone terrace amused me, though Blue Tits seem less inclined than others to alight on the ground for the birdseed scattered there. Gourmands, no doubt.

An early December morning. Downstairs to start our tea and breakfast, carrying the wicker laundry basket full of clothes for washing, in the kitchen I open the pine door to the utility room-cum-larder, and am greeted by a noisy scratching and rustling. I freeze in my tracks, thinking a rat or mouse has found its way inside. *Damn.* My pulse accelerates. Just then, a distressed chirping adds to the commotion coming from the area near the sink. Is it a bird outside the window? Not yet stepping into the room, I crane my neck and listen carefully from around the corner. No, the bird is definitely inside the house. I set the clothes basket on the linoleum floor and inch forward stealthily, peering around the small, second fridge we have placed on the counter in the workroom.

A Blue Tit peeps loudly and hurtles itself against the square panes of glass. On the outer side of the window, its mate cheeps loudly in reply, each trying to reach the other but confounded by the invisible barrier separating them. For a minute, I'm thunderstruck with astonishment, suddenly flooded with empathy, the previous flustered anxiety vanished.

How on earth did this chap get inside? The window is perpetually locked shut and we have no key, thus I cannot simply set the bird free. A baffling mystery. Deliberating briefly, I turn and walk to the front door, opening it wide to the frigid morning, giving myself an unobstructed path to escort the trapped visitor outdoors. Returning to the kitchen, I pause and inhale a deep breath, filling my entire being with love and the spirit of gentleness. Then I step calmly into the laundry room and move things from the windowsill—liter-sized, green glass bottles of sparkling water, cans of San Pellegrino *limonata*—the wee one repeatedly crashes into.

196 ♦ WHERE TWO WORLDS TOUCH

Cans and bottles removed, I spread fingers outward to form a loose cage and slowly move my hands toward the glass. Scooping the Blue Tit into cupped palms, I curl them around him protectively, tickled by the teeny taloned feet and thrum of blue wings, my own heart fluttering like rapid wingbeats. The peck of his beak doesn't hurt, merely part of the sweetly curious experience. I cradle the tiny bird next to my chest for a short cadence of seconds, then walk to the living room.

Dressed for work in suit and tie, Robert descends the stairs just as I am heading out the front door.

"I have a Blue Tit in my hands!" I gush with joy, brown eyes wide and a smile lighting my face.

Upon reaching the entryway, the blue and yellow bolt explodes from its fleshy cage, rocketing through the open door and out into the tall, conical cypress beside the fishpond on the edge of the terrace. Following the meteoric flight, I step out into the chilly air of the cloudy morning, nearly a slap across my face, the flagstones freezing beneath bare feet.

The liberated captive zooms upward from the tree, joined immediately by its counterpart arriving from the rear of the cottage, and they disappear across the drive into the band of bare woods opposite. I linger another moment or two, still grinning, then step back inside the warmth of the house and close the door behind me. Robert shakes his head with a wry smile and tired eyes.

"Oddly, I'm not surprised to come downstairs and the man I live with is holding a bird in his hands. What does it say about our life that this seems *normal* to me?"

"He was trapped in the laundry room, pecking at the window with his mate on the other side, so I caught him and set him free."

"But how did he get in there?"

"I have no idea," I shrug with raised eyebrows, a note of incredulity in my voice. "Just a bit of feathered magic and mystery."

"Trapped in the utility room, pecking at the glass to escape. That's basically the way I feel about banking right now."

He sighs heavily, already cloaked in grey to match the burdened day outside.

"By any chance is there a scone to take with me this morning? I'm late ...kind of a rough night and a slow start."

"Yes, I'll wrap one up for you."

After my companion has gone, driving away to his battles, I reenter the laundry room to start the clothes washing, still lightly trembling with happiness. Replacing bottles and cans removed from the windowsill, a miniature, blue-grey feather rests next to the glass. A perfect present and memento. I will place the little gift beside various others I've collected on my altar in the Sky Kiva.

Buzzing from the visitor in my hands, utterly puzzled by the unexplained occurrence, I set to brewing some spicy, warming chai in a saucepan on the stove. Opting not to make my usual warm porridge, instead I pull from the cupboard a box of organic muesli, and catching the irony, a smirk turns up the corner of my mouth. The cereal is called Early Bird.

Magic happens, I know. Yet when some enchantment mysteriously occurs, our agnostically inclined minds quickly dismiss it away. Considering the inexplicable encounter, thankfully a Blue Tit appeared in the utility room. Had I walked in and found a barn owl banging against the glass, I would have messed my pants.

⌒

Late December. Days are impossibly short. Nights are interminably long, dark, and frigid. I've decorated the cottage for the holidays in a low-key fashion with some ornaments and unscented candles placed about.

At the florist shop on the High Street in Haslemere, I purchased a handmade wreath of leafless vines and twigs, charmed by its rustic simplicity and winter austerity. I've tarted it up with a classic gold bow, as well as small, crimson glass pinecones and stars. Placed upon the front door as a traditional symbol of welcome—even if not made from customary evergreens—it's lovely. I have also bought a few pretty baubles; two boxes of green and red orbs, stenciled attractively with gold scrollwork. Affixing

198 ◆ WHERE TWO WORLDS TOUCH

them to filigree ribbons, hung from the ugly, industrial wall sconces downstairs, they make a quirky bit of décor.

Highfield Cottage is now officially *festive*. Let the holidays commence.

For various reasons, we haven't had a traditional cut tree in years. We don't even own a stand for one.

"I'd really like to get a live tree in a pot," I suggest, "if we can find one."

Easily enough, we locate a three-foot spruce at a garden shop in nearby Godalming, and back at home, I place our little conifer on the low, coffee table in front of the glass doors in the main reception. The unattractive, black plastic container makes an eyesore, but a swath of gold fabric does a suitable job of concealing it.

As the decorator, I weave a string of white fairy lights through the fragrant branches and adorn the stubby green limbs with a few precious ornaments—the sentimental sort, each with a story. The one Robert made as a child: a golf-ball-sized Styrofoam round, coated in red and gold glitter, with a small photo him smiling, his hair platinum blonde. And a similar one of my own: the lid of a canning jar, fitted with a black and white photo of me as a little boy, my belly pushing out the button of a plaid flannel shirt. Here and there, a couple more baubles and trinkets, accompanied by handmade German ornaments from the Black Forest where Robert spent his youthhood.

"It's kind of a Charlie Brown Christmas tree, isn't it?" he remarks, arms crossed across his chest as he considers our holiday addition.

Indeed, the top is a bit crooked, and one side is decidedly fuller than the other, but who cares. The Tree of Life, I call it. Not only because the dwarf evergreen is alive and growing, but as celebration of the mythic, and a nod to Celtic cosmology.

Robert's mom comes to visit from central Florida. She lives in a massive retirement community where people drive golf carts to the grocery store and the public square for nightly drinking and dancing. A diminutive woman with a Southern accent, addicted to Coca Cola and thick applications of hairspray, with the exception of last December, she has joined us at the year-end holidays since her divorce more than a decade ago. Generally cheerful, overly talkative, she's mostly harmless. Friendly to a fault. Her visits tire me, but things could be much worse, I remind myself, *so* much worse. Given the international flight, along with my partner's desire for his mum to have an extended holiday in England, she stays three weeks or longer. A period during which Robert conveniently goes to the office, leaving me at home with her.

"Very opportune of you," I mutter dourly as he prepares to escape to the bank for another workday.

"Isn't it? You're a bloody saint. Bless you, love."

No doubt I'm earning sainthood points. I endeavor to be kind, jovial, and patient, faring better at times than others. Half-listening as she gabs about people I don't know, individuals I will never meet. Another story from her past. As a man who prefers trees to people, even relatively quiet folks, I feel steadily worn down as the days tick by. And I will face another three weeks entertaining her in June when she comes for the wedding. More sainthood credit. Bucketsful.

Normally, I don't drink wine at lunch even though it's common practice in Europe. Playing host to a mother-in-law for an extended period, however, my mood and outlook lighten noticeably with a lunchtime glass of medication.

I appreciate her vocal enthusiasm for my cooking. Parked in the kitchen, Laura Jane observes, asks questions, and talks nonstop while lunch and dinner manifest. After years of visits, she has learned the chef doesn't delegate tasks nor does he desire assistance, but she insists on asking if I want her to help with anything. A Southern thing, apparently.

"Just sit there and relax," I direct, understanding the word is subjective. She thinks she's relaxed and unwound, but her mind and mouth rarely stop moving. Once, I listened to her talk for almost two hours without stopping other than to breathe. Astounding.

Each year on the holiday visit, we endure her audible lament that our house, no matter where it may be on the globe, is woefully under-decorated. And although she enjoys visiting England for its Old World charm and change of scenery, she complains daily and redundantly about the cold.

200 ◆ WHERE TWO WORLDS TOUCH

Repeatedly, she voices her wish we might come to her Florida house instead; a residence stuffed chockablock with Christmas clutter, every inch of open space on tabletops and elsewhere occupied by decorations. In her view, I do not fully understand the holiday spirit, and am somewhat mean-spirited about Christmas in a Scrooge-like fashion. The gay Grinch, perhaps.

Confessedly, *cheer* seems a tall order during the "holidaze," and I find it easier when I keep things simple. As with most elements of my life, *less is more*. I'm hardly a minimalist, but I prefer a modicum of something special and elegant to a surfeit of mediocre, thank you.

In the Northern Hemisphere, the December solstice, usually on 21st December, marks the longest night of the year. Darkness reaches its fullness. Nearly a decade ago, unable to subscribe to any notions or celebrations regarding the alleged birth of Jesus, and seeking to make the holidays more personally meaningful, I began hosting an annual winter solstice feast at our house. An intimate sit-down dinner for close friends, an all-out affair employing fine porcelain and the silver from my deceased, adoptive mother. At a festively decked table, I delivered a brief speech about the pagan origins of the solstice, the Roman holy days of Saturnalia and Sol Invictus celebrating the sun's return, and how Pope Julian the First moved the Christ Mass from springtime to coincide with the largest pagan holiday of the year, arguably to gain more followers for Christianity.

Through the initial years of celebrating my chosen winter holiday, Robert and his mother gave me something modest at solstice, with primary gifts on Christmas Day, *their* holiday. I grumbled a preference to receive main presents on *my* holiday, but December 25th remained the principal exchange until the year before we moved to London, when, on the winter solstice, Robert presented me a beautiful, two-foot high, hand-carved wooden statue of Quan Yin, the Goddess of Compassion. Elegant and poised, jade green, she stands upon a shawl of gold silk draped over a wooden cabinet, attended by candles, a Tibetan bronze bowl, and an incense burner. Ever since her arrival, two proper holidays exist in our house, with the agreement each of us receives his gifts on the day he prefers.

Too much time has passed since our well-traveled dining table hosted the revelry of clinking wine glasses and bright voices in gaiety, and I'm hungry for such things once more. I would dearly love to stage a solstice feast this year, a gathering more celebratory and social than merely me, Robert, and his mother. Yet as nomads and outsiders, we've no one to invite, other than a fox or two passing through the garden. *C'est la vie.*

Haslemere regrettably lacks a good butcher shop. The one in the newer part of town doesn't impress, and shopping there involves getting off the bus a long way from the High Street where I do the rest of my purchasing, then waiting at least half an hour for the next coach to arrive. Even when I have the car, my predilection is for Midhurst where both butcher shops are superior. Ahead of the date, I ordered some partridges to cook for solstice dinner, one per person, and fetched them yesterday.

"What is that terrible smell?" Robert asks when he opens the fridge in the utility room.

"It's the birds," I reply, nonplussed, intent on my task of mincing vegetables into tiny *brunoise.*

"That can't be right. They must be spoiled."

"No, they're just game birds. Very ripe."

I keep on with my knife, neatly diminishing the vegetables on the hefty bamboo cutting board. My mate remains dubious, secretly convinced the carcasses have gone rancid and we're all going to die of food poisoning either at the table or shortly afterwards.

"You're *sure* they're okay . . . ?"

"Yes, dear. Positive."

The naked birds will be wrapped in thick, streaky bacon and placed in a roasting tin. I have only prepared partridges once before, ages ago, so I've glanced at recipes for guidance. Suggested times vary widely, thus I'll take a middle figure and check on them, allowing more time if needed.

While I set the table for this evening's holiday meal and attend to my list of tasks in the kitchen, Robert and his mother head off for last-minute

202 ◆ WHERE TWO WORLDS TOUCH

gift shopping in Guildford. Happy to let them brave the crowds and have a few hours of quiet time home alone, I put on some favorite Christmas music. With a crystal flûte of dry, classy Taittinger conveniently to hand, the bubbly notes of pear, almond, and toast tickling my nose, all is well.

The sky glowers dark and threatening all day. In the afternoon, snow begins to fall; large, wet flakes in a steady flurry, the sort you want to catch on your tongue with a smile. By the time the two shoppers return, a frosting of white decorates the lane and garden. An hour later, a solid inch covers the ground with more accumulating steadily. A child of Southern California, land of sunshine, frozen winters do not win my affections nor warm my heart. Yet, the snowfall looks pretty and slightly magical, perfect for a holiday night. Secretly, I am thrilled. The cottage is aglow with two dozen candles, the table laid for our intimate feast, and it's snowing outside. Here in England, my winter fête feels nearly Dickensian. And I am not Ebenezer Scrooge.

For our ordinary suppers, even something mundane as pasta, I plate dishes in the kitchen and bring them to the table, chef-style. When entertaining, or special occasion meals, we dine in courses, as the French do. Tonight, a vintage Blue Willow platter holds a wheel of warmed Camembert, topped with roasted wild mushrooms and walnuts, surrounded by toasted garlic crostini. Dipping the crisp toasts into warm, oozy cheese and the sautéed fungi is compulsively addictive, requiring repeated samplings, and one must fight the temptation to simply have this be dinner itself.

Red brocade covers the table, with an ornately embroidered runner, gleamingly accented by the good silver. Pinecones sit down the middle, along with gold ribbons, fragrant mandarins with shiny dark tongues of leaves still attached, glass baubles, and handmade, Bavarian heirloom snowflakes crafted from shaved curlings of spruce or birch. The tall, beeswax tapers flicker timelessly. We dine first on soup made with puréed fennel and pears, topped with crushed hazelnuts and feathery fennel fronds, and when our bowls of palest green, creamy *potage* stand empty, a winter salad of curly frisée, apples, dried cranberries, and best-quality blue Stilton. A pleasing contrast of crisp bitterness paired with sweetness, tartness, and the pungent

English cheese.

The partridges will be served atop a parsnip and apple mash. The minute I pull the birds from the oven, irrespective of choosing the middle mark for time, they are overcooked. Dismay floods through me like a swirl of cold water. How could I be so very off the mark? Is the small oven at fault? An error in temperature? I curse myself for not checking them earlier, and for not soaking them in a brine solution which would have helped. Game birds, typically lean, are unforgiving. Alas, nothing can now be done to remedy the situation. *Quel désastre.*

At table, the birds are tough as leather. I have mostly learned to not apologize when a dish doesn't live up to my expectation, but tonight I feel gutted over the bacon-wrapped-stones-cleverly-disguised-as-partridges.

"Well, you can't go wrong with bacon," says Robert, kindly looking for the proverbial silver lining. "Everything is better with bacon!"

Bless him. Even with the overcooked birds, dinner can hardly be called a travesty. And dessert is still to come. My professional cooking philosophy is things may fall apart in various ways, but how a meal culminates is essential. People always remember the finale.

Our small-scale feast ends with a decadent confection of bittersweet ganache in a chocolate and cinnamon-laced crust, dusted with unsweetened cocoa, a dollop of whipped cream on the side. Serving the tart at the table, I glance out the dining room window to observe the ongoing thick snowfall, illuminated by the warm glow of the cottage lights. Precisely at that moment, a red fox crosses the far edge of the terrace, stepping gingerly through the freshly fallen blanket. A fingertip traces up my spine and neck, sending a shiver through me. What a perfect blessing of wildness on a special night. The visitor has already slipped out of sight. I say nothing but simply smile, a glistening of emotion in my eye.

Cheered by the clink of sterling on porcelain plates, with candlelight reflecting on crystal glasses, the treat of fine Champagne, a gentle goodness calmly overcomes me. Robert's vast improvement from a year ago is immeasurable. Gazing across the table at my dear man, animated and jolly, his troubles at work are briefly at bay. Despite lacking friends to share a

204 ◆ WHERE TWO WORLDS TOUCH

spot of merriment, this may be my favorite solstice ever. Last December, returning to Britain, I never expected—nor could I have even guessed—I'd be here, living with Robert in the English countryside. One cannot fathom the Mystery, and none of this grace do I take for granted.

The day I departed Seattle with Kona for London, a dear friend came to the airport to see me off. She shared her decision to start a *gratitude journal*, which she recently learned about while watching Oprah's television show. I already kept a dream journal but, listening to her, decided to undertake the new twist; jotting and recording random things I feel thankful for. Since then, the practice has seen me through good times as well as darkly challenging passages. The small, gold-rimmed ledger rests upon my altar in the Sky Kiva, where every so often I pick it up, then fill a page with a list of details and people I'm currently most appreciative of. Wild ones like foxes and birds, too. Anything which echoes in my heart with goodness, I write it down. Simple but profound.

The little journal has taught me something important: gratitude is one of the most powerful spiritual practices to embrace. Shifting one's focus opens us—*openness* being the prime directive for a conscious life. Amid any drama, distractions, or despair, seeing the small diary provides the visual cue to stop and pause, to reframe my experience. Inhale a full breath and anchor my feet on the earth. Let go. Lean into yes instead of a resistant no.

Perspective is everything, determining the world we inhabit.

On a snowy winter solstice, unquestionably I have a page full of things for which I'm grateful. Deep appreciation for the miracle and mystery of life. A wealth of blessings bestowed.

Just like Tiny Tim says at the end of Dickens' *A Christmas Carol*, "A Merry Christmas to us all; God bless us, every one!"

~

Christmas Day finds us still under snow. The shops in town have been mobbed, not only due to the usual holiday crush but the added factor of a blizzard. Harried people hurriedly gathering provisions for several days because everything will be shuttered through Boxing Day—an additional bank holiday following Christmas. The lane is barely passable, especially given the hill, and our two trips to Waitrose, Robert driving us along the slushy, slick roads, left me mildly shattered. Graciously sheltered at home, the two small fridges and utility room-cum-larder stocked full, feels like a blessing, indeed.

Short on refrigerated space, I've stashed a box of vegetables in the garage knowing the cold air will keep things fresh, the risk of hungry little visitors notwithstanding, yet given my inclination for feeding nature's creatures, I won't be overly distraught if some produce gets nibbled on. Even with a mother-in-law at the house, I'm merrier than I've been in years, relishing the rituals of a hand-crafted life, which in winter are mostly domestic and indoors.

Following breakfast, we gather in the reception where an impressive fire roars upon the hearth, occasionally popping and shooting sparks. A holiday album by Loreena McKennitt plays softly while we open the stockings and wrapped presents tucked around the Charlie Brown-style Tree of Life. Robert and his mum are cozily on the green loveseat, chatting, while I sit removed from them on the teak Balinese bench, when a loud knock at the window prompts me to turn, startled by the sound. A gorgeous vermillion fox crosses the white expanse of buried lawn. A Christmas photograph in motion, a daylight version of my sighting on solstice night.

"Look!" I point, smiling.

Laura Jane claps her petite hands with delight. She adores most wild animals when she sees them, provided they are not too close, and are not rodents. Or armadillos. Or raccoons. Or have teeth, in general.

"Did you hear that loud knock?"

"What knock?"

"The loud rap on the window prompting me to look up and see Mr. Fox outside."

My beloved smiles at me with raised eyebrows, a familiar and knowing look, shaking his head.

"Apparently, only *you* were meant to hear it. Someone wants your

206 ◆ WHERE TWO WORLDS TOUCH

attention."

I turn back to the bay window just as the visitor disappears beyond the hedge to cross the landlords' drive. Increasingly, the spirit world feels very near, the veil between realms gossamer thin. Much as I try not to, I sense it distinctly. A host of subtle, somatic clues signaling a shift from ordinary awareness. Flickers of energy and a shimmer in my own energetic field. Movement in my peripheral vision, and occasional disincarnate voices. Awakened by thunder or lightning in the middle of the night when no storm reportedly exists, and then receiving a download of information and cosmic insight. A knock at the window. Colorful agents of mystery, such as little birds appearing in the laundry room. So it goes, living at the threshold where worlds touch.

Later in the afternoon. Robert and Jane rest upstairs, and tranquil silence holds the house. Wearing my French linen apron, I feel ready for a break from the work of preparing Christmas dinner. My suggestion was to cook a goose, but today isn't my holiday, and the other two voted for a roast. The brined pork loin sits air-drying so its thick layer of fat will crisp into bronzed crackling. Time to stoke the fire in the main room, the morning's blaze long since burned low to glowing coals and ash. Contemplating a trip to the garage for more oak logs, I stand at the windows, aimlessly gazing at the winter landscape with its low, menacing sky. The noble Wishing Tree rises tall and elegantly bare at the center of the snowy garden. As if retracing steps from earlier, a large fox walks delicately along the fence line and then crosses the buried lawn. Such impeccable timing. For an instant, my breath stops, like always with magical encounters.

The sparkling snow. A lustrous fox. An indelible moment for my soul to treasure.

The canid pauses and turns its head as if detecting my gaze, ears at the ready. I wave with a grin through the glass.

"Blessings to you, wild one."

The bushy-tailed transient trots on, slipping from view around the edge of the fishpond, headed towards the neighboring cottage. And while the dwindled fire demands my attention, the repeated serendipity of life stirs me to musing.

Despite wishing circumstances or things were different, what if existence plays out *exactly* as meant to, orchestrated by some larger and mysterious force. Increasingly, it seems so. And if I am precisely where destined to be—in this moment, with each breath—regardless of limited perception, might it be possible *everything* is actually perfect, even the challenges, losses, and heartache?

Snow and Christmas foxes. Our humble cottage smells temptingly of caramelized apples from the warm *tarte tatin* resting on a glass cake stand in the kitchen. Soon the roast, rubbed with spices, chili, and cocoa, will be in the oven, accompanied by a tumble of organic, baby potatoes cooked in duck fat, and the house will smell irresistibly good. The promise of delicious things to come. Enough work for this cook. For now, anyway. Time for a cup of tea, to sit and savor the curious magic of our first winter holidays at Highfield.

Bless us all.

On the day in early January when Robert's mother departs, another snowstorm bears down on southern England. Driving to the airport, we are uncertain whether her flight will be able to leave, and snow already falls lightly. The plane takes off as scheduled, however, one of the last out, and before we return to the cottage, Gatwick Airport has closed to all travel.

"I'm glad she's off safely," Robert says, navigating the snowy motorway at reduced speed, his brow furrowed with concentration as he grips the steering wheel. "I love my mom, but she's exhausting. I'm looking forward to some quiet time with just you."

"Likewise, love. Maybe we can finally have sex?"

"You *know* I can't have sex when she's in the house, right down the hall!"

"Yes, I've dealt with this very unfortunate phenomenon for years. She arrives and you become a prude, prim Victorian. I'm pretty sure she knows we have sex. I was ready to put her on a plane a fortnight ago. All I'm saying

208 ◆ WHERE TWO WORLDS TOUCH

is that you'd better give it up when we get home."

He laughs out loud, close to a snort, placing his hand on my knee in well-acquainted gesture.

"Let's have a nap first, I'm so tired I really need to lie down."

"Okay, a sex nap. Brilliant. I love those! Drive a little faster, why don't you ... "

The skies have turned black, and the air swirls thick and white. We're traveling through a giant snow globe. More than a foot accumulates by evening, and when morning arrives on frozen breath, nearly another foot of glittering alabaster has fallen. A silent wonderland enfolds all. In a modern world shorn of mystery and magic, nature has suddenly opened the door into a forgotten realm.

Beneath an icy blue sky, enchantment sparkles in the air with invisible static. I half expect if I went out walking, hearing only the crunch and squeak of snow under my fleece-lined boots, I'd find a lone lamppost, encounter a faun named Tumnus, and discover I have stumbled upon Narnia, all the land under the spell of the White Witch.

With the lane impassable, we're not going anywhere, but the driveway must be shoveled. At least a path wide enough for the car to get in and out eventually. Given his vertebral damage, Robert's back won't tolerate lifting or twisting, thus the sizeable job falls to me alone. Body warmed by the physical effort of hoisting heavy, wet snow, I mostly enjoy my muscles working in non-ordinary ways. The task takes an hour, and my still-less-than-able companion emerges from the house from time to time, bundled in a puffy jacket, cheering me on, and gives a thumbs-up from the office window adjacent the kitchen.

With yesterday's shopping trip to Waitrose on the way home from the airport, and a timely veg box delivery from Abel & Cole, we are well-sorted with provisions. I have barely finished shoveling when our neighbors two houses down—*next door but one*, as Brits say—whom I have met in a passing fashion, come by to enquire whether we need anything. Foreseeing the lane's steep hill might become completely insurmountable with ice and snow, they parked their four-wheel drive vehicle near the crossroads. Garbed colorfully in woolly hats, gloves, scarves, and boots, towing a toboggan and a round, red plastic sled, they are about to trek back to the car, hoping the main road is cleared enough to get to town. Provided they can reach Midhurst, and if the grocery store is open, they will pick up supplies. Upon return, the plan is to leave the SUV parked once more at the crossroads and haul everything back using the sleds. In light that we are barely more than strangers—foreigners, no less—their offer strikes me as a gesture of extraordinary kindness and goodwill. Score a point for the English.

David is a soft-spoken, dark-haired handsome fellow, slightly soft around the middle. From our brief exchanges when I've passed their house walking along the lane, he seems to have a pleasant disposition. A stay-at-home dad, he works remotely and oversees the children, while his pretty wife escapes to an office somewhere. Poor bloke, I don't envy him.

"Do you need bread? Milk? Wine?"

"I think we're well set, really, but thank you so much for thinking of us," I smile appreciatively.

His suggestion that wine ranks amongst necessities isn't lost on me—daddy has children, after all. Thankfully, not only am I child-free, but I've got a couple of nice Rhône vintages tucked away, brought back from Provence. We'll get through without too much angst.

Food or wine aren't my primary concern, but rather *heat*. The oil in the large garden tank has dropped perilously low, and I hadn't thought ahead to order a delivery. For two Americans accustomed to air-forced furnaces, the setup of oil heating a *boiler*, which in turn heats the water in the radiators in each room, comprises a new facet of life. No oil, no warmth. The Wimbledon townhouse had radiators and must have had a boiler—likely the contraption in the closet under the stairs next to the washing machine, which I assumed was some sort of arcane water heater—but there wasn't an oil tank. Possibly, it's a rural thing, I don't know. Upon ringing the local oil delivery company, the woman on the phone informs me that they are overwhelmed with orders due to the cold weather and snow, and it will be at least a week, possibly two, before they can get to us.

The utility room has an electric, stand-alone water heater, and I console myself if we run out of oil to heat the house, we will still have warm water for bathing. So long as the power stays on, of course. A large supply of firewood sits piled in the garage, and we have two plug-in, portable radiators. We will be very frugal, shutting off heat in the guest room, second bath, and the loft with its pink bathtub where Robert soaks every night.

Irrespective of miserliness, in the days ahead, the tank drops to empty and the cottage goes cold. Barely warmer than an icebox. Hopefully, the pipes won't freeze. The main salon becomes our primary den, and I maintain a welcoming fire on the wide hearth, regardless that most of the heat vanishes up the chimney. Together, we snuggle up on the loveseat, wearing bulky sweaters, knitted caps, wool socks, and thermal underwear beneath our clothes. Wrapped in the thick French duvet from our bed, we plug in the radiator close at hand, and I keep the logs burning.

"Someday, we're going to look back on this and laugh," Robert grins, holding a cup of warm tea, a tasseled beanie rolled down past his ears.

"Provided we live through it, you mean, and they don't find us dead here in the spring when they stop by to see why we haven't paid the rent."

"You are so dark, sometimes. Funny but *dark*."

"I think that goes alongside 'brilliant but scary', doesn't it?"

Lifted from one of the Harry Potter movies, my mate likes to paint me with the phrase. *Brilliant . . . but scary.*

At night, we lug the two heaters upstairs, placing one in our bedroom and the other in the bathroom. The rest of the cottage is a refrigerator. For the first time in months, despite the arduous trial he faces, Robert almost feels thankful to go to his Farnham office during the day, though he's concerned for me back at the igloo. For my part, layered warmly and in love with my charcoal cashmere scarf, I brew pot after pot of milky chai, with warming cinnamon, clove and ginger, ever so lightly sweetened. Couch and coffee table drawn close to the robust fire, my trusty fountain pen and A4 notebook in hand, in the hushed cottage held in the silence of a snowy world outside, I continue writing chapters for the emerging book manuscript.

This is just part of the adventure, I tell myself, a steaming cup cradled in my hands. So much for my earlier, transcendent awareness of life being perfect.

Whatever the case may be, divine precision or cosmic joke, I will never again forget to check the oil tank during winter.

STANDING STONES

THE FROZEN WORLD finally thaws. England reverts to sodden green and heavy grey, and even in the cold depths of winter, unless the day is utterly foul with pouring rain, my countryside walks continue.

The American early Modernist painter, Georgia O'Keeffe, at her adobe compound on the mesa in Abiquiu, New Mexico, played a game of sorts with her gardener, moving various, hand-sized stones set atop the wooden cover of the well in the central courtyard. He would move one or two to a different position during his rounds or passing through the patio, and sometime later in the day, O'Keeffe, as she crossed between the main house and her studio, would rearrange the rocks in a different position. His move, her move. Repeat.

Such is how the gate in the tall, deer fence plays. Because the deer pass through the hedge along the lane, or walk gracefully up the driveway, grazing in the garden almost daily, I see no point in keeping the portal shut. The Rumi gate, I call it. When the gardener comes, he shuts and fastens the access I've propped open, whereupon, when heading out on my rambles or returning, I leave the entry ajar once more. His way, my way. Repeat.

Roving through the living realm surrounding Highfield, observing its gradual changes as the frigid, dreaming season rolls on, I'm cognizant of my deepening relationship. Swaddled in layers, coat, and cashmere scarf in the bleak of midwinter, following familiar paths strewn with withered leaves and chestnut hulls, or leaving the track altogether, my senses cast wide, I sink steadily into a poignant relating with these fields and naked

STANDING STONES ♦ *213*

woods. The Wild Beloved greets me with each step. Drawn alluringly into communion, realizing the interconnectedness of *everything*, enraptured by the wordless but audible song of the world—the harmony weaving all together—I don't wish to live where that music cannot be heard.

Rather than being *from* a place, like Somerset or California, what does it mean to be *of* a place? Unquestionably, I am too nascent an arrival to be *of* this region, but the earth doesn't consider me an outsider, each of us inhaling the other's breath as lovers do. In the smallest of ways, perhaps I'm beginning to belong, yet to do so *fully* means to stay and grow roots.

My restless spirit yearns to park our painted gypsy caravan beneath some sheltering trees beside a singing stream, and let the wheels rot off. The desire for a kitchen garden, tended by my own hands in the rich dirt, planting prayers along with seeds, grows stronger. A profound wish for an intimate bond with land and place, deeply connected, in bones and breath, as if wedded in a sacred union. I would like to appreciate a locale and terrain through changing seasons and years, as a beloved, feeling a resonance in my soul, opening outward through an unlocked heart. I long for rootedness, entwined with a natural community, both human and *other*, even if remaining an outsider—which beyond America's borders I will always be. An adoptee shortly after birth, I may never know the kinesthesia of *heritage*, but the sense of home I've long sought, those contours become clearer and more defined. Moreover, nature surrounding me, as here in this lovely corner of England, provides the essential frame, I know.

Confessedly, forging a long-term life here seems difficult to imagine. The tranquil charms of our existence on an oak-shaded lane will eventually fail to balance the scales if Robert doesn't make a career change. He wishes more than anything to escape the dreary world of banking, but options are slim at this point. For us both, any small desire to return to the States lessens monthly. Most everything about Europe suits us better. We'll never be *from* here but possibly we could be *of* here.

Chop wood and carry water, I remind myself. Keep toiling with the manuscript, despite the full scope exceeds what I can accomplish. So what if I remain invisible in the world and have little of concrete value to offer on

214 ◆ WHERE TWO WORLDS TOUCH

a larger scale. The opportunity remains to say *yes*, to dive headlong into the transforming process of relationship as a spiritual, soulful path. Lean into supporting my beloved in all the ways I can, even if that means somehow holding up the moon to provide illumination for him on a dark journey. Most especially then.

⌒

Occasionally, I think of Robert as one of those characters in stories unwittingly transported to another realm and time. A gallant, medieval knight trapped among the glass and steel towers of modern day. Distinctly out of place. Unsure how to return to the world where he once belonged. He endeavors to build meaningful, supportive relationships with his team of managers, encouraging rather than criticizing. While he doesn't really give a damn about the corporate world anymore, he deeply enjoys coaching people, one of the things he does best. Banking needs a bit of heart like his— likely an entire heart transplant—but the secret druid hasn't discovered his true calling yet. Whatever that may be, it certainly isn't finance.

"I don't know how you do it," he says one rainy, dark evening, seated at the dining table in our standard way, wearing his blue Hamburg jumper after work. Weariness etched on his face.

Dinner tonight is fishcakes with a homemade tartar sauce spiked with capers, gherkins, and fresh herbs, accompanied by a crisp green salad of baby rocket, as usual. A reassuring, satisfying meal in the bleary depth of January.

"Sitting home alone all day in silence, just writing. No distractions, no friends. I'd go crazy."

"For what it's worth, I wouldn't last two days in your world. I'd quit, walk out the door and not look back, then go find a job as a florist or gardener or a farmer, dealing with lovely plants instead of people."

"You've always preferred trees to humans."

"Except you, darling," I smile at him, fork and knife in hand, cutting into a round, golden patty, pushing it through the green-flecked sauce.

STANDING STONES ♦ *215*

"Sometimes, you prefer trees to me, too. I've said it before, it's like I married Thoreau, a man who would rather be out walking somewhere wild and lonely."

"It's anything but *lonely* in nature. I'm never alone. I find quite a convivial solitude outdoors. There's actually so much going on, it's mind blowing."

"Well, I admire you," he dips his head in a little bow of acknowledgment.

"Mutually, love. You inspire me. I watch you get dressed, putting on a conservative tie and cinching it up, shuffling out the door to a job that's a millstone around your neck, facing impossible expectations and a horribly unsupportive boss. Living with chronic pain. It's your effort and paycheck that makes my own undertaking even possible . . . I couldn't do it without you. There's a sacred reciprocity playing out here, for sure."

The beeswax tapers burn low, golden rivulets dripping down the candlesticks. Chewing a bite of his food, Robert considers the plate before him, his brow slightly wrinkled.

"There's something different about these fishcakes . . . a smoky taste."

"They're mackerel. You don't normally like the oily sort of fishes, but I thought *smoked* might be worth a try."

"Delicious."

My partner is tired and dejected, struggling to rally at mealtime, to engage in meaningful conversation, when he would prefer to simply disappear. Probably a good thing alcohol doesn't tempt him nowadays.

"I hate that it's dark when I go to work in the morning and dark when I come home, and I'm inside a fluorescent lit office all day. I actually sort of *like* my branch visits, because at least driving around I see daylight and the living world. Except for a few good souls, I'm beginning to think banking is the land of the undead."

Hearing him, my own countenance and gaze softens with empathy, wishing to console somehow, even when there's nothing I can do. Robert needs a guiding star. He also needs more yoga and stretching to help his back, as I'm frequently urging, but movement of contracted tissue feels painful, so he avoids doing so. The discomfort keeps him from his own

216 ◆ WHERE TWO WORLDS TOUCH

rehabilitation, locked in a downward spiral.

As with his declining mood and depression, his stalled recuperation affects both of us. Beyond a weekly massage and plying him with probiotics to help restore his gut microbiome, decimated by the antibiotic regime in hospital, I seek other ways to bolster my companion. The inclination to merely take care of him is an old pattern, one necessary to reframe, but I grapple with how or whether to push him to take accountability for his healing.

One grey day, listening to him complain about stiffness and pain, censoring myself from recommending yet again he find a yoga class, or swim at one of the indoor pools, like at the leisure centre on Kings Road, inwardly embroiled in conflict, I speak my truth.

"I can't be the one who 'fixes' you, Robert. That isn't my responsibility or role. You have to step up to your own self-care."

"Right now, I'm just trying to survive," he whips trenchantly, eyes grey and hard, his jaw clenched in restrained anger. "And I'm under so much stress, it's all I can do. The last thing I need is a partner nagging at me to do yoga or go swim."

I bite my tongue, lips pursed tightly. Daily, I strive utmost not to pester or be a harpy, instead to find the elusive balance between encouragement and pushing. A gentle challenger, not a persecutor. Agitation, heated and prickly, rises in me at his comment, and I take a deep breath. Exhale audibly in a discharge.

"I don't *nag*, Robert. I see you spiraling further into your pain and darkness, and I know from experience, both my own as well as clients—to say nothing of us living together for so long—you must take care of *yourself* or everything else falls apart."

We both recognize his well-worn strategy of placing work ahead of his own well-being, even in front of our relationship, working hard to earn respect and admiration from those above him on the ladder. The Good Boy Scout. And I do acknowledge, lately this pattern is something more than mere *approval*; for him, berated daily he is failing, his survival feels truly at stake. Robert isn't accustomed to failure. His body pays the toll, however, and isn't healing as it should, becoming steadily more rigid.

For much of our relating, we've upheld the principle—occasionally a half-joke—there isn't a right or wrong way to do anything, rather only *his way* versus *my way*, both with their respective merits, drawbacks, and potential lessons. As a paradigm shift, at times, this can be a challenging perspective to live by, especially when triggered, angry or hurt, or any way tangled in subconscious expectations and attachments.

Criticism doesn't build love, even less so during a difficult passage, and I struggle to balance my opinions and expectations regarding how he undertakes his healing process or doesn't. Trying to drop my attachments to his journey or the outcome when his choices impact us both daily. Wishing his suffering would ease but accepting, ultimately, the changes must come of his own volition.

Regardless of not labeling as *right* or *wrong*, I selfishly want him to heal, so that his lack of well-being impacts our relationship less than it currently does.

Yet I know very well that shadows exert a personal gravity; holding us firmly in habitual, clever ways of avoiding our core material—those wounds we carry like skeletons in the closet. Ruts in a track, our patterns guide us to the same, familiar destination and nowhere else. Shifting the entrenched and outworn strategies, recognizing their somatic components, like restricted breath and contracted postures, and breaking out of the grooves of established conditioning, forms the ongoing work of personal evolution. If we wish to change and grow, that is.

Invariably, we see another's shadow far more easily than our own. Again and again, I soften my judgments and try to place myself in Robert's shoes, looking honestly in the mirror—reminding myself that love is never punitive or vindictive. Shadows are always difficult to dance with. Phantom-like, they require being held gingerly, with deft fingers which gently support and stretch, holding firm when they contract reflexively against touch. Somewhere in their murky, protected depths, a mysterious gift awaits discovery, like a glossy pearl within the tightly closed oyster.

Undoubtedly, buried and disguised gifts await us here, if only we can

218 ◆ WHERE TWO WORLDS TOUCH

find them.

〜

The cold and rain of January weigh upon us like a blanket of wet, heavy wool and despair. I hunger for signs of new life, but all of Britain is chilled and barren. Beneath a sheet metal sky, even the evergreens seem burdened.

A Saturday morning finds the two of us unhurriedly enjoying a late breakfast of toasted homemade bread, eggs, and orange juice. Requisite strong coffee for my weary man, and amber, unmucked-with English Breakfast tea for me.

"Let's go to Stonehenge," suggests Robert. He has wanted to visit the Bronze Age monument since we moved to Sussex, and I too have desired to go, but we haven't yet made the trip. The famous stone circle stands barely more than an hour drive from here.

"Nice day for it," I frown, crunching another bite of toast, looking out the window at pewter clouds and bare trees bending in an icy wind.

"Well, it won't be crowded . . . " my partner counters hopefully, a lilt to his voice. Coaxing lightly but not pleading.

A valid point. For a second or two, I search his face, seeing he really wants to go, needing an escape from his struggles. Despite the freezing weather and my disinclination, a soggy day heaviness in limbs and spirit, no greater good will be served being a stick in the mud and staying at home. If life in England depended upon fair weather, we'd never go anywhere but for two weeks in the summer.

Just say yes.

"Alright then," I acquiesce. Robert's face lights up with a smile, and he sits taller in his chair, suddenly energized.

We wash the breakfast dishes and then change our clothes for an outdoor ramble, grabbing hats, scarves, gloves and whatnot. The gloomy day outside is a melancholy piano sonata in a minor key, hardly inspiring for the picnic hamper, so I stash provisions in a canvas tote: local organic apples, potato crisps seasoned with sea salt and vinegar, my perpetual bag

STANDING STONES ◆ *219*

of raw almonds, a couple of San Pellegrino *limonatas* from the fridge. We'll find a proper lunch somewhere. Less than thirty minutes after Robert's suggestion, we are underway, cruising comfortably through the stark winter landscape. Naked trees waving in a blur as we pass.

Conversation drifts to June, our wedding still largely unplanned. My partner wishes to get married in a lovely formal English garden, possibly a grand house in the background.

"Surely, we can locate such a place to rent. Maybe one of the National Trust sites we've been to. Or we find a new place around here . . . somewhere in the South Downs."

I can't summon to mind any place we have visited where I would want to exchange vows, and a burden of reluctance settles into my bones, heavy as clay. Never mind nearly everyone does it, the idea of renting a venue for a wedding feels odd to me. Impersonal and soulless, like a banking transaction. My wish is a ceremony imbued with *meaning*, ideally including some sort of connection to the place we will gather. Yet perhaps these aims are unrealistic. Ironically, not so long ago, I would have contentedly signed a document at our local council office, no friends or family present, but now such an idea rings hollow and anonymous. As two men, our union makes a statement about equality.

Both of us decidedly belong in the spiritual-but-not-religious camp. Not for a heartbeat would we consider getting married in a church. Far too conventional and too Christian. On this we agree, at least.

"We could have a pagan wedding at Stonehenge," Robert chuckles, amused at the thought. Turning to him as he drives, my flat-faced expression says you-have-got-to-be-kidding. No way. Even if the English Heritage site allowed such things, I've no interest in our event having unknown spectators and tourists looking on.

As if on cue, the world's most famous standing stones appear upon the horizon.

On a weekend late morning, a mostly empty car park greets us. A quiet sigh of relief lightens my spirit, thankful for the blessedly few visitors, and regardless of the cold, gladness finds me that we spontaneously undertook

220 ♦ WHERE TWO WORLDS TOUCH

this outing.

Surreal, as an American, to reside just over an hour from the enduring Neolithic landmark. Many have commented the stones aren't as large as they expected, and how tragic the motorway so close by. Departing the visitor centre, approaching the circle, I'm not disappointed by their size and stature; if anything, a discreet excitement ripples through me. My primary disenchantment is the road a couple hundred meters distant with cars zooming by; the noisy, rushed, and soulless modern versus the silent, immovable, and ancient sacred.

Handset pressed to his ear, Robert listens to the audio tour he rented at the visitor centre as we stroll towards the circle. Recorded commentary is generally interference, and I prefer to simply wander, observe, and contemplate. In the unsolved puzzle why this site was constructed so many miles from where the stones originated, a place that when the pillars were erected wasn't a plain but part of the great forest covering much of Britain, some conjecture *ley lines*—meridians of energy encircling the earth like underground streams—meet here to form a vortex. Our ancestors, more highly attuned to the subtle forces of earth and nature, likely detected the subterranean magnetic currents. Various mystics and healers claim the energetic lines strengthen us, amplifying our own bioelectric energies, conducive for health and well-being. Curious whether I will feel anything as a *sensitive*, I'm tracking my bodily impressions despite the January wind buffeting me.

The great stones are cordoned off, visitors restricted to a curvilinear path on the perimeter, which is surrounded by a low, mounded earthen henge enclosing the entire site. Immediately upon crossing through the circular embankment, a slight tingling occurs at the front of my forehead, the spot popularly known as the "third eye" or brow chakra; a sensation I'm well-acquainted with from meditation and expanded awareness. Differently than usual, however, I feel a mild pressure where the nasal cartilage meets frontal bones.

Quelle coincidence. Except, I don't believe in that. And the body doesn't lie.

Robert walks on, listening to the audio device, but I turn and retrace my steps out of the earthen circle. The sensation ceases immediately. Reentering the outer henge, the activation lights up again and persists when in the vicinity of the stones, intensifying the closer I get to them. Simultaneously, my chest expands, like a dilation of the heart.

I've fallen behind my counterpart. He realizes I'm distracted by something and returns to where I stand. Noting the puzzled expression on my face, pausing his audio tour with the push of a button, he looks at me enquiringly.

"Can you feel it?" I ask, my dark eyes curious and smiling.

"Feel what?"

I describe the phenomenon, pointing to my forehead and bridge of the nose, then indicating the outer earthen circle that somehow forms an energetic boundary.

"It's fascinating . . . I've never felt anything like it."

My dear man is a good sport and very accommodating of his odd, highly perceptive mate, and he's far more empathic than most people. We turn and walk back, moving around the oncoming tourists with their handsets in various languages, stepping across the low, grassy henge—the threshold where the activation in my body promptly switches on and off. Crossing over, Robert shakes his head, mildly disappointed.

"I don't feel what you're talking about," he shrugs, "but you're more sensitive than I am, especially about earth, nature, and spirits."

"That's true, but maybe the sensation is dulled by your pain medication."

No one passing by appears to notice anything or pause. Just as with life, in general, few people pay attention to anything but the blatantly obvious. Close again to the menhirs, standing at the edge of the roped path, my frontal facial bones are mildly activated and buzzing. The stones stand like the Pillars of Wisdom, and I long to wander into the inner circle, laying hands upon the monoliths themselves. What would I feel at the center of the ring? Would the whirling in my forehead grow exponentially stronger, some sort of attunement and an increased sense of power?

"You know," Robert sighs, slipping the handset over his wrist and

222 ◆ WHERE TWO WORLDS TOUCH

switching it off once more, "it's actually much more pleasant to simply be here and take in the stones, rather than listening to someone speaking about why they *think* things happened here . . . when nobody *really* knows."

Pulled back from my unspoken reverie, I nod in agreement, followed by a conspirative wink.

"The only plausible explanation is the extraterrestrials built it."

"Strangely, that doesn't sound less plausible to me than prehistoric people rolling and dragging sarsen stones weighing twenty-five tons, twenty miles from Marlborough through a forest. And the bluestones coming all the way from south-west Wales." He shakes his head, crowned with the wool derby cap he wore to Ireland. "Anything is possible, I suppose."

The grey sky leans heavily upon a near-distant horizon. Walking beside my companion, grateful for the thin crowds, I casually observe the other visitors all bundled up against the blustery wind of the Salisbury plain, speaking various languages, audio tour handsets glued to their ears, snapping photos, and generally *tuned out*. Even with their presence, I'm alone in my private, somatic experience of curious energetic activation. A foot in two worlds, as usual.

Coming to Stonehenge, I prepared myself for an underwhelming experience, expecting to find its magic long gone. A mysterious monument now relegated to merely a tourist attraction like so many other sacred, powerful sites. And whilst far from mystical, the not-so-subtle stimulation of energy gates in my body genuinely surprises me. My embodied assessment is the stones mark a remarkable junction of Earth's energies, and this was a healing, powerful place—even today, for those who can feel it.

Were the day not so cold, biting at our ears, we might be tempted to linger, but we've had enough. We can always come back. Akin to how I felt in rugged Connemara, a resonance of affinity hums in my bones, awakening something timeless and elemental. The ageless circle would indeed be magical if the tourists and motorway were gone. Passing through the low earthen henge a final time, the frontal pressure in my head ceases, and a soft blue wave of sadness courses through me. Humans have created a world of chaos and noise, completely enslaved to our machines and distractions.

The sacred has vanished from most of our lives, and religion isn't an equal replacement. People fail to recognize Earth is more than simply *alive* as a sphere of interwoven ecosystems—if they even acknowledge that—but a living, psychotemporal entity. We've lost the connection—the understanding—*it* is *us*. Human soul as part of the greater soul of nature and the earth itself. Inseparable.

Grateful for the warmth of the car and heated seats, we drive to nearby Salisbury for a reviving lunch in the old centre of town, afterwards wandering briefly into the historic cathedral Robert wishes to visit. Untethered, my thoughts keep drifting across the plain to the surprising circle of stones, as if called by some forgotten dream.

Holy, holy.

Driving back to Haslemere, beneath the low, somber clouds, our shared mood feels subdued and pensive. Rearranged and unexpectedly altered in a way not yet apparent. Longing for something we didn't know was lost, likely never to be found.

Such a sad mystery. The great monoliths stand silently, while everyone is headed to the shopping malls, or glued to their electronic devices, credit card in hand.

⌒〜

The oppressive gloom of English winter feels relentless, beating down my spirit with cold rain like the saturated earth itself. February marks the lowest point, the nadir of despondency. We haven't seen the sun in weeks, and I'd give anything to board a plane or train for an escape to sunnier, brighter realms. The Mediterranean has never called to me as strongly as during these dark days, and, predictably, I daydream of Provence, à la Cézanne, a painted sky of endless blue, and the Côte d'Azur.

As weak daylight fades in the late afternoons, I find comfort at the hearth; both the crackling fire in the main room, and the warm, soul-nourishing goodness cooking in the oven or simmering pot. Thick, hearty stews. Silky, soothing risottos. Savory pies topped with flaky, golden

224 ◆ WHERE TWO WORLDS TOUCH

pastry. A free-range chicken with crispy, bronzed "roasties" alongside. Yet even with the solace and grace of the table, winter's darkness seems interminable. I cannot fathom living farther north this time of year. No wonder Prehistoric people erected stones and monuments to clock the return of the sun, illuminated at solstice or equinox. Ancient calendars, of sorts. Creating the human agreement of *time*. Still today, their compelling constructions remain unrivaled reminders of the cyclical nature of life, and the seasons of rebirth, growth, and abundance will arrive once more.

Heeding the email suggestion of rainbow-clad Sara, Robert and I make a trip to Avebury in Wiltshire, another Neolithic henge monument, the largest stone circle in Britain. Unlike Stonehenge some twenty-four miles away, visible for ages, the stones at Avebury were toppled and buried in the medieval period, and a small village built near the center of the site. Preserved by the English Heritage organization, considerable excavation has restored the henge and circles to the extent possible, but many of the original ninety-eight sarsen stones are missing, destroyed by early Christians encouraged to believe the pagan monoliths were satanic.

Like a blessing from the old gods, the day shimmers clear, and while certainly not *warm*, not freezing. Nor is the wind blowing, which makes our wandering outdoors pleasant enough. Lacking the fame of Stonehenge, and given the frigid time of year, we have the site nearly to ourselves. Detailed maps and diagrams indicate the layout of a spectacular complex ages ago, impressive in scale, originally contained within a giant chalk embankment. Two avenues lined with column stones led up to the outer circle of monoliths, as well as two smaller circles, north and south.

The place is nowhere near as powerful or evocative as Stonehenge, however. Energetically, I feel no activation in my body, no unusual sensation or subtle current. Possibly, the broken up, segmentation and discontinuity of the circle interferes or subdues the energies. Perhaps the ley lines do not form so strong a junction here, or I am simply not close enough to the actual convergence point. Regrettably, the houses and buildings near the center of the henge, along with the village pub, further diminish any awe or grandeur.

STANDING STONES ◆ 225

Avebury's redeeming factor is visitors can walk among the monoliths. One may lay hands upon and sit beside them. In the open field, I do just this, standing beside a silent grey giant, palms on its rough, cold skin. Listening. Feeling. In the Old Ways, stones are keepers of memory and story, blessed with an unimaginably long life. My sense is the great stones mostly sleep, likely forever. Few celebrate or sing to them anymore; people merely meander around these inanimate objects which defy the rational brain and easy explanation. Gone are the days of bonfires and magic. Only the sun-bleached ribbons dangling from a nearby barren tree yield evidence that any still remember, yearn for, or honor what the upright rocks represent.

The sarsen stones are uncarved and naturally shaped, distributed over a wide area. Hands resting upon a 40-ton menhir, I feel trivial. Humbled. Slightly melancholy, too, a misty finger of grey-blue tracing up and down my spine.

Across the wide ring, I watch the secret druid while he wanders about, dressed warmly, scarf knotted around his neck, standing next to certain stones as if examining them. Here and there, he touches one. What does he feel or sense? How good and restorative for him to be outside under the pale sky, breathing fresh air, with yielding earth underfoot. Connecting with nature. The soul of the world, perchance. He needs something larger than the limiting story of pain and work holding him in a dark embrace.

"Do you feel anything here?" he enquires when our paths rejoin, searching my face with an earnest look.

"Not really. An openness in my chest, a slight expansion in my body, but not the distinct sensations at Stonehenge."

"This must have been so truly impressive when it was intact, when the avenue was standing..."

A wistful note in his voice echoes the same mistiness trailing me like lonely spirits. Hands stuffed into pockets of his black wool coat, he stares across the empty circle of dormant, unmown grass with its array of massive, upright, irregular pillars.

"Sometimes I feel like I was born in the wrong age. It makes me sad, really. Our modern world, what are we creating? We're just destroying the

226 ◆ WHERE TWO WORLDS TOUCH

planet, it seems."

"We're not good at creating beauty anymore. Or rather, we've lost the appreciation it's important," I sigh, tilting my head back to look skyward, watching a large hawk trace spirals high over the open field.

"I should have been in a world where there is magic."

"I'm sure you *were* in that world in another lifetime. Probably many lifetimes. Maybe that's why you miss it, especially when you're quiet, connected, and paying attention. There's still magic . . . but not in the way people expect or wish for. Personally, I think 'magic' is just a higher functioning of reality, like miracles."

Withdrawing one hand from the warmth of a pocket, Robert reaches out to me. Clasping his hand in mine, I squeeze it with an I-love-you message, and both of us smile. Irrespective of an indigo longing, a lightness and ease radiate around him, burdens lifted from his shoulders at least for now. Here, in the broken circle of giant stones, like our forgotten ancestors, we will look for the return of life-giving light and warmth in days ahead. Something to hope for.

We have honored winter long enough.

⌒

Crocuses sing gaily in the garden and along the lane, little gold and purple cups of joy. Life reemerges from the long, dark tunnel of hibernation, one bud and blossom at a time. On my countryside rambles, ascending the heath to the summit of Blackdown, gazing out over the green South Downs toward the distant sea, inspiration strikes with the irrepressible energy of spring.

"What do you think about getting married up on Blackdown?" I query Robert over a plate of fresh-baked, cranberry ginger scones, our respective strong coffee and tea alongside. Who cares if scones don't constitute breakfast fare in Britain, they suit fine in our house. Both of us are relaxed, glad for the weekend, my companion casual and not dressed for work. A welcome blue sky smiling outside, cheering us gently.

"We could drive up on the Haslemere side with our guests in a couple of cars, and then walk out along the main trail. There are so many beautiful spots. The whole space looks over the countryside to the coast."

Looking at me across the dark wood table, he considers my words for a minute.

"Where would people sit?"

Always an eye for practical details, this man.

Popping a bite of still warm, lightly sweet scone into my mouth, the tartness of the cranberries plays against the sugar of the crystalized ginger root. Delectable.

"Each person could carry a folding chair."

He has heard the story years before, but I recount the wedding attended as a youngster with my mother in the 1970's, an overnight campout in Joshua Tree National Monument in California. A catered dinner was served in a great tent like a pavilion, the first time I tasted caviar, followed by dancing and then sleeping in individual tents. The early morning ceremony unfurled with a dawn processional from the campsite to a ring of massive boulders overlooking the desert, where the couple's vows took place. For a child, the wonderfully exotic experience was almost The Arabian Nights. The vast landscape, with its inconceivable darkness and million twinkling stars, its astounding silence in the early morning, enchanted a city boy.

"I still remember the processional to the wedding. The cool dryness of the dawn air, the crunch of the gravelly dry sand under my shoes as we walked wordlessly among those giant boulders, alongside my mom in her white, embroidered cotton dress from Greece and laced-up sandals."

Marrying on the wild heath seems very *us*. Far more appealing than any rented, formal garden. In light of how I've come to know the summit's open space on my walkabouts, Blackdown seems nearly like my own glorious unkempt estate.

"As long as it's not too far a walk. No River-esque rambles across the countryside. Your stepmom has a bad foot, and I won't be able to carry much . . . "

A flicker lights his irises. The idea intrigues him. He agrees to drive to

228 ◆ WHERE TWO WORLDS TOUCH

the car park near Tennyson's Lane for a walk, a scouting trip for possible places which might suit. Sipping coffee from his preferred, hand painted Deruta cup, setting it back on the saucer, Mr. Blue Eyes glances at me inquisitively.

"What would a Celtic wedding be like?"

His British roots and heritage increasingly interest him, along with Old World spirituality, feeling a tug to explore Wales and the West Country—the more magical and wild places remaining in Britain. Connemara awakened this, I think. Or the standing stones. A mysterious joint conspiracy, perhaps.

"Not sure, really, but we could do a *hand-fasting*; an old pagan custom of holding the other's wrist and then binding them together with a ribbon or cord."

"I love that!" he smiles, eyes flashing like sunlight on the sea. "Yes, I want something very nontraditional tying us to the ancient histories of this land."

Brilliant. We are inching away from prefabricated notions and stale models into a more soulful realm, free to create what we choose. Whatever we fashion will be distinctly earth-centered, original, and organic. In coming months, as spring bursts forth with vivid color and fresh inspiration, every tree clad in electric new growth, we will create our vows, and crystalize the elements of our ceremony we wish to include, like music and poetry.

"Personally, I want our ritual to symbolize new life and possibility," I offer, feeling slightly buoyant with optimism. "A renewed commitment. The mystery and grace of being alive and walking side by side on a journey."

"I'd like that too. And I'm confident you'll come up with exactly the right framework and words for that, my pagan witch," Robert grins tenderly, gaze still twinkling. "Especially as the wordsmith and master of ritual you are."

"I'm not a witch, I'm something else. Sara is a witch. A fourth-generation one, no less."

"Green Man, then."

I cock my head slightly, reflecting for a moment, thoughtfully rubbing my chin with its close cropped beard.

"Not that I couldn't be a male witch, or a 'green witch'—ones who focus on plants and healing, like with my essential oils and potions—but I find all the convenient labels are just too confining. None of them fit. I'm something more. And different."

"Granted, but you're pretty spooky sometimes."

My eyebrows arch in surprise at the word.

"That's what Paul says about Sara, did you know that? She's 'spooky'. It's the word he uses for anything mystical, paranormal, or otherwise out of his tightly closed box . . . though really, he's secretly curious."

"It's a good word, *spooky*."

"I prefer *unhinged*, myself."

Robert reaches for another bite of cranberry-studded scone on the small, handmade plate beside his Italian coffee cup and saucer, chuckling.

"The Brits think most Americans are unhinged, in general. We're too emotional, too upbeat, too optimistic, too this or that. Personally, I vote you're *spooky*. And if people knew you, that's likely the word they'd choose too."

Maybe, I shrug nonchalantly.

"Good thing I'm basically a recluse. Most likely, people would think I'm just very odd or slightly mad. The irony, of course, is the rest of the world is basically insane. Totally disconnected from nature and the earth and their bodies, living an unsustainable consumer lifestyle, addicted to gadgets and technology, blindly chasing money like the most important thing. A global, collective delusional disorder. I'll argue that I'm actually one of the sane ones . . . more or less."

"More or less."

A friendly smile passes between us, a comfortable, energetic acceptance of each other. Intimate and good. The warm depth of our relating. The place where our two worlds touch.

"On the other hand, there's a distinct chance this is just a fool's journey, and I am simply barking, *spacking* mad. Who can say?"

"All I know is you're beautifully peculiar."

"You charmer," I grin and wink, playfully.

Beautifully peculiar. For a non-conformist, reluctant mystic, surely, it's one of the loveliest compliments imaginable. I should kiss him for that.

Marry him, too.

THE FIELD OF POSSIBILITY

THE FIRST OF May. Beltane. A year ago tonight, I stood in a wheat field in Kent, casting intentions and offering myself to the Moon, then met a glistening fox in the lane. This evening, the celestial light has not yet risen in the sky, and in the darkness, I am with Robert outside the cottage, warmly dressed with wool caps on our heads and soft scarves wrapped round necks. The night feels only cool, not cold, but my mate would say otherwise, perhaps.

Departing the sanctuary of the house, we cross the lawn and pass the Wishing Tree with its new raiment of emerald, then pause at the gate in the deer fence, propped ajar until crotchety old Alan closes it again.

"I call this the Rumi gate because, when I step through it, I'm reminded of his poem about the field . . . you know the one."

Taking my partner's hand, I recite the words aloud from memory.

"Out beyond ideas of wrongdoing and rightdoing, there is a field. I'll meet you there. When the soul lies down in that grass, the world is too full to talk about. Ideas, language, even the phrase *each other* doesn't make any sense."

"I love that one," Robert smiles back. "You amaze me with the way you recall poems so easily. Your memory is much better than mine."

In my customary way, I squeeze his palm with an I-love-you message, three quick clasps in succession.

"It's a soul practice. Just like moving beyond ideas of wrongdoing and rightdoing, and feeling for the soul of the world." I turn toward the open

232 ◆ WHERE TWO WORLDS TOUCH

gate. "We're crossing the threshold, leaving the so-called real world behind us. If only for now, we are venturing into a different, less-human domain. You're entering the Field of Possibility, where the quantum becomes the physical. Step into it with intention."

Following my lead, we pass through the fence portal and walk into the openness of the southerly field. The earth has been raked into clunky clods of dark soil by a tractor, and the entirety of the furrowed hill is a carpet of ankle high, green shoots. Traversing the rough grooves of ground, we crest the field's high point and descend the slope until the cottage lights, the only manmade illumination, disappear. Still farther we go into the shadowy expanse of sprouting wheat glimmering in the night.

"I don't know how you see in the dark," mutters Robert, clutching my hand and squinting his eyes, staring down at the ground, trying to determine his steps. "You're like a cat. I can *never* see like you do."

"More an owl than a cat."

Squeezing his hand reassuringly once more, I lead him forward, boots crunching the chunks of dirt as we tread the silvery green ground.

"Once upon a time, you would have just gone off and done this by yourself."

"I still go off and do this on my own . . . but I *also* want to include you. It's Beltane, the celebration of the union of the Wild God and Goddess, the sacred masculine and the divine feminine. The veil between realms is thinnest tonight, same as Samhain, what we call Halloween, six months opposite on the calendar wheel. Traditionally, this is a night of magic, when worlds overlap, but whatever your belief system, *shared* intention is always more powerful than solo."

As if summoned by my earlier comment, an owl calls from the blackness of trees somewhere beyond the field's borders.

Whoo, whoo, whoo . . . are you?

I am the reluctant mystic, with my human beloved alongside me.

"I remember May Day from my childhood in southern Germany, the village celebration and dancers round the May pole with long ribbons. The local women all had flowers braided in their hair or round their heads. I didn't understand what any of it meant but I loved the pageantry and sense of community . . . the festivity."

We have reached roughly the center of the field, where I halt.

"Here, this seems good."

I sit down cross-legged, gesturing for Robert to do the same. Once he does, we hold hands and sit facing each other, two solitary figures in the night. From pockets, we withdraw the items brought along: a small sachet of dark red corn kernels; a votive candle in a glass holder; a stick of resinous New Mexico piñon incense; a pea-sized garnet, and an inch-long piece of opaque green tourmaline; a cigarette lighter; as well as two small slips of paper with handwritten words in purple ink.

The two of us are co-creating a modest ritual on an auspicious night. Robert cups his hands protectively to block the wind, and I flick the thumbwheel until the lighter sparks to life, igniting the incense and wick of the small votive. The candle flame dances erratically but stays alive, sheltered by the glass holder, radiating a sphere of light in the darkness. I place the resin stick in the dirt, its glowing orange tip birthing a thin snake of fragrant smoke, curling upward and immediately dissipated, snatched away by the night's invisible hands.

Mirroring me, Robert holds his piece of paper to the candle flame and sets it alight. The folded slip of written words symbolizes the thing or pattern in life each of us feels most ready to release, to relinquish carrying as emotional and psychic baggage. Our parchments burn down to grey ash, a sacrifice to the firmament, immolated by the spirit of fire and transformation.

Together we sing softly, a chant for beauty and gratitude, improvised on the spot, two baritone voices blending and playing in the stillness. As an offering, we tuck the semiprecious stones into the soil between us and cover them, along with the red corn. Just as when I have scattered these heirloom seeds previously in solitary rites, I've zero expectation the ruby kernels will sprout and grow. More likely, they'll end up in a pheasant's gullet. Like stepping mindfully through the Rumi gate into the field, the action is merely another symbolic gesture. Considered another way, a token act of deliberately giving something back to the earth from whence so many of our blessings arise—a humble nod of sacred reciprocity within the living realm of oneness and interconnectivity.

Loosely holding hands, seated opposite each other, the creaturely night breathes around us, stirring a faint rustle amid the distant dark trees, slowly coming awake to itself. Inhaling the quietude and cool air, we've stepped out of time and place. We might be anywhere, in another lifetime of a different age, waiting for the moon to rise above Troy.

In my heart, tonight's ritual is less about making magic than simply creating a conscious ceremony with each other. Here is a moment to pause, to invite and make room for the sacred; to tenderly celebrate the arrival of spring and new beginnings. Welcoming possibility and unforeseen blessings, supporting each other's readiness to drop whatever limits and no longer serves our highest good—individually as well as our relating itself. Embodying *conscious* relationship and commitment. Appreciating the mystery of one's beloved.

If only real change were so facile a gesture as burning a scrap of paper and letting it go. As humans, we weave and stitch our conditioning deep into the psyche, binding it fast. Yet genuine spoken intent carries power, and as an indication of awareness, like a vow, makes a good first step. Alas, our subconscious resistance runs much deeper.

A few weeks hence, Robert and I will publicly enact another ceremony, witnessed by family, circling back to the seeds of intention planted here and now.

Tonight, waiting for the moon, is just for us.

We do not sit long. My companion's back won't tolerate it, despite his brave front and general good nature. For a few minutes more, the blue-eyed, secret druid and I linger in the dark expanse of the field, holding hands. Senses flung wide. Breathing in, breathing out. I close my eyes, listening, but hear no ultrasonic, wordless exultation. Will I ever experience that elusive gift of highly expansive awareness again? I dearly hope so.

The stiffness of Robert's pose calls my attention. He's chilled.

"I love you," I smile, blowing out the small white candle.

THE FIELD OF POSSIBILITY ◆ *235*

"And I, you," he grins back in the darkness.

"Thanks for venturing into the Field of Possibility with me."

"I always value that you offer me these sorts of things to feed the soul. I respect the way you make time to do them."

"They matter. To live a conscious, embodied life, it's essential to pause, to intentionally disconnect to *reconnect*. Like going outside at night and looking up to see stars and moon, glimpsing the bigger picture instead of only the minutiae and grind of day-to-day life."

"I'm glad we live where we can see the stars . . . when it's not raining, I mean. And not that I step outside enough to see them, but they're so beautiful."

Above us, a fistful of diamonds flung across the inky blue velvet, twinkling in priceless hues of blue and white. The sun's paramour still plays coy and hides, but the night grows brighter, and she must nearly be rising.

"Do you know what binary stars are?"

He grins again at me, recognizing a preamble to an explanation.

"No, I don't."

"A beautiful phenomenon found throughout the cosmos. They are pairs of stars, each with its own center of gravity, orbiting around each other, held by the other's pull. It's cosmic, celestial allurement, and together they spiral through the universe."

I wait for him to make the connection. A stream of heartbeats slips by. The pieces click.

"That's what we are . . . binary stars."

"Yes. You and me, each with our unique composition, destiny, and individual light, but traveling together as a unit along the arc of time and space."

"I don't know where you learn this kind of stuff, or how you hold it all in your elephant-sized brain, but it's beautiful and I love you for it."

He whispers the term once more, softly, as if weighing and considering it. Or simply making a wish as the night breeze rustles the far trees in a murmuring whoosh.

"Sort of clunky for a cute little nickname, though . . . 'yes, my binary

236 ◆ WHERE TWO WORLDS TOUCH

star."'"

"Fair point. It's definitely not as endearing as *pumpkin* or *mon petit*."

"My back hurts and I'm cold. Let's go back to the cottage."

Standing, I reach out to assist, pulling him to his feet with a steady tug, and then into my arms for a kiss.

"Cup of tea, love?"

"Lovely. Eros?"

The scented, black tea blend from Mariage Frères in Paris, redolent of rose and pomegranate, we both share as a favorite. Too intensely aromatic for breakfast, we often enjoy a cup after dinner. Caffeine be damned.

"Of course, what else would lovers drink?"

"Oh, yes, please. And cake, too?"

"*Naturellement*. The Beltane Faerie Cake awaits."

"I know, I've been waiting all day for it! Did you make the rosemary-honey-infused whipped cream to go on top?"

"*Mais oui*. Just for your Lordship."

The salutation makes him laugh, and he hugs me tightly, both of us bulky in our thick coats.

Walking back across the roughly uneven dark field, hand in hand, ascending the rise, the cottage comes into view, framed in shadows of English oaks along the lane. Candles aglow in the windows, Highfield looks homey and inviting, the way a house should, I think. The sight triggers a warm and pleasant upwelling, a sense of well-being in the world and our hearts. Stepping through the Rumi gate, crossing some mystic barrier from an enchanted realm to the denser sphere of everyday reality, I squeeze his hand tightly once more.

I would know this hand anywhere.

Such wonderful certainty, a swirl of bright joy spreading through my chest, a lotus blossom unfurling.

Like jeweled beads strung together, life is made of these precious moments. Surely, the goodness of our days arises from an ability to recognize, appreciate, and savor things as little celebrations of grace. The ordinary sacred is everywhere, in every breath: our lover's warm hand in ours, the pale roses blooming gaily even in the rain, twittering birds in the garden, the zesty citrus aroma of peeling a fresh mandarin and its tartly sweet juiciness on the tongue. The feel of bare earth underfoot. The towering, energetic presence of a venerable tree. A pot of soup simmering on the stove on a cold, grey day stirring our hunger. All the humble, intricate delights, too many to count or name.

No question, some passages are more difficult or stormy than others. Robert and I still navigate a rough crossing, finding our way through his ongoing dark night of the soul. Both of us seeking our true self and a worthy, valid calling in the world. Shadow crawling. Life repeatedly brings us opportunities to venture into the places we're frightened of, confronting a legion of fears. Situations where we draw back into resistance and false security, our breath shallow and tight, but only in stepping out of our comfort zones, into uncertainty, do we grow and evolve. Chaos loves to overturn the tidy apple cart. Yet, beyond all setbacks and seemingly wrong turns, disappointments and losses, the heartache and unfulfilled longing, what a priceless gift to be alive.

Crossing the night-platinum lawn towards the house, the shimmer of a breeze in the Wishing Tree, rising majestically in shadow at the center of the garden, speaks to me.

You have been loved.

Instantly, my breath deepens, knowing the truth of this.

Once we were young, beautiful, and blithe. Glowing with fire and shiny dreams. Some element of that magnetism still endures, now softened at the edges and embellished with etched lines and wrinkles of character. With any luck, we are like good wine, maturing from overly fruity brightness and harsh tannins to something richer, earthier, and complex. *Beguiling*, if very charmed.

As for the fire and dreams, I feel them mellowing to a gentle flame burning steadily. My ardent hope is simply to be planted in a place that nourishes on all levels of body, mind, and spirit, to have more of *this* which enfolds us here. Because *it* is *us*. How exhilarating to roam the globe for adventure or searching for home, but how lovely to be *of* a place, striving

238 ♦ WHERE TWO WORLDS TOUCH

to fashion something of beauty and value to the world—until the day we finally surrender our vessel of a body and return to the earth from whence we came.

Beauty fades. Love too, more often than not, blighted by expectations, attachments, wounds and defenses. As the secret druid and I approach the cozy cottage, hand in hand, I know one thing: how good to love and be loved in return in the open arms of vulnerability.

Like the endless spiral of seasons marked by the great standing stones, our love goes on. Broken open and melted down, we've lost the shape, identity, and precious things we thought defined us, only to discover we are something much larger. More authentic and vital. Alluring.

Together, we are greater still.

Everything is relationship. Created through a string of impossible, million to one chances, the universe exists in order to experience life, even the most commonplace moments in an ordinary day, like a shared meal together. A walk outdoors. A cup of tea. If we strip away any distinction between the ordinary and the sacred, the mundane and the magical, then everything is exquisite. Beauty becomes its own excuse for being, and perfection exists in every moment as the days fly away.

How trite to proclaim life a miracle, but what other suitable word exists? Only *mystery*, perhaps. And the invitation is to say yes, to trust in the unfathomable intelligence and creativity at the heart of everything, co-arising, guiding us to unknown destinations and destiny.

Imagination is evidence of the Divine.

The silver coin of moon rises above the slopes of Blackdown. We've traveled so far to be here in our painted gypsy caravan, rolling and bumping our way along the winding road. The Magical Mystery Tour, indeed. Our respective worlds overlapping, sharing the grace of the table, and the touch of each other's hand. Reaching the stone terrace, just before stepping into the circle of illumination thrown by the porch light, feeling a curious tingle up my spine, I pause, my eyes scanning the inky darkness along the distant hedge by the neighbor's house. Possibly, I'm imagining, but someone watches me. Fox, most likely. Or spirits on this night when the veil is only a whisper of thought.

Before bedtime, I will place a slice of Beltane Faerie Cake at the foot of the Wishing Tree as a modest offering and oblation. Nature spirits won't really want it, they don't consume human food, but my friend the fox will. Oh yes. May all be fed.

Robert has gone into the house to get warm, his figure held in the doorway by a corona of light.

"Are you coming in?"

Turning my face upward to the night's stars, smiling wistfully at the incandescent moon, I draw in a deep breath of gratitude. Quietly in awe of the cosmic imagination. Feeling and listening for the song and soul of the more-than-human world. Ever the reluctant mystic, always a foot in two realms, tending the hearth fire at the threshold where worlds touch.

"Yes, love. Coming now. I'll put the kettle on."

What mysterious, sweet grace, this life. Following a path at our feet or blazing one's own way forward, nowhere to be other than present, learning all true journeys begin and end in the heart.

Just say *yes*.

240 ◆ WHERE TWO WORLDS TOUCH

ACKNOWLEDGMENTS

Marlena de Blasi ("Chou"), my appreciation for your lushly gilded memoirs of a life in Italy, which comforted me during my time as an outsider living in England, and inspired the original draft of this story. Thank you too for the brief gift of your friendship and the admonition to find my own voice. *Grazie mille*.

Merissa Bunton, who braved the first draft of this narrative and generously taught me about the most overused word in the English language ("it"), and to never begin a sentence with that common noun. Six years and a dozen full-edits of the manuscript later, bless you for reading the resuscitated version and giving me a chance for redemption.

Katie Boyer Clark, book designer, who once again conspired with me to fashion the most beautiful offering we could manage. Thank you for your ever-willing good nature, keen sense of design, and humoring my perfectionist obsession with little details, dear.

Robert, *mon petit*. The painted gypsy caravan rolls ever onward, searching for home but knowing it's always in our hearts. What a gift to grow older together, gracefully surrendering the things of youth. Such a grand adventure, my love, wrapped in beauty and touched with mysterious grace. Boundless gratitude for the endless support and always being my champion.

242 ◆ WHERE TWO WORLDS TOUCH

ABOUT THE AUTHOR

River Faire is a body-centered therapist, an *intuitive*, a Paris-trained chef-turned-holistic-wellness coach, and a multi-award–winning author. Formerly known as L.R. Heartsong, his eloquent, lyrical books invite readers on a journey that will nourish the soul, touch the heart, uplift the spirit, and inspire the mind.

Discover his various offerings (books, podcast, literary blog, coaching, and more) at RiverFaire.com

Printed in the USA
CPSIA information can be obtained
at www.ICGtesting.com
JSHW020940261123
52633JS00003B/12